# After Prison

# After Prison

## Navigating Employment
## and Reintegration

Rose Ricciardelli

*and* Adrienne M.F. Peters, editors

WILFRID LAURIER
UNIVERSITY PRESS

Wilfrid Laurier University Press acknowledges the support of the Canada Council for the Arts for our publishing program. We acknowledge the financial support of the Government of Canada through the Canada Book Fund for our publishing activities. This work was supported by the Research Support Fund.

Library and Archives Canada Cataloguing in Publication

    After prison : navigating employment and reintegration / Rose Ricciardelli and Adrienne M.F. Peters, editors.

Includes bibliographical references.
Issued in print and electronic formats.
ISBN 978-1-77112-316-7 (softcover).—ISBN 978-1-77112-318-1 (EPUB).—
ISBN 978-1-77112-317-4 (PDF)

    1. Ex-convicts—Employment—Canada. 2. Criminals—Rehabilitation—Canada. I. Ricciardelli, Rose, 1979–, editor II. Peters, Adrienne M. F., [date], editor

HV9346.A38 2017            331.5'10971            C2017-902945-2
                                                C2017-902946-0

Cover design by David Drummond. Text design by Angela Booth Malleau.

© 2017 Wilfrid Laurier University Press
Waterloo, Ontario, Canada
www.wlupress.wlu.ca

This book is printed on FSC® certified paper and is certified Ecologo. It contains post-consumer fibre, is processed chlorine free, and is manufactured using biogas energy.

Printed in Canada

Every reasonable effort has been made to acquire permission for copyright material used in this text, and to acknowledge all such indebtedness accurately. Any errors and omissions called to the publisher's attention will be corrected in future printings.

# CONTENTS

# Navigating Employment Post-Release
## An Introduction

Rose Ricciardelli, Don Evans, and Adrienne Peters

I mprisonment for any length of time gives rise to diverse experiences of strife, stress, and grief. With incarceration, an individual is removed from society, and their potential participation in educational programs or the labour market is at least temporarily—but too often permanently—stayed. Recognizing, however, that occupational positioning or student status is a core identifying characteristic of any individual, how can society expect successful community re-entry after incarceration for individuals lacking education or consistent (if any) employment experience? Indeed, successful community and employment reintegration for former prisoners—parolees, probationers or simply releasees—is a long noted concern across provinces, territories, states, and countries. In Canada, from 2010 to 2011 approximately 163,000 adults were in custody each day and of these prisoners 77 percent were released back into the community (Dauvergne, 2012). Thus, community and employment reintegration is a reality negotiated by well over 100,000 adults annually in Canada alone. Looking to our neighbours to the south, the situation is even more sombre; as staggering numbers of prisoners are released into the community, we see the movement away from mass incarceration to mass supervision, leaving millions of adults in the United States trying to find employment as they navigate probation and parole. Securing employment is, in many cases, essential for releasees to successfully reintegrate and desist from crime (Harding, 2003; Visher, Winterfield, & Coggeshall, 2005).

Researchers have reliably demonstrated that employment provides releasees with heightened self-esteem, feelings of independence, financial stability and pro-social responsibility (Rahill-Beuler & Kretzer, 1997; Rosenfeld, Petersilia, & Visher, 2008; Uggen, 2000). However, employment is hard to come by for former prisoners, and finding gainful employment is even more challenging (Visher, Debus-Sherrill, & Yahner, 2008). After incarceration, men, women, and youth must navigate the effects of the stigma attached to their criminal past, gaps in their employment history or a complete lack of law-abiding employment experience, negligible social networks to rely on for assistance in finding work, the demands placed on them by their parole/probation conditions, as well as the demands of programming and treatment, and changes in technology and societal living when seeking work. Recognizing the multifold challenges shaping employment re-entry for releasees, this edited collection was born to provide insight into the realities of creating, seeking and finding work after imprisonment.

This collection of contributions had its beginnings in the observations and experiences of two of the editors who had access to the development and implementation of a day reporting centre in a large Canadian city. The reporting centre was established, largely drawing on experiences of Don Evans in his prior roles as a social worker, community corrections researcher, probation/parole officer, editor, and in government, to assist with parole supervision by providing additional services. The overall objective of the day reporting centre was to assist parolees as they strove to successfully complete their sentences and create a pathway to a crime-free life. The referrals to the centre, for a variety of reasons, represented more difficult situations in terms of both the parolee's risk of reoffending and in establishing a stake in conformity. One notable reason is simply that the centre tended to take referrals of high-risk parolees who were assessed as requiring additional supervision, beyond that of the normative parole officer visitations. Of course, it has been argued that such assessments have been designed under the presumption of keeping society safe from the parolee, rather than with the well-being of the releasee in mind (see Hannah-Moffatt, 2012).

The day reporting program is informed by the risk–need–responsivity (RNR) model developed by Andrews, Bonta, and Hoge (1990), although the practitioners in the program developed a specific need-focused approach in terms of developing interventions specific to the parolees referred to the program. Crucial to this need-focused approach is an awareness of the importance of getting the parolee stabilized in the community, which includes the two major activities of securing housing and employment. With these needs stabilized—or at this level of stabilization—it then becomes possible for case workers to work with releasees toward more long-term goals that will assist in the integration process and eventually result in desistance from crime. Daniel Mears and Joshua Cochran (2014), in their book *Prisoner Reentry in the Era of Mass Incarceration*, go beyond the normal discussion of "punishment" as being the prison sentence and look more broadly at what they call "invisible punishments" that are the result of imprisonment; punishments that create specific problems for released prisoners. These include challenges with regard to disenfranchisement; housing; finances and employment; family reunification; drug use, addiction, and mental health treatment; welfare benefits; and supervision. Each of these "punishments" are examples of challenges facing parolees upon release from prison worthy of book-length discussions.

We, however, have chosen to focus on the role of employment in the reintegration and desistance process, as with employment, the possibility for housing increases and parolees are able to make strides toward resolving many of the aforementioned challenges. Further, employment reintegration is one area where we have witnessed parolees undergo countless struggles with serious implications for their sense of self and their willingness to remain in the community. Employment (i.e., the search for employment, lack of skills or pre-employment training, or inability to maintain employment) has been a source of devastation, fear, concern, and lack of confidence; consequently we feel this edited collection's focus on the role of employment for releasees makes a valuable contribution to knowledge, discussion, and policy. Indeed, in our society, popular public thought is to always punish the "offender"; however, we also want offenders to become contributing members of society and as such pay off their dues. These two issues are inherently contradictory, and cannot be resolved until the realities of employment reintegration are understood and efforts are made to help individuals (re-)enter the labour force after prison.

In this book, our focus lies in exploring the issues and challenges related to the role employment plays in reintegrating released prisoners back into society and setting them on a pathway to desistance from criminal activity. To this end, we begin by providing a brief comment on these two processes, reintegration and desistance. Next, we discuss community stabilization, employment and education, aspects of the current labour market and the associated bifurcation of the released custodial population, all to provide the context of employment reintegration in a way that situates the contributions of diverse authors. We conclude the collection with a discussion of the developmental aspects of employment approaches and a summation of the diverse contributions that follow.

## REINTEGRATION AND DESISTANCE

Various definitions of reintegration exist throughout the criminological, sociological, and other literatures, but for our purposes the process contains elements of an official recognition that the individual reintegrating has been deemed "rehabilitated" by justice personnel and demonstrated that they have undertaken moral reform and, when appropriate, reconciliation. Thus, they are ready to rebuild or restore their social capital and develop their human capital and resources. The chapters in this collection offer examples of frameworks, programs, and policies that attempt to meet some of the objectives of the reintegration process as tied to employment. It also must be recognized that this process is part of the development of a new identity and narrative for the former prisoner as they leave behind their "offender" status and become desisters from crime.

Desistance is generally understood as the "process by which offenders give up criminal activity and become law-abiding citizens" (Laub & Sampson, 2001; Maruna, 2001; Weaver & Weaver, 2013). However, there is no substantive agreement among researchers on an inclusive definition of the process. Initial studies exploring why or how offenders exit from criminal activity were largely re-examinations of earlier studies on "delinquent" behaviour focused on what happened to offenders when they were older (Laub & Sampson, 2001; Sampson & Laub, 1992; Sampson & Laub, 1993). In these studies authors suggest that people age out of criminal behaviour as they develop stakes in conformity, through community ties such as employment, or marital and family ties that encourage desistance (Moffitt, 1993). But marriage and employment alone do not solidify pathways for desistance; other researchers suggest desistance depends on the strength and quality of an offender's relationships, commitments, and self-identity. Together these constitute structure and self-monitoring that, when coupled with emotional support, is the foundation for desistance.

Following from these results, Maruna (2001) employed narrative theory to examine the psychology of desistance beyond the age-out theory. He discovered that successful prevention of recidivism depended on the personal narratives individuals developed. Specifically, desisters create redemption scripts that claim their past criminal activity resulted from external factors beyond their control, while recidivists develop condemnation scripts that embody a fatalistic viewpoint and doubt their ability to change. Desisters also feel they have a role to play in the reformation process. For former prisoners, it would be prudent for criminal justice policy to clearly highlight the *end* to their punishment and provide some means of signalling their redemption and re-inclusion within their communities. This concept of redemption is explored by Maruna (2001) who discusses "redemption scripts" and the process of "making good," where the ex-offender is able to rewrite their past into a necessary prelude to a productive and "worthy" life. This self-reconstruction is not a deletion of one's history but rather a reinvention of one's self—the creation of a new identity.

Current understandings support that desistance from criminal activity is related to managing key risk factors such as criminal associates and substance misuse to name but two (Andrews & Bonta, 2010). Recent work of researchers in this area has recognized that desistance involves changes in lifestyle and opportunities *and* a renewed interest in rejoining the community, which includes the development of human and social capital (Maruna & LeBel, 2010). It is in this context that we highlight a few general themes and the challenges inherent to understanding and providing services that assist released prisoners in their stabilization, integration and desistance from crime; each a critical element in reducing reoffending and maintaining parolees beyond their supervision experience. Reintegration and desistance are complex processes that occur over a period of time and there is much we do not yet know. It is our hope that this collection will further our knowledge of the role of one key aspect, the importance of employment, in contributing to a former prisoner "making good" (Maruna, 2001) in society.

## Community Stabilization

After release from prison, individuals generally find themselves facing specific challenges that, if not overcome, can have a destabilizing effect on their capacity to successfully meet their warrant expiration date/supervisory period without a return to prison or criminal behaviour. This initial process of stabilization includes providing assistance in securing identification documents such as a birth certificate, driver's licence, health card, and so on; finding appropriate and affordable accommodation; navigating parole conditions, especially any that might interfere with finding a job; managing the stigma of having a criminal record; securing employment or upgrading educational/vocational certificates; and assistance with navigating technology or acquiring at least basic computer skills. Meeting these stabilization needs is further challenged by the fact that when prisoners are released from institutions they lack a number of assets—from material possessions like basic clothing, money, an address, even shelter or food, to positive social connections—the lack of which are a major barrier to their reintegration. This poverty of social capital combined with general poverty requires supervising agencies to provide assistance that could otherwise have, possibly, been received from families and friends.

Recognizing that releasees tend not to have a social network that can be mobilized on their behalf, the work of support falls, of necessity, to the community and government agencies involved in their supervision. The difficulty in the current economic climate emerges when the agencies responsible for reintegration services are underfunded and understaffed. In consequence, these agencies are too under-resourced to meaningfully undertake activities of support. The minimal resources and services are even more stretched as a result of releasees continuing to use these services even after they reach warrant expiration since they are often the sole venue of support available. Efforts on the part of these agencies to meet releasees' needs have led to some interesting, innovative, and helpful strategies such as pooling resources and creating networks with other service providers outside of the criminal justice system. These emerging pioneering partnerships include reintegration hubs or reporting centres that involve collaborative approaches where a number of services unite to manage these early re-entry challenges. There is, however, a limit to how far the staff and services of these agencies can be stretched, particularly as the demand for service keeps growing. These invaluable services are precursors to releasees finding work, the reason for our emphasis on exploring the role of employment in reintegration and stabilizing the individual in the community.

## Employment and Education

Researchers indicate that immeasurable value and benefit can be realized from employment (Graffam, Shinkfield, & Hardcastle, 2008; Petersilia, 2007; Sampson & Laub, 1997). Employment generally contributes toward an increased likelihood of an individual successfully completing the supervisory period; a decreased possibility of a return to prison for a technical violation or even a new offence; and it signals an individual's stability and progress toward desisting from a criminal pathway (Nolan, Wilton, Cousineau, & Stewart, 2014; Uggen, 2000; Visher et al., 2008). Notwithstanding the established value of employment in promoting reintegration and eventual desistance from crime, there are a number of barriers that inhibit access to meaningful work, which are discussed throughout the diverse contributions in this collection. These include having a criminal record; access to suitable work clothes and equipment; and dealing with employer perceptions and expectations. However, beyond these more personal or individualized barriers, there are also systemic challenges that releasees face. These systemic challenges are often omitted from discussions about employment re-entry yet need to be accounted for if genuine efforts are to be made to overcome the effects of these challenges. Three of these challenges currently need our attention, as they relate to securing employment for released offenders: they are changes in the labour market, the aging of released offenders, and the developmental needs of former prisoners seeking employment.

The first, *changes in the current labour market*, is marked by the recent economic downturns in North American and European markets that have led to closures, reductions in the labour force, and wage depression. Said realities impact the general population and, as a result, have made the securing of meaningful work for released offenders even more precarious. This is compounded by the constant accounts in the media and academic literature of the new shape of work, a derivative of technology, robotics, modernization of manufacturing, and cutbacks in government services that lead to new forms of work and service arrangements. Recent discussions of the shared economy and the "uberizing" of many jobs add to the complexity of finding work for all unemployed individuals, including released offenders, and particularly persons without experience and skills in technologies. Some agencies, in response, have turned to creative efforts in an attempt to find alternative ways to assist releasees with finding employment opportunities. An example of such a venture includes the consolidation of efforts among re-entry service providers who then together solicit the government for funding to help develop and execute a social enterprise (see KLINK, 2015). These social enterprises are designed to provide employment and pre-employment training or other work-related developmental activities to releasees that may result in self-employment. Other work creation efforts include exploring ways to provide financial support to releasees, for example through interest-free loans, that can be used to purchase necessary equipment or certifications, or the building of a social network that can assist releasees in finding and maintaining employment. Across all of these creative ventures one thing always stands out: the fact that "one size does not fit all" when it comes to individuals' reintegration needs, and employment reintegration needs in particular. There is a genuine need for differential approaches to employment programming that together address or at least take into consideration the many different needs of the former prisoners seeking assistance in finding and securing employment.

Another aspect underpinning the need to individualize the approach to finding employment for former prisoners relates to the fact that the *released population is bifurcated by age*. An overview of those being released from prison in Canada quickly reveals that a larger portion of older releasees (over the age of 50) are likely to be paroled in comparison to other incarcerated persons (see Grant & Lefebvre, 1994). Young releasees have a good chance of entering the labour market and staying in it for a period of time, while the older releasees have a more difficult time acquiring employment or are already over the retirement age of most jobs. Further, the larger the gap in employment experience—a direct result of being in prison—the harder it is for any person to find employment.[1] Of course, among both the older and younger parolees, there are those who by reason of mental health issues or other disabilities will find themselves to be considered unemployable and seeking disability pension from local welfare services. Most of the programs in such sectors are geared towards the younger releasees, more likely to be employable, rather than towards the reintegration of the older or disabled releasees. For these latter offenders, research into what can be done to meet their needs must be encouraged—assistance in reintegration must be directed toward meeting a range of individual needs if desistance from crime is to be a genuine possibility for all releasees.

The latter systemic challenge, *developmental aspects of employment approaches*, arises from the recognized need for differential approaches when working with releasees searching for employment. In this context, it would be wise to consider the developmental aspects—the age, educational experience, and employment history—of each releasee in order to better understand how we can adequately assist releasees in becoming job ready. Beyond the aforementioned factors, developmentally there is also a need to distinguish releasees by length of time served, which can impact how much catch-up needs to be accomplished before the releasee is ready for labour-force re-entry. The catch-up may involve renewing certifications, understanding new technologies employed in their previous work environments and appreciating the new barriers facing them as a result of incarceration (see Holzer, Raphael, & Stoll, 2002). What is required is a thorough assessment of the individual, which includes their academic and vocational history, their degree of motivation, their employment history—including type of work while in prison—and their long- and short-term goals relative to a possible career. The notion of having a career path also helps create a link to desistance from crime by fostering hope for the future and an acknowledgement that despite the criminal record and the time spent in prison, life is not over. This type of assessment also serves to make community corrections workers more effective in their interactions with releasees and more desistance focused in their work. Moreover, possessing the knowledge that such assessments would provide about releasees can assist community corrections employees in uncovering any learning, developmental, or physical disabilities, and identifying transferable skills, vocational or academic interests, and suitable occupational options. If such an assessment could be conducted prior to sending releasees to pre-employment training where the instructors tend to stress resumé writing, interviewing skills, and suitable dress, individuals attending the class may be more motivated and optimistic. Under these circumstances, they would be aware of their interests and recognize that their service providers are trying to match their interests to the labour market. Unfortunately, more work needs to be done in this area, particularly with a focus on those identified with disabilities severe enough to warrant disability pensions. A second area of focus must be on older releasees who need to learn how to cope without work and could benefit from guidance to appropriate leisure activities similar to programs for those retired from the workforce.

This book is our effort to stimulate both academic and practitioner thinking about how to best apply our knowledge from research and practice to a desistance-focused approach of releasee supervision. In the pages that follow, we seek to show diverse ways that releasees can reconnect with society, acquire a stake in conformity, and reengage with the community through the social stabilizing effect of employment.

## OVERVIEW OF BOOK

The intention here is to provide a brief overview of the chapters. As demonstrated in this edited collection, the experiences of former prisoners during the re-entry process can be challenging, particularly where employment re-entry is concerned, given they lack many of the skills and experiences necessary to acquire gainful or, indeed, any employment. In recognition of these difficulties, researchers in sociology and the interdisciplinary field of criminology have focused on themes relevant to this process from within theoretical, legislative, and policy-related frameworks.

This edited collection is divided into four sections. In the first, the contributors explore the significance of employment in contemporary society; the stigma of a criminal record, incarceration, as well as mental illness; and the relationship between incarceration, reintegration, and gainful employment. In the second section, the contributions focus on criminal record management in Canada versus other Western countries; parolees' experiences of re-entry as linked to employment reintegration; and the role of work in the process of successful re-entry. The third section comprises four chapters on specific programs and case management practices designed to assist releasees' in their transition into free society as labour market participants. The contributors reveal the provisory successes of former prisoners in employment ventures, as well as the challenges they face and difficulties that arise when evaluating employment reintegration programs. In the fourth and final section, barriers to employment experienced by specific populations during employment re-entry are presented.

## Section 1: The Employment Re-Entry Enigma/Dilemma

We begin Section One with "Work after Prison: One Man's Transition" and invite the reader into the life of "James,"[2] a former prisoner, who served a life sentence and who has faced countless employment-reintegration-related hardships and successes since his release, one often leading to the other, as he continues to reintegrate into society. He describes a steady and repeated process of applying, being interviewed, being hired, training, working, losing his job, and recovering. This process can be daunting, and for those who are less successful it requires unremitting resilience. In this context, James's story shows how once someone becomes "institutionalized" by personnel in the system, the reversal process can be arduous and lonely, if the reversal is even possible. James's story reveals that, as in his case, former prisoners may return to the community feeling naturally fearful, but simultaneously excited and confident because they may possess a strong drive and particular skill sets. Yet, they may not be afforded the same opportunities or level of trust as other potential employees who have not incurred a criminal record or experienced incarceration, especially if they have served a life sentence. James Young also writes, in line with other contributors, that the job opportunities available to former prisoners tend to be precarious or require lengthy commutes, pay low wages, and leave the employee working long or poor work hours in less than ideal conditions. James also describes his experiences in training programs which offered little to no pay but which he needed to complete with a positive attitude if he was to be "successful." He highlights other barriers experienced during his employment re-entry, including the stigma of his criminal record and his "lifer" label, and lacking a social network to help him secure work (i.e., he acknowledges that much of the labour market is oriented around "who you know"). James's is a story of resiliency. Throughout his journey, he maintained a sense of optimism and determination to persevere.

In chapter 2, "Employment and Desistance from Crime," Kemi S. Anazodo, Christopher Chan, and Rose Ricciardelli unpack the relationship between employment re-entry and desistance for former prisoners on parole. The authors start the process—a process that continues throughout this edited collection—of establishing employment as central to desistance from crime and to overcoming the stigma of incarceration. The contributors explain how various labels or "marks" are applied to releasees that may inhibit their ability to acquire employment. In dedicating a portion of their chapter to their consideration of a series of established constraints that former prisoners encounter, the authors show how each can severely impact their likelihood of gaining employment. These constraints include: perceived personal shortcomings and anxieties, residential instability, limited social support, lack of access to education and training, loss of drivers' licence, release conditions/restrictions (e.g., mobility, visitations), having a criminal record, and limited job skills and/or qualifications. They, however, always return to the fact that employing former prisoners can be in society's best interests. It serves to reduce crime and, in effect, reduce costs for the government and taxpayers. Anazodo and her colleagues continue by emphasizing the benefit employment can have on reducing former prisoners' likelihood to recidivate, thereby increasing public safety. By providing releasees with resources, training, skills, and employment, the authors demonstrate that the attitudes that citizens have toward former prisoners can also be improved. After prison, releasees begin a new life phase, often with hopefulness, as they work to become labour market contributors, desist from crime, and reconstruct their identity away from that of an offender.

In the final chapter of Section One, "Employment and Criminal Offenders with Mental Illness," Krystle Martin extends the risk–need–responsivity (RNR) model to the reintegration of prisoners with mental illness. Recognizing that stigma is an often unavoidable element in reintegration for those returning to the community, it must be noted that former prisoners with mental illness face multifold stigmas during re-entry. As Martin—by means of extant literature—reveals, persons with mental illness comprise a notable proportion of the prison population and, thus, of the re-entry population. The obstacles encountered by releasees, such as poor education and employability, stigma, interrupted and limited social networks, and strict hiring policies and legislation are further aggravated by psychiatric symptoms. This compounding of factors, Martin suggests, necessitates more specialized clinical interventions for this population; specifically strategies based on individual strengths (as also explored in chapter 9), supported employment practices (see also chapter 8), and that manage former prisoners' employment expectations, attitudes, and openness concerning their pasts. Through the presentation of secondary research including interviews with offenders with mental illness, as well as with practitioners working with these offenders, the chapter provides support for a shift in thinking about the dually stigmatized group of releasees with mental disorders. Martin concludes her contribution by calling for more effective reintegration-employment practices, spearheaded by trained and experienced specialists who serve to educate potential employers about the realities of mental illness and its link to offending, as well as advocate on behalf of, and better manage the distinctive needs of, this population.

## Section II: Criminal Histories, Employment Prospects, and Moving Forward

Section Two begins with a contribution (chapter 4) from Samantha McAleese. In "Job Search, Suspended: Changes to Canada's Pardon Program and the Impact on Finding Employment," McAleese explains that after prison, releasees begin the often arduous process of reintegrating into the society from which they had been absent, whether for a few days, months, or years. This time away from family, friends, work, and free society can be overwhelming and possibly demoralizing for them as well as for those from whom they were absent (such as family and employers). While former prisoners are expected to actively re-engage with society, they face barriers doing so, the greatest of which perhaps is their criminal record. McAleese highlights how Canada and many other countries have enacted legislation to manage these records and, in effect, assist offenders in removing the associated stigma by removing various records from their file over time. These records include formal court conviction and sentencing records, as well as police records and any special conditional/restrictive records, which can all severely hinder a former prisoner's employment prospects. McAleese outlines the Canadian approach to these records: the pardon program, referring to the practice in Canada of recognizing continued desistance as a measure of long-term success, thereby sanctioning the sealing of a former offender's record. Some offenders are, however, not currently eligible to receive a pardon, namely sexual offenders, violent offenders, and chronic offenders. Furthermore, pardons, once granted, can be revoked. However, as a result of the *Safe Streets and Communities Act*, Canada most recently amended the model outlined in its *Criminal Records Act*. In consequence, the newest record suspension program, introduced in 2012, has raised a series of new complications that include further extending the wait period for record suspensions, and precluding select groups of former offenders (i.e., those convicted of chronic and sexual offending) from ever receiving a record suspension. McAleese provides a comparative assessment of the approaches used in other countries to outline other strategies to facilitate what Shadd Maruna (2011) termed "judicial rehabilitation." She further recognizes that a simple reflection of alternative penal policies is not sufficient to inform further amendments to Canada's criminal record statutes and that continued research is needed. Nevertheless, she suggests that Australia, England, and Spain's versions of an automatic "spent" process for select criminal records (i.e., the complete clearance of the punishment and criminalization process) may be a model warranting closer examination in Canada and elsewhere.

This section ends with Rose Ricciardelli and Taylor Mooney, in chapter 5, "Vulnerabilities and Barriers in Post-Release Employment Reintegration as Indicated by Parolees," discussing the benefits, as well as protective factors, experienced by releasees that are attributable to employment. These include self-esteem, financial stability, connectedness, involvement with or time spent in pro-social endeavours, and in positively contributing to society. Turning to the work of Goffman (1963), the contributors explore the contradictory image of the former prisoner who is often characterized as a "less desirable kind" (p. 3) and who must continually bear the stigma attached to this label which too often interferes with and threatens the influence of the above listed employment-related positives. Agamben's (1995) "homo sacer" is also applied to expand on the stigma and isolation felt by many prisoners during reintegration. Ricciardelli and Mooney then analyze the results of interviews with a sample of paroled men and women to include their experiences in a discussion of the education- and work-specific challenges releasees encounter (e.g., low-paying, low-skilled, seasonal or part-time, and precarious employment, as well as limited work history and hiring policies). Attention is specifically drawn to the ways respondents felt their employment search was affected by the stigma of incarceration or a criminal record; too often respondents described being told directly that their criminal past prevented their hiring. This barrier was compounded by their lack of work experience and pre-employment readiness (i.e., they did not know how to compile a resumé, conduct themselves in an interview, or acknowledge the gap in their employment history), and their parole and residency conditions. In light of these findings, the authors call attention to several target areas for individualized correctional and reintegration programming, such as post-secondary courses, foundational technology-oriented courses, and various vocational/pre-employment preparedness courses.

## Section III: Employment Reintegration Programming: Supportive Strategies and Related Outcomes

Owing to the numerous challenges experienced by many releasees as they re-enter free society, Section Three is composed of four chapters, where each is oriented toward work programs or case management practices developed to assist former prisoners in surmounting this barrier to reintegration. The first chapter, "Is Criminal History at the Time of Employment Predictive of Job Performance? A Comparison of Disciplinary Actions and Terminations in a Sample of Production Workers," written by Mark G. Harmon, Laura J. Hickman, Alexandra M. Arneson, and Ashley M. Hansen, centres on much needed policy amendments (such as the "Ban the Box" movement in the

United States that seeks to remove criminal record screening from hiring practices), employment programs, and employment. Harmon and colleagues continue by examining Dave's Killer Bread, Inc. (DKB), located in Oregon, USA; a company with a long-standing commitment to hiring individuals with a criminal history. The DKB philosophy is that by exhibiting an openness to hiring those with a criminal past they can attract individuals who may have had criminal justice contact, but who have experienced a turning point in their life as Laub and Sampson (1993) have labelled it, and play a role in directing them away from a criminal trajectory. Drawing from a sample of 425 male and female employees who worked in operational positions at DKB between 2012 and 2015, the authors address whether individuals with a criminal record (i.e., felony conviction) incurred prior to their employment at DKB exhibited differential work-related performance outcomes. Said another way, they studied if former offenders were more likely to receive disciplinary action and employment termination than non-former offender employees at DKB. They found that individuals with a previous felony conviction neither incurred significantly more disciplinary action than employees without a criminal history, nor were they terminated at a significantly higher rate. The authors underscored that a small majority of their sample, both those with a felony record and without, sustained their employment at the company at least until the end of the study. In discussing potential explanations for their findings, Harmon and colleagues make a valuable contribution to the empirical research on employment outcomes for former prisoners, shining a light on the lack of statistical differences that exist between persons released from prison and individuals without such a past experience. They further show that companies such as DKB provide a promising "second chance" opportunity for the reintegrating population, and could easily be adopted by other organizations that are open to pursuing similar recruitment and hiring protocols.

Christine Hough's chapter, "Transforming Rehabilitation: A Critical Evaluation of Barriers Encountered by an Offender Rehabilitation Program for South Asian/Muslim Offenders within the New Probation Service Model," addresses the United Kingdom's recent amendments to its criminal justice policies under the title of Transforming Rehabilitation, where voluntary agencies (also referred to as third-sector organizations) are receiving reduced government support for their organizations and associated services. Hough focuses her chapter on South Asian/Muslim individuals involved in the criminal justice system in North West England, highlighting their need areas, including those based on their specific cultural traditions and those arising from obstacles that the population disproportionately faces. Examples of the latter include being stereotyped as drug dealers or members of extremist/

terrorist groups in prison and damaging their relationships with family and close friends (due to perceptions of having dishonoured the family or community more generally). She explores the changes felt by ReachingOut, a mentoring program offered by the agency Arooj, to work exclusively with justice-involved South Asian/Muslim individuals, the most pronounced of which is the loss of program referrals, despite the growing numbers of South Asian/Muslim individuals in the system, because of the new Transforming Rehabilitation (TR) agenda, corporate ownership of probation services, and system of payment by results (PbR). Anecdotally, Hough shares how these services benefited South Asian/Muslim prisoners and their families, both during their incarceration and during subsequent community integration by assisting them in their job search, application, preparation, and attainment. Service users are also presented with resources to aid them in beginning their own business ventures or in volunteering with Arooj. Yet, Hough reveals how small, yet potentially promising, programs are gradually being "downsized" and possibly phased out, unfortunately precluding any evaluation to assess their influence on former offenders'/prisoners' rehabilitation and reintegration. She advises governments to speak to local representatives before revising policy and introducing new offender management strategies, based on a neo-liberal, business framework that could threaten the successful reintegration and future employment/societal contributions of these individuals as she ponders if "we" truly care about achieving rehabilitation, or if it was a political rhetoric that is now being replaced by a system marketing one product, but delivering another.

Turning to youth programming in chapter 8, "Promoting Employment Opportunities through Mentorship for Gang-Involved Youth Reintegrating into the Community," Adrienne Peters details a justice-based community program offered to gang-involved youth in British Columbia, Canada. Premised on the mentoring framework of offender rehabilitation, the Career Path program model is a variation of a mentor–mentee relationship, designed to assess and foster individual youth's employability and work needs. In this context, recognizing the strong ties that develop between youth involved with criminal organizations (gangs), Peters highlights how Career Path aims to replace the negative values and activities of young people with pro-social ones, through connections with their employer and their other employees. Detailing how employers and colleagues act as role models for the young person, she reveals how youth can learn from such positive mentorship opportunities as they are given opportunities to become increasingly autonomous. Beyond earning wages in the program, youth are shown that they are valued employees and that program coordinators and staff are committed to them, despite any minor or major setbacks they encounter, such as job loss, poor temperament, or lack of interest. The focus is offering opportunities to youth participants in Career Path to take on more responsibilities in the future, as an incentive for their hard work and a reward for dedication. Workplace advancement is central to many employees' feeling valued and committed to the organization, thus employers benefit from offering such opportunities to all their employees, following steadfast work and perseverance, irrespective of the youth's past. Peters then concludes the chapter with a program template for those interested in helping similarly profiled youth during employment-based rehabilitation and reintegration activities.

This section ends with Ashley Brown's contribution, "Barriers to Community Reintegration: The Benefits of Client-Centred Case Management and Pre-Employment Skills Training," where she speaks to her experiences as a case manager of a client-centred program that combines risk–need–responsivity (RNR) and the Good Lives Model (GLM) in Toronto, Ontario. As a provider of services to former prisoners, some voluntarily availing themselves of the program's services and others not, Brown underscores the importance of developing relationships for successful case management practices. Detailing five stages in her case management process, she advocates for compassionate responses to participants' personal values and goals, and a need to modify case management strategies as relationships develop and the releasee progresses. Releasees often first have needs tied to basic community stabilization (e.g., shelter, food, and safety) that must be met before they can direct attention to employment needs. Brown speaks to the value of pre-employment training for individuals that includes interview preparation, networking, resumé writing, and work-related problem solving, and how employment—be it continued vocational training or an actual job—contributes to sustaining basic community stabilization needs. Brown argues that the success of any employment program lies largely in case management practices that support releasees' reintegration needs as determined by their individual strengths, resources, and desires, combined with established evidence-based rehabilitation models.

## Section IV: The Employment Reintegration of Unique Populations

The final section begins with a contribution from Dale Spencer, "'Between a Rock and Hard Place': How Being a 'Convict' Hinders Finding Work in the Neo-Liberal, Late-Capitalist Economy," Spencer addresses the deleterious impact present post-industrial, capitalist, neo-liberal societies can have on reintegrating former prisoners who are also homeless—a too common secondary obstacle during re-entry. Homeless persons too are dually stigmatized, first by their incarceration and then by their homelessness. Spencer applies a "Homo Economicus" lens to explore how formerly incarcerated, homeless men are excluded from labour force participation and thus occupy an inferior position in such power structures. Drawing from 70 semi-structured interviews with homeless men, aged 16 to 65 living in Chicago and Winnipeg, Spencer seeks to understand the events in these men's lives that contributed to their experiences and current unemployment. Persistent emergent themes, Spencer reveals, include a lack of education/training, the availability of only low-skilled, longer-term jobs, and in some cases, job offers that were rescinded when a participant's criminal history was revealed. For this reason, irrespective of one's inclination to desist and avoid further incarceration, a temporary placement may not be a reasonable option when there are, as Spencer notes, continuous "pulls" toward and opportunities for criminal activities. An additional barrier on the path to employment for these men, beyond the lack of a permanent address or suitable interview attire, was the challenge of shelter life for these men who were expected to leave early in the morning, transport all of their belongings, and in consequence, exacerbate an already dishevelled image. Spencer attests that many of the homeless men he interviewed felt they did not have a voice, and there is thus a very real need to work toward strengthening their self-worth.

An issue that should not be overlooked is the experiences of individuals who have been wrongfully convicted. In Kimberley Clow's contribution, "Does the 'Wrongful' Part of Wrongful Conviction Make a Difference in the Job Market?," she draws attention to existing initiatives that address wrongful conviction, such as Innocence Projects, while acknowledging that the precise number of individuals affected by such miscarriages of justice is virtually impossible to enumerate. In spite of convictions having been reached erroneously, Clow contends that these individuals encounter the same stigma that is felt by "true offenders" during re-entry. To test her hypothesis as it relates to employment, she assessed potential employers' response to letters of employment interest from individuals with varying criminal histories. Mailed letters represented one of four conditions: no suggestion of a criminal record, criminal record disclosure, falsely obtained criminal record, and out of work for some time without a reason provided. The responses from employers revealed that applicants were discriminated against most often based on their past, whether they had been truthfully or wrongfully convicted. That is, employees without a record received the greatest email response rate (even in the second control case of those who had been unemployed for a lengthy period of time) and both the wrongly convicted and the rightly convicted had lower response rates that were not statistically different from one another. Clow, ending this section, advocates for future research in the area and for the expansion of reintegration programming and support services for wrongly convicted persons as they navigate employment and post-exoneration success.

Our edited collection concludes by drawing on prominent classic and contemporary theoretical perspectives to demarcate the nexus between employment and (non-)offending. We also present the results from leading empirical studies corroborating these relationships and highlighting the role employment plays in the lives of individuals before, during and after incarceration; particularly as they strive to reconnect with family and their communities and desist from crime during re-entry. We assert, based on the presented research, that employers, organizations, and society can likewise benefit from the employment of former prisoners; therefore, pre-employment and supported employment programs and policies are essential investments that precede more successful offender reintegration.

Finally, we would like to acknowledge the fact that without the cooperation and collaboration of all involved in this project this book would not have materialized.

## NOTES

1  Uggen (2000) indicates that employment preparation/reintegration programs are more effective for older releasees; however, the focus here is not on persons near or in their retirement years.
2  James is a pseudonym being used to protect the contributor's identity.

## REFERENCES

Agamben, G. (1995). *Homo sacer: Sovereignty and bare life.* (D. Heller-Roazen, Trans.). Stanford, CT: Stanford University Press.

Andrews, D. A., & Bonta, J. (2010). *The psychology of criminal conduct.* Cincinnati, OH: Anderson.

Andrews, D. A., Bonta, J., & Hoge, R. D. (1990). Classification for effective rehabilitation: Rediscovering psychology. *Criminal Justice and Behavior, 17,* 19–52.

Dauvergne, M. (2012). *Adult correctional statistics in Canada 2010/2011.* Ottawa, ON: Statistics Canada.

Goffman, E. (1963). *Stigma: Notes on the management of spoiled identity.* Englewood Cliffs, NJ: Prentice-Hall.

Graffam, J., Shinkfield, A. J., & Hardcastle, L. (2008). The perceived employability of ex-prisoners and offenders. *International Journal of Offender Therapy and Comparative Criminology 52*(6): 673–685.

Grant, B. A., & Lefebvre, L. (1994, May). Older offenders in the Correctional Service of Canada. *Forum on Corrections Research, 6*(2), 10–13.

Hannah-Moffat, K. (2012). Risk and punishment. In J. Simon & R. Sparks (Eds.), *Handbook on punishment and society* (pp. 129–151). Thousand Oaks, CA: Sage Publications.

Harding, D. (2003). Jean Valjean's dilemma: The management of ex-convict identity in the search for employment. *Deviant Behavior 24*(6): 571–595.

Holzer, H. J., Raphael, S., & Stoll, M. A. (2002). *Will employers hire ex-offenders? Employer preferences, background checks, and their determinants.* Madison, WI: Institute for Research on Poverty, University of Wisconsin.

KLINK. (2015). *Social value.* Retrieved from http://drinkklink.com/social-value .html

Laub, J. H., & Sampson, R. J. (1993). Turning points in the life-course: Why change matters to the study of crime. *Criminology 31*(3), 301–325.

Laub, J. H., & Sampson, R. J. (2001). Understanding desistance from crime. *Crime & Justice, 28*, 1–69.

Maruna, S. (2001). *Making good: How ex-convicts reform and rebuild their lives.* Washington, DC: American Psychological Association.

Maruna, S. (2011). Reentry as a rite of passage. *Punishment & Society, 13*(1), 3–28.

Maruna, S., & LeBel, T. P. (2010). The desistance paradigm in correctional practice: From programs to lives. In F. McNeill, P. Raynor, & C. Trotter (Eds.), *Offender supervision: New directions in theory, research and practice* (pp. 65–89). Cullompton, UK: Willan Publishing.

Mears, Daniel P., & Joshua C. Cochran (2014). *Prisoner reentry in the era of mass incarceration.* Thousand Oaks, CA: Sage Publications

Moffitt, T. E. (1993). Adolescence-limited and life-course-persistent antisocial behavior: A developmental taxonomy. *Psychological Review, 100*, 674–701.

Nolan, A., Wilton, G., Cousineau, C., & Stewart, L. (2014). *Outcomes for offender employment programs: Assessing CORCAN participation* (Research Report No. R-283). Ottawa, ON: Correctional Service Canada.

Petersilia, J. (2007). Employ behavioural contracting for "earned discharge" parole. *Criminology & Public Policy, 6*(4), 807–814.

Sampson, R. J., & Laub, J. H. (1992). Crime and deviance in the life course. *Annual Review of Sociology 18*, 63–84.

Sampson, R. J., & Laub, J. H. (1993). *Crime in the making: Pathways and turning points through life.* Cambridge, MA: Harvard University Press.

Sampson, R. J., & Laub, J. H. (1997). A life-course theory of cumulative disadvantage and the stability of delinquency. *Advances in Criminological Theory, 7*, 133–161.

Uggen, C. (2000). Work as a turning point in the life course of criminals: A duration model of age, employment, and recidivism. *American Sociological Review, 65*(4), 529–546.

Visher, C. A., Winterfield, L., & Coggeshall, M. B. (2005). Ex-offender employment programs and recidivism: A meta-analysis. *Journal of Experimental Criminology 1*(3): 295–315.

Visher, C. A., Debus-Sherrill, S., & Yahner, J. (2008). *Employment after prison: A longitudinal study of releasees in three states. Research Brief.* Washington, DC: Urban Institute, Justice Policy Center.

Weaver, A., & B. Weaver (2013). Autobiography, empirical research and critical theory in desistance: A view from the inside out. *Probation Journal 60*(2): 259–277.

# Section I

The Employment Re-Entry Enigma/Dilemma

# CHAPTER 1

# Work after Prison
## One Man's Transition

James Young [pseud.]

I am a lifer. I went to prison as a teenager, was tried as an adult, and spent more than 20 years in prison. Despite my youth, my skills and experience in computers, bookkeeping, and administration made me a valuable commodity to the prison administration. The prison system has a ladder of employment mirroring that of the community. There are many jobs available that require little skill to master or perform. Some of these jobs require working the whole day, while some require as little as 30 minutes. The jobs that require the most skill often have the longest hours, and it can be hard to find an educated prisoner willing to work harder than the rest because everyone is paid the same regardless of the effort required. Therefore, positions that require a greater level of skill entice workers by offering perks (recognizing the feeble pay) that take the form of time off, food, clothing, and ability to recognize and take advantage of grey areas within the rules.

In my area of expertise, computers, the personal restrictions are many. Since 2001, no prisoner has been allowed to buy a computer or bring one into the institution, and prior to this we were only allowed to buy a computer that would run Windows 98. Further, we have never been allowed access to the Internet. So, if I had entered the job market after 2010, knowing only how to use Windows 98, I could not have considered myself competitively up-to-date on recent technologies. The job opportunities that I availed myself of while incarcerated allowed me to use Correction Service Canada (CSC) computers with newer operating systems and software and to remain current with advances in the community. This is where the aforementioned "grey area" comes into play, as employers would allow me access to software and even purchase software that I wanted to use, despite policies restricting such access for prisoners.

I, fortunately, was one of the most sought after employees in my prison. I could basically pick and choose from any job and felt confident that I would be hired if I applied. During my incarceration, I spent a year and a half managing the million-dollar food budget for the entire penal population; two years as one of the top data-entry technicians where I was able to quadruple my salary through incentives; and more than five years tutoring adults earning high-school diplomas. I also spent a year as the elected committee chairperson where my responsibilities included writing proposals, managing money, and advocating and negotiating with the administration on behalf of the population for various events and activities. I reached the point that five hundred criminals were willing to trust *me* to listen to their most personal problems, spend their money wisely, and negotiate with the Warden on their behalf. Thus I felt certain that, by any objective standard, I possessed the necessary skills to find employment in the community. I felt a strong sense of pride in my accomplishments, I believed in my skills and abilities, and I was motivated. I have always had a burning desire to work, which was particularly strong when imagining the possibility of working in the community, where I could begin to establish my life post-incarceration. Having gone to prison as a teenager, my release placed me in the situation of looking for work for the very first time.

Prior to my release from custody, I proactively created three separate resumés: one detailing my computer installation and repair experience, another explaining my work with bookkeeping, and a third for administrative positions. I crafted cover letters, and constructed a database of several hundred different introductions, bodies, and closings that could be mixed and matched for composing the "perfect" cover letter, specific to the job for which I would apply. This way I felt I could readily compose a cover letter for any employer. I learned about all the "best" websites for job hunting, the most effective strategies for entering information on these sites and when filling out job applications, and I created a spreadsheet I could use to track potential employer information, as well as the status of my job application and the progress of my candidacy.

In almost every possible way, I felt I was ready for life in the community and convinced that success would rapidly be mine. I believed that during my job interviews, employers would see my skill set in the same way that every employer in the prisons had, and I thought I surely would quickly be hired.

In the first six months that I spent living at a halfway house I submitted over 500 resumés. I spent time at employment resource centres, registered on every local job-hunt website that I could find, subscribed to every possible employment opportunity notification, and even paid to have my resumés professionally revised. I felt that I had done everything possible a person could do to acquire some form of employment. Despite all of these efforts, I think I was invited to a total of three job interviews. The frustration left me screaming into a black hole with only silence as my answer.

I watched as guys with different skills, mainly in the trades, were hired into different positions. Oftentimes, these former prisoners used personal contacts to obtain these jobs, which unfortunately was not an option for me. I had chosen to move to a city I had never lived in before, and had no family or friends nearby to help me.

I was baffled and confused. The difference between my expectations and reality was immense and overwhelming. Even by chance, I had expected that I would have been called for a few interviews, but instead, every avenue I approached met me with that same deafening silence. In the absence of any, let alone meaningful, feedback, I was not able to adapt my application package and, as a result, I didn't know what I should modify and what I could leave the same. I talked to everybody that I could—anyone that would listen or could help—and after talking to me and reading my resumé, they shrugged and said, "I don't get it either."

## THE COFFEE PROGRAM

As my job hunt continued, with little success, I gradually expanded the fields in which I was job-searching. I had been hearing about people from the halfway houses who were participating in a program that allowed them to work for three weeks in a coffee manufacturing plant. Although in the early stages of the program they were agreeing to work for free, they were gaining valuable experience, a job reference, and in some cases, the plant would hire individuals whose work they liked. The idea of working for free was a sticking point for me. I then learned that the program had connected with a local employment agency and, regardless of whether you were hired at the end of the three weeks or not, you would likely still be paid. This seemed like a reasonable outcome to me and would provide me with net earnings of about a $1000. So I signed up.

The three-week work program also included an extra week of unpaid preparation, where participants would discuss job skills, work expectations, and how to overcome any likely obstacles that presented themselves. At the end of this first week, the coordinator facilitated the three-week placement.

I was already familiar with many of the topics that were covered during the first week, but still felt that a review could always help. Many of the other participants in my group were learning much about employment processes, so recognizing my knowledge base, I too helped when I could and tried to focus on the benefits of the three weeks of paid work that were impending.

On the last day of the training portion, the coordinator explained that he would now contact the coffee company and provide them with information about each of the participants, including me, to begin the hiring process. I felt an initial spike of fear. I then confirmed with the coordinator that, up until this point, the company had not been given any information about the participants. I asked if, in my case, as a lifer, that would be a problem. The coordinator felt certain it would *not* be a problem, as other lifers had been placed, and even hired through this program. I finished filling out my paperwork while he spoke to the employer on the phone. At one point, I could hear his raised voice in the office although I could not make out the words. It didn't matter. I knew that it was trouble. When he came out of his workspace he quickly spoke to the other participants and sent them on their way. Then he pulled me into his office. He began by apologizing and then explained that the company did not want someone with my record working at their plant, even for three weeks.

|  |  | |  |

An important point in this account is that some of the coffee that this plant was processing was being sold by the organization hosting the program. It was essentially an attempt to close the circle. In other words, the organization sold the coffee, paid a coordinator, who trained employees, who then manufactured the coffee. The whole point of the plant's primary objective in hiring people with records was to generate money to pay for more people with records to obtain jobs. The plant had committed to this plan and was excited about participating, at least, I felt, until I had come along; although I later learned I wasn't the first or the last who has been refused participation.

I counted the week in pre-employment training as a loss and, after pushing away my disappointment, returned to my search for work. During this period of time I had been pursuing my education at a local college where I focused on improving and certifying my computer skills. After I proudly finished the A+ Certification I added it to my resumé and decided to try some door-to-door job hunting instead of exclusive Internet job hunting. As always, I did my research and identified around 40 computer stores in the area in which I lived.

I spent a few days canvassing the stores with no results. I doubt I have to explain how frustrating it is to walk into a store, hear that they need someone, and never hear from them again. It was becoming harder and harder to reconcile my belief in my own abilities with the complete lack of results that I was experiencing.

## THE COMPUTER STORE

Finally the door-to-door job hunt paid off (months later, of course), although not in the way or for the reasons I had expected. Instead of impressing the employer with my computer skills, it was the interest section at the bottom of my resumé that had caught his attention. The experiences listed centred on my volunteer work at a church where I had been participating in an early-morning breakfast program for people who were homeless. The owner of the store had reviewed my resumé, dismissed my hard-earned (and expensive) A+ Certification with an "Everybody has that now, it doesn't mean anything," and then noticed the volunteering. After asking a few questions he said that he really liked someone who volunteered and offered to hire me two days a week for $7/hour (minimum wage at the time was $10.25), with a commitment to increase this once I completed the training. I accepted the offer immediately and began working.

I remained in this job for six months; even as I found other work, I was able to make time to work at the computer store. To this day, I remain grateful for the opportunity I was given to practise my skills in a real work environment and for the many things I learned from the owner. During these six months, I eventually reached $8/hour.

## THE SKATING RINK

In the fall, the coordinator of the coffee program approached me with another job opportunity. I think he was feeling a bit guilty about the outcome of my last experience and wanted to do better. There was a local skating rink that hired Rink Guards during the winter season. Although it was seasonal work, there was a strong likelihood that this opportunity would continue during the summer months through other positions within the organization of which the skating rink was just a small part. Although this was not the type of work that I wanted to do, had envisioned myself doing, or that used my skills—I hadn't been on skates in at least 15 years and the job required two–three hours of skating a day—I felt that I could do the job and, quite honestly, I did not have any other options.

The coffee program coordinator scheduled an interview for me and several other former prisoners. I was the only one who attended the meeting with the Rink Manager. He quickly looked at my resumé, and then asked how long I had been in prison. I told him. He followed up with, "For what?" I gave him a non-specific summary, but was honest about the type of conviction I had, given I was lifer, and thus had been convicted of murder. He was fine with that and asked me not to talk to the other employees about it because they were young and wouldn't understand. I followed his advice; however, it turned out to be mistaken and when the position later collapsed, the only part I was able to salvage was a couple of friendships.

The duties of the job were simple: sharpen skates, rent out skates and accept payment, skate on the ice and enforce the rules, and clean. Easy. It took a little time to learn some of the procedures, but sharpening skates turned out to be rather simple once I learned how. The cash register was programmed in an unusual fashion, which occasionally led to erroneous entries, but the task was still readily learnable. The skating itself was the hardest part, but also quickly became a favourite part of my day, as I renewed my old skills and practised new ones. Cold days, warm days, freezing days all passed by and I learned my job and worked as hard as I could.

I also don't mind hard work; I never have. But I do prefer to work smarter rather than hard; nonetheless, hard work is sometimes the only way to get a job done. I quickly realized that I liked the job and the people, and that I wanted to prove my worth during the winter period, as well as earn a summer spot for myself. If there was a dirty job, I was there. If something needed to be lifted and carried, I was there. If something was sitting in a corner or in our way, I moved it. Soon after I started, I made a joke of my work habits to let them know what I was like, stating "Somebody is my middle name"—a play on the phrase "Don't worry about it, somebody will do it," as I was that "somebody" and I would get the job done. I never realized how much it had caught on, and how much the others noticed I was doing until one day after a late night I came in and said, "I'm not doing much today, I'm tired and taking a break. Unless it's a big deal, let's leave it until tomorrow." One of my co-workers turned to me in shock and said "But, you're Somebody. You're the guy who does stuff." "Not today," I replied, simultaneously pleased that my efforts had been noticed.

As the season progressed, Christmas and New Year's Eve loomed as big events. The number of guests climbed higher and higher during those days and many of us employees worked longer or extra shifts. In addition to the Rink Manager, there were three supervisors, who alternated so that there was one working per shift. As the new guy, I was working on several different shifts, sometimes overlapping with other shifts, and during one of these shifts, I was approached by one of the supervisors to work New Year's

Eve. This would normally have been a day off for me. They needed me for a 16-hour shift in order for the rink to remain fully staffed and open until after midnight. Of course I agreed to work, and I worked myself into the ground to make sure everything moved smoothly that evening.

The following week the Rink Manager found a quiet moment and pulled me aside. He told me that my work had not gone unnoticed; in fact, he specifically said that of the dozen or so people working there, in his mind I was one of the top employees. This was after only slightly more than two and a half months of my employment at the rink. He then asked if I was interested in continuing with the organization in the summer and, amused by the enthusiasm of my reply, told me he would make it happen.

Two weeks later, those words were ashes in my ears. While at the computer store working at my other part-time job, which I had scaled back to one day a week, I received a phone call from the coordinator of the coffee program. He told me that someone had learned more specific details of my offence, and had bypassed the Rink Manager and approached the Board of Directors of the organization. Although they knew that the Rink Manager occasionally hired individuals with criminal records, the fact that I am a lifer was a surprise to them. They immediately contacted the Rink Manager and the coffee program coordinator and told them that I must be terminated immediately. I could not even return to work.

Without warning, thought, or reason, except my past—an event from 20 or so years prior—I lost the job I had worked so hard to secure and maintain. Once again, the interpretation of my teenage actions overshadowed a phenomenal work record and strong set of job skills. I went from "one of the best" to *persona non grata* overnight, and the only thing that had changed was what my employers knew.

At first, I didn't know what had happened, or the details of why I had been fired. Then, surprisingly, some of my co-workers started texting me. I thought that having learned about my past I would be rejected not just by my employer, but by everyone I associated with. Instead, these co-workers reached out to me, not simply by providing gossipy information, but on a personal level to invite me into their lives outside of work.

From them I learned that the supervisor, who had asked me to work the extra shift, had looked me up on the Internet. It turned out to be a known, an unkept "secret," that people hired through this agency had criminal records. Everybody knew, and as long I was doing my job they didn't care about the details. This supervisor felt differently and raced to tell the Board of Directors what he had learned. Ironically, I also learned that, a few weeks after I was fired, the CEO called the rink office excitedly claiming that he had seen me walk into the skating rink (clearly, I was not to return and clearly not welcome there). It wasn't me. He didn't even know what I looked like.

## THE EIGHT-HOUR JOB

After getting fired from the skating rink job, I spent a few weeks moping around, trying to get over another loss that had nothing to do with my abilities as an employee. Although the halfway house where I was staying did not allow residents to use computers, owing to my school work I was able to spend the majority of my days (from about 8 a.m. to 10 p.m.) at school, using the school's computers as I desired. Indeed, I had been looking forward, for a long time, to spending some free time playing some of the new games that were unavailable in prison. I had just purchased a copy of *Fallout: New Vegas*, a game I was excited to try. Since the school didn't care how we used the computers, each morning I went to school, installed the game and spent the whole day exploring the wasteland. This occupied me for about three weeks while I was moping.

Indeed, I recognized that when I was in prison I really developed my skills in time-wasting. I watched the same movie 20 times and read the same books over and over. There are novels and even entire series of books that I have read more than ten times just because there was nothing else available. Over the years, these behaviours develop into habits and thinking patterns. For example, when I was first released from prison I bought a number of DVDs, happy that I could own something important to me that I could use over and over again. This is an attitude learned from living in scarcity. But in the community there is no such scarcity. I can borrow a lifetime's worth of books or DVDs; I can rent ten new movies every day; there is downloading, streaming, Netflix ... a world of opportunities awaits.

But all the programs inside and all the "help" that a prisoner is given never touch on these sorts of realities. CSC is quick to label anyone who has spent more than a few years inside as institutionalized. This can take many forms, but the help they offer is very specific and does not deal with the types of issues I experienced. That means that each of us, sometimes with the support of those who have gone before, has to recognize our own coping patterns, fight to break them, and purpose to be the new person we want to be in the community—all on our own.

I knew that playing computer games wasn't going to move me forward; I knew it wasn't going to help me land a job. Still, the pain and frustration of getting fired was debilitating and it was hard to move on. Ironically, the very supports that are in place for people being released can work against us, instead of for us. As a lifer, basically as long as I do not break the law, I can live (rent free) for years in the community at a halfway house. They provide food and a small living allowance and anytime things become too difficult, the temptation to huddle in a corner can be hard to resist. Ironically, as a lifer I have it better than most parolees. At least I have a safety net. The question is then, what need do I have for a job if all my necessities are paid for?

From a survival standpoint, there is none. I haven't allowed myself to want more than what was right in front of me for decades; I haven't had a "want" for more than 20 years. A job is not just a chance to purchase some of the luxuries general community members take for granted. Luxuries like tape, scissors, shoes that fit, movies, books, DVDs, digital watches, or post-secondary education. I'm lost trying to even describe greater luxuries than those because those are the things I've dreamed of for years. A job is a chance to break out of a cycle I know is holding me back. To live a life that is about more than just getting through the next month or the next year. So, in my mind, the need for a job is not about survival, it's not about meeting needs or wants. It's about who I am and who I want to be tomorrow.

|||| 

As I sat, playing games, all these thoughts percolated in the back of my mind, but I knew that pushing myself through these feelings was more harmful in the long run than simply allowing them to pass. I waited for the intensity of my feelings to subside and, eventually, I pulled myself together and started looking for work anew.

After another month passed, I was contacted by a company that was located outside of my permitted travel area (as a parolee, I have restrictions on where I can travel without a special travel permit). I made sure I read the directions carefully to ensure I could get to the facility and be there while still abiding by all of the rules that govern and dictate how I live.

Travel time would be about an hour and forty-five minutes each way, with a very tight morning commute; I would have to catch the earliest subway train. It would be tough, but doable. Thus, I went to the job interview and, after a quick test of my skills, the interviewer told me that they were hiring for a warehouse position. Not the best news, but at least it was with a computer company. The interviewer also explained that with my skills there was the possibility for me to easily advance in a few months to other positions within the company; positions with less physical work, higher wages, and the opportunity to use my computer skills. Over the course of the interview we even briefly touched on my criminal record, but she explained it would not be a problem. Everything sounded great.

I quit my part-time job with the computer store, spoke with my parole officer and began to organize the paperwork for my travel permit. I also spent a week going to bed early to prepare for my first day of work. When that day came, I arrived and attended the orientation. I understand that some people may not read the fine print when signing on to a new position, but, given my experiences, I read every word, every detail, then I researched and asked questions. The job contract read, basically, that the employer may occasionally change the work scheduling for operational reasons. I made an error and misunderstood what this could mean. I thought that this meant the employer could modify my work timetable, so that some weeks, I would work at an earlier or later time. This was not a big deal as far as I was concerned. On my first day following the orientation, there was a big sign posted indicating that all shifts from Monday to Thursday would start 30 minutes earlier and last an hour longer, while Friday would stay the same, and that this would be in effect for the next four months.

I calculated the implications: four days a week working nine-hour days with an eight-hour work day on Friday equalled a 44-hour work week—the maximum hours per week legally allowed without the employer needing to pay me overtime. Including the three and a half hours of travel time daily, these would be long work days on which I could no longer take the subway in the morning given the earlier start time. Thus, it would take at least two hours to get to work each morning and 15 hours of my day would be devoted to work.

Literally, with my other parole responsibilities, it would now be impossible for me to keep the job. Regular employees could struggle for the month, move closer, or buy a car. They didn't have a curfew, the mandatory meetings required to meet parole conditions, or a parole officer to check in with regularly. But I did. So I had to quit after my first day. I sent the employer an email explaining that I would not be able to work there after all with those hours.

I recognize that the free rent and living allowance are pretty important; this was one situation in particular where the halfway house was a huge advantage. Without it, I would be on the street. The biggest thing I'm afraid of is how the halfway house and my parole officer are going to react to my inability to find employment. But, surprisingly, they don't seem worried at all, so I've put that concern away for now. Given I wasn't yet attached to this job, it was easier to lose and I'm stronger after having just been fired from the skating rink.

So after 15 months in the community I still don't have a job. My new plan is the same as the old one, but with more discipline. I get up at seven, spend the morning at an employment agency, return to the halfway house at lunch, and then go to school until supper. I might not be working, but I try to replicate a working schedule. Evenings are for exercising and relaxing.

I've applied at Tim Horton's, Dollarama, Chapters, grocery stores, call centres, sales and retail jobs, and warehouse jobs. I've walked into 50 computer stores to drop off resumés.

It's just figuring out what is next and not giving up. I'm optimistic that things will improve. They have to, don't they?

CHAPTER 2

# Employment and Desistance from Crime

Kemi S. Anazodo, Christopher Chan, and Rose Ricciardelli

G ainful employment, in essence, provides the foundational "building block" that former prisoners require to transition successfully into society post-release (Visher, Winterfield, & Coggeshall, 2005). Employment, beyond a means to sustain a lifestyle in free society, is a central source of identity (Luyckx, Schwartz, Goossens, & Pollock, 2008; Uggen, 2000). It can be seen as a positive way for individuals to contribute to society and develop a sense of purpose and meaning in the world. Stable employment, in particular, enables individuals to provide for themselves and for their families post-release and, as such, has been identified as an important factor of successful reintegration (Petersilia, 2007). Thus, it is important that justice systems and social structures be supportive of individual endeavours to secure employment and desist from crime since most people who were formerly imprisoned eventually return to the community (Andress, Wildes, Rechtine, & Moritsugu, 2004; Travis, 2005; Visher & Travis, 2003).

Individuals face several constraints as they transition from a correctional institution to society, such as overcoming depression, anxiety, or any negative self-perceptions that have been internalized (Gausel & Thørrisen, 2014). Former prisoners also face specific constraints that will vary across social and cultural contexts. These constraints may include a lack of access to housing, a lack of access to public assistance (e.g., disability, welfare), an inability to vote, difficulty obtaining student loans, and revocation of a driver's licence (Hoskins, 2014; Luther, Reichert, Holloway, Roth, & Aalsma, 2011). Reflecting on the numerous challenges and barriers that former prisoners face, we explore the relationship between employment and desistance from crime post-release. This chapter is divided into five sections. In the first section, we unpack understandings of desistance from crime and then, in section two, the stigma tied to serving time in prison for men or women post-release. In the third section we consider social limitations to obtaining employment post-release; and in the fourth section, we probe what we call "structural constraints"—the numerous barriers to employment former prisoners experience, which include pre-employment screening and employers' unwillingness to hire individuals who were formerly incarcerated. In the final section, we explore the social benefits of broadening hiring polices to include former prisoners, followed by concluding remarks.

## DESISTANCE FROM CRIME

In the early 1990s, criminologists started to explicitly explore why or how offenders stopped participating in crime (Sampson & Laub, 1992, 1993, 1995). Although these early studies were largely a re-examination of earlier studies on delinquent behaviour, the focus was oriented toward following offenders in order to reveal what happened to them as they aged, i.e., whether they continued to participate in criminal activity or whether they eventually stopped. Sampson and Laub (1992, 1993, 1995) suggest, in light of their findings, that individuals age out of criminal behaviour, because as individuals age, they develop stakes tied to conformity in mainstream society. For example, they acquire employment, marry, or start families, and these events or investments are tied to their desistance. From this perspective, these events are recognized as turning points for individuals that can promote a movement away from crime. Of course, marriage and work alone would not necessarily create a pathway that encourages desistance. Instead, desistance depends on the strength and quality of the person's commitments and relationships over time. However, these events and commitments do constitute structure and self-monitoring activities that, when coupled with emotional support, provide a foundation for desistance from crime.[1]

Following from these studies, other researchers started to question why offenders "quit" offending; among them was Maruna (2001), who employed narrative theory to examine the psychology of desistance. Using this approach, Maruna discovered that individuals developed meaningful narrative identities through the use of personal life stories. Simply said, he revealed that "desisters" created *redemption scripts*, which were used to claim that their past criminal activity was due to external factors outside of their control, and which also described their role in their reformation and movement away from crime. On the other hand, people who continued to engage in crime, the recidivists, developed condemnation scripts that embodied their fatalistic viewpoint and doubted their ability to change. Maruna (2001) further put forth that desistance was a maintenance process—a desister had to continue to abstain from crime repeatedly "in the face of life's obstacles and frustrations, that is, when 'everything builds up' or one receives 'some slap in the face'" (p. 26). A desister then is an individual who is "going straight" or "making good" as part of their continual life-long experiences: they cannot quit desisting (Maruna, 2001, p. 26).

Thus, it is not simply an event that triggers desistance—it is both a process and a decision coupled with experience. Specifically, Maruna, LeBel, Naples, and Mitchell (2009), drawing on primary and secondary deviation as put forth by Lemert (1951), defined primary desistance as the "absence of offending behaviour," whereas "secondary desistance refers to a change in identity consistent with a reformed ex-offender" (see Maruna, 2011, p. 79). Some scholars (e.g., Giordano, Cernkovich, & Rudolph, 2002; Maruna, 2001) give greater heed to the salience of the offender's cognitive transformation—secondary desistance—across social contexts as the driving motivator in processes of desistance. To this end, Giordano and colleagues (2002) identified four cognitive transformations that they believe are of most value for any person desisting from crime. These are: (1) the desister must be open to change; (2) they must be exposed to and receptive to the prospect of change; (3) they must be able to envision a new self; and (4) they must view deviant behaviours as undesirable or, at minimum, not personally relevant to their identity and lived experiences. What leads to desistance, in this context, is constructed as the individual's ability and willingness to change. A consensus has, however, emerged among scholars, identifying successful desistance as a result of both the interaction of social factors and cognitive transformation or agency (Bottoms & Shapland, 2011; Bottoms, Shapland, Costello, Holmes, & Muir, 2004; LeBel, Burnett, Maruna, & Bushway, 2008). Of course, as cautioned by Bottoms and colleagues (2004), although agency is the central component of desistance, agency must always be considered within the social context of the desister.

Overall, then, desistance from crime is generally accepted to be "the causal process that supports the termination of offending," particularly representing an individual's continual "state of non-offending" (Laub & Sampson, 2001, p. 11). "Termination" is used by Laub and Sampson (2001) to describe the specific point in time (i.e., the event) in which criminal activity ceases, while desistance itself is an ongoing process rather than a single event. Not surprisingly, desistance is an important part of social reintegration following incarceration (Davis, Bahr, & Ward, 2012). The hope is that individuals can desist from crime on a permanent rather than a short-term, intermittent, or even long-term basis (Maruna, Lebel, Mitchell, & Naples, 2004). Here, there is no substantive agreement among various researchers as to an inclusive definition of when one is confirmed to have desisted. For some, desistance is the permanent cessation of criminal activity, while others accept that periods of reoffending may occur (McNeill, Farrall, Lightowler, & Maruna, 2012). This variance in perspectives has led to debates about how best to measure desistance and how best to apply research findings from desistance studies to practise and to program development.

In this context, a key debate relates to whether the employment of former prisoners truly promotes desistance (i.e., reduces recidivism). Some researchers have found a significant positive relationship between employment and desistance while others have questioned the validity of the relationship between these two variables (Davis et al., 2012; Tripodi, Kim, & Bender, 2010). In Canada, based on a sample of individuals who had served federal sentences, employed former prisoners were found to be less likely to return to crime in comparison to those who were unemployed (Nolan, Wilton, Cousineau, & Stewart, 2014), thereby supporting employment's association with desistance from crime. Similarly, based on a national work experiment with former prisoners in the United States, Uggen (2000) found that employed former prisoners were significantly less likely to reoffend than those who were not employed. In particular, regular, stable employment was determined to be an important resource for individuals who were previously incarcerated.

Conversely, based on an extensive literature review, Homant (1984), for example, noted that while employment was an essential aspect of successful reintegration post-release—in particular, parole success—it did not invariably result in an individual refraining from engaging in criminal behaviour. It was argued that prisonization and self-esteem were crucial in understanding reintegration success. Relatedly, a study of recidivist males in Norway found that those former prisoners who had obtained employment had already desisted from crime *before* transitioning into employment and, in consequence, there was no causal link between being employed and recidivism (Skardhamar & Savolainen, 2014).

Although the nature of the link between employment and desistance continues to be challenged, several authors have underscored the importance of sustainable wages, good working conditions, and stable employment for desistance (Finn, 1998; Graffam, Shinkfield, & Hardcastle, 2008; Harrison & Schehr, 2004; Uggen, 1999). At work, individuals are exposed to informal social controls that can be seen as an essential component of desistance from crime (Davis et al., 2012). These informal social controls include accountability for work responsibilities and consistent monitoring. As captured in reports from the United States and England, most former prisoners are especially keen to improve themselves and their image; therefore, some former prisoners demonstrate a higher level of commitment, loyalty, honesty, and reliability compared with people without a criminal background (Devaney, 2011; Gardiner, 2012; Gill, 1997; Jolson, 1975). Work environments give former prisoners the opportunity to associate with law-abiding peers, and their commitment to maintaining their job may also constrain their associations with deviant peers or the pressures to resort to crime (Davis et al., 2012).

## THE "MARK" OF INCARCERATION

After serving time in prison, individuals do tend to be aware of the importance of finding a job (Harding, 2003) and recognize that finding legitimate, ideally gainful, employment after release is paramount to their long-term success (Scott, 2010). Even from the perspective of Correctional Service Canada, parole conditions tend to revolve around the need for employment; thus, finding a job, or at least working toward securing employment, is typically a component of abiding by parole conditions (Correctional Service Canada, 2003). A wealth of research has shown that employment provides former prisoners with a sense of self-esteem, independence, financial stability, responsibility, and contributes to desistance from crime (Laub & Sampson, 2001; Rosenfeld, Petersilia, & Visher, 2008; Uggen, 2000). Recognizing this, many former prisoners place a great deal of importance on obtaining gainful employment post-release.

Although employment is an essential element influencing former prisoners' ability to desist from crime (Davis et al., 2012), they typically face several personal challenges, such as physical and mental health concerns (Dwyer, 2013; Griffiths, Dandurand, & Murdoch, 2007; Hammett, Roberts, & Kennedy, 2001; Scanlon, 2001), health issues associated with substance abuse and addiction (Griffiths et al., 2007), behavioural problems (Fletcher, 2001), and negative or naïve self-perceptions (Atkin & Armstrong, 2013; Fletcher, 2001; Maton, 2012). Without the necessary resources to overcome these challenges, this may interfere with individuals' ability to obtain and maintain employment. Former prisoners are, in addition to their personal challenges, tasked with navigating a labour market filled with numerous barriers, which include: legal restrictions (e.g., in the acquisition of housing, public assistance, student loans, and driver's licences), occupational licensing requirements, mandatory criminal records checks, and credit bureau investigations (Graffam et al.,

2008; Holzer, Raphael, & Stoll, 2003; Laub & Sampson, 2001; Visher & Travis, 2003; Travis, Solomon, & Waul, 2001). Former prisoners must adapt to continuous lifestyle changes while facing numerous obstacles. Their response to these adjustments post-release will eventually determine their success and commitment to community living (Gill, 1997; Scott, 2010).

Some past research seems to suggest that a criminal record is in itself, rather than any deficits in personal skills, the main constraint on an ex-offender's ability to secure employment (Graffam, Shinkfield, Lavelle, and McPherson, 2004; Pager, 2007; Waldfogel, 1994). Individuals who have been labelled "offenders" because of their criminal record will likely experience social stigmatization with negative effects for both employability and employment (LeBel, 2012; Waldfogel, 1994; Western, 2002, 2007; Western & Pettit, 2005). Their social stigma results from the collective prejudicial attitudes and discrimination oriented toward those with criminal histories (Corrigan, Larson, & Kuwabara, 2010). Social stigmas create social distance between the stigmatized and non-stigmatized groups, which may result in stigmatized individuals experiencing discrimination (Link, Cullen, Frank, & Wozniak, 1987). Maruna (2001) revealed that an individual's experiences of conviction and subsequent incarceration often fuelled their negative views of and detachment from society. In a similar vein, the strategies people use to cope with stigma may also have personal consequences (Link & Phelan, 2001). In their study of 112 Black males working in North Carolina, USA, James and colleagues (1984) found that these men sought to cope with and overcome stereotypes associated with their race by overworking themselves, which led to hypertension.[2]

Former prisoners' responses to stigma tend to be influenced by lived experiences post-release, such as how they are treated and how they perceive other citizens view them in society. This shapes their perception of the social stigma, and in turn, structures their social identity as a former prisoner (Corrigan et al., 2010). The extent to which a person accepts the stereotypes associated with their former prisoner identity will then determine if and to what degree they feel devalued (i.e., to what degree the stigma is internalized) (Vogel, Bitman, Hammer, & Wade, 2013). Goffman (1963) used the notion of actual versus virtual social identity to explain the consequences of stigma on individuals. Specifically, he explained that the virtual social identity that individuals hold—which their audience imposes upon them—discredits any and all attributes beyond those informing the stigma attached to an individual. The person's actual social identity—the attributes and qualities outside of the criminal status they possess—is ignored or nullified in favour of their virtual social identity (i.e., an identity based wholly on their criminal history). The former prisoner identity becomes salient in this context, together with the power to reshape how one views oneself, including one's perception of self-worth, social positioning and, as a result, one's ability to have the confidence to successfully pursue any opportunities that are presented.

While a criminal record alone can limit one's employment opportunities, barriers to employment are heightened for individuals who have received custodial sentences compared to those who have not. While some individuals may be able to obtain employment post-release, the "ex-convict" label substantially affects the type and duration of employment (Harding, 2003). That is, irrespective of work-related experiences, availability of resources, and intellectual or psychological challenges, when offenders are released from prison, the most defining aspect of their employability is their identity as a former prisoner. Past researchers have suggested that individuals who have been incarcerated have reduced access to steady jobs, and that their abilities to earn higher wages are limited in comparison to someone without a conviction (Waldfogel, 1994; Western, 2002).

## SOCIAL LIMITATIONS

In addition to barriers to labour market participation based on the stigma of their criminal record, former prisoners also face challenges related to the time they have spent outside of the workforce, such as lost social network connections (Western, Kling, & Weiman, 2001). Periods of incarceration lead to gaps in employment history, which can be a red flag to employers, thereby limiting employment prospects for former prisoners. Using data from a sample of 3,000 businesses across Atlanta, Boston, Detroit, and Los Angeles, Holzer, Raphael, and Stoll (2006) found that several employers were apprehensive about hiring applicants who had gaps in their employment history based on the assumption that these gaps may have been attributed to time spent incarcerated. Relatedly, relying on the results of surveys administered to employers within the food service and restaurant industry in Arizona, Decker, Spohn, Ortiz, and Hedberg (2014) gender, and employment: An expanded assessment of the consequences of imprisonment for employment found that the chances of success in progressing through the employment process were adversely affected for applicants who had "limited skill sets and little employment history" (p. 61). Since most former prisoners have been absent from the labour force for an extended period of time, they are often not up to speed with new workplace practices or technologies (Decker et al., 2014) and may face challenges throughout the employment process (e.g., as a result of a lack of familiarity with the application, submission, and interviewing process).

Reliable social networks can improve an individual's ability to find stable employment, including former prisoners', either by providing actual employment opportunities or references for employment (Graffam et al., 2004). Even individuals with a tainted reputation and few qualifications (i.e., work history, education) may benefit from social capital when seeking employment (Lin, 2001). While incarcerated, however, individuals' social networks often deplete, which makes it especially difficult to find persons who can provide suitable references for employers post-release (Moore, Stuevig, & Tangney, 2013).

Lin (2001) identified four distinct ways that social capital promotes the likelihood of job attainment. First, through the flow of information from their social ties, individuals may learn about job opportunities. Second, having social capital may influence key decision makers within an organization. Third, the quality of a candidate's social network, and resources generally, may outweigh any deficits in their personal qualifications or reputation. Finally, a person's association with particular social groups may serve to positively enhance others' perceptions of their reputation. Applied to prisoner reintegration and employment: if someone gives a former prisoner a chance or vouches for them, others are also more likely to do so. Individuals on parole may have access to personal support staff at a halfway house, a day reporting centre, or through other correctional support services, which may help increase their accessibility to social capital. However, individuals who have completed their sentence and no longer qualify for services provided by Correctional Service Canada, will likely encounter more difficulties obtaining a suitable reference or accessing networks/opportunities (i.e., acquiring additional social capital).

## STRUCTURAL CONSTRAINTS

Structural discrimination, whether intentional or unintentional, within processes, systems, and institutions includes governing laws and organizational policies that ultimately restrict certain individuals from participating in an organization or society in some way (Corrigan, 2005). For example, former prisoners face barriers obtaining and securing employment although their incarceration and past criminal activities may have nothing to do with their abilities as workers. Employers generally perceive former prisoners as untrustworthy and are thus reluctant to hire them (Holzer, Raphael, & Stoll, 2004, 2007). In this way, the stigma associated with incarceration comes as a collateral cost to their successful reintegration (Dominguez, Alvarez, & Loureiro, 2012).

Occupational requirements and corporate policies may also exclude former prisoners from entry into particular occupations (Harris & Keller, 2005). Depending on the occupation and service provided, organizations may request a criminal background check (Connerley, Arvey, & Bernardy, 2001; Holzer et al., 2004) and/or a credit bureau investigation (Bonanni, Drysdale, Hughes, & Doyle, 2011). For example, someone who had been convicted of fraud may find it difficult, if not impossible, to apply for a job in a financial institution or in a position that requires the handling of money. In some cases, former prisoners may struggle under restrictive parole guidelines, such as curfews and geographic boundaries for permissible travel that complicate successful reintegration (Richards & Jones, 2004) and access to employment opportunities.

In effect, incarceration often excludes former prisoners from the mainstream economy, which forces them to turn to secondary markets and informal economies where they are more vulnerable to reoffending (Western, 2002). As a result, career development is much less accessible to former prisoners (Vernick & Reardon, 2001). Researchers have found that it is within secondary-sector industries that employers are most willing to hire former prisoners post-release (Lichtenberger, 2006; Nally, Lockwood, & Ho, 2011). Lichtenberger (2006) examined the earnings records of former prisoners in Virginia, USA, over the course of a five-year period (1999–2003) and found that industries that had hired the greatest number of former prisoners during this time period were the manufacturing, construction, and mining sectors. These were followed by accommodation and food services, administrative and support services (which included temporary employment agencies), as well as transportation and warehousing services. Industries that were the least likely to hire former prisoners were in the areas of finance and insurance, scientific and technical services, public administration, and health care (Lichtenberger, 2006). Nally and colleagues (2011) found similar trends in Indiana, where organizations in the manufacturing, construction, trade, and retail industries were among those identified as typical employers of released prisoners.

Industry trends seem to support the presumption that former prisoners typically face limited job prospects compared to those without a criminal record (Holzer et al., 2003). This translates into many former prisoners settling for temporary, low-skill and low-income employment (Harding, 2003). In this way, former prisoners are more likely to be taken advantage of by employers. For instance, they may be overworked (Purser, 2012) or dissatisfied with their pay (Visher, Debus-Sherrill, & Yahner, 2011). Given that former prisoners tend to be more or less desperate for work, while having limited employment opportunities, they are an easy population to exploit (Atkin & Armstrong, 2013; Purser, 2012). With a lack of opportunities and potentially low-paying work, over time there may be little incentive for former prisoners to remain employed and they may be enticed to return to the perceived benefits of crime (Gill, 1997; Waldfogel, 1994).

In spite of the low participation of former prisoners across various industries, academics, policy-makers, and practitioners have expressed disagreement over the extent to which involvement in the criminal justice system directly leads to negative consequences in subsequent employment. To address this disagreement, Pager (2003) used an experimental audit design to assess the hiring process of former prisoners across a range of entry-level employment in Milwaukee, Wisconsin (USA). The author isolated the effect of a criminal record on employment outcomes by having matched pairs of individuals apply for real entry-level jobs, each using four distinct conditions. In each condition, favourable work histories were allocated to each individual. Three of the conditions included a history within the criminal justice system, while under one condition the applicant did not have a criminal record. All three criminal justice conditions were associated with less consideration by employers relative to the noncriminal control.

Relatedly, based on a sample of male former prisoners who had served in federal institutions in the United States, Nagin and Waldfogel (1998) examined the effect of incarceration on lifetime income and found that first-time conviction was positively related to income for individuals under 25, and negatively related to income for individuals over 30. Any subsequent convictions (i.e., two or more) were found to negatively affect income for all age groups. In a later study, Graffam et al. (2004) conducted semi-structured interviews in Australia with convicted former prisoners and correctional service professionals and found that for individuals who had criminal records, employers were often more concerned with this than with what training or education the ex-prisoners possessed. Ultimately, the stigma of being a former prisoner affects employer perceptions of an individual's employability, and consequently limits the choice of pursuable occupations and job opportunities.

## PRE-EMPLOYMENT SCREENING

The job application process typically involves candidates being screened to determine their suitability and eligibility. These are assessed through a variety of employment tests, interviews, and background screening (Cavoukian, 2007). Individuals who are successful in the assessments are considered for employment; after that, they may, however, be asked at some point during the hiring process to indicate if they have ever been convicted of a crime. In

Canada, although it is not illegal to leave this question blank, there is a clear moral component involved in determining how to respond to the inquiry. Basically, a former prisoner faces the difficult choice between three answers. By answering "*No*," a former prisoner is dishonest, which may be undesirable for someone working to disassociate themselves from the stigma of moral ineptitude associated with "criminal identity." Indeed, too often being convicted of a crime leads individuals to embody the identity of an untrustworthy and dishonest "criminal" (e.g., Waldfogel, 1994). Yet, by saying "*Yes*" the applicant may lose the job opportunity, as they are then tainted with the stigma of a criminal identity. The final option would be for an individual to refrain from answering, which may be seen as suspicious to an employer who may simply equate not answering to an admission of criminal history.

Organizations are increasingly using pre-employment screening tools to decrease the chance for poor hiring decisions (Adler, 1993; Wang & Kleiner, 2000). Pre-employment screening is intended to: verify the accuracy of the information an applicant provides; uncover potentially concerning information (e.g., violent behaviour and theft); limit uncertainty about potential candidates; demonstrate due diligence in hiring; and deter applications from individuals with a "questionable past" (Rosen, 2002). The criminal background check may be performed as a form of due diligence, which organizations often claim to conduct in the interest of protecting their employees, customers, and other stakeholders (Clay & Stephens, 1995; Giguere & Dundes, 2002; Raphael, 2011). Pre-employment screening tools include: interviews, skills test screening, reference checks, criminal record checks, bureau investigations, and education verifications (Wang & Kleiner, 2000). For former prisoners, each of these screening tools can significantly limit their ability to secure employment. Being honest about their past, for example, could trigger the hiring manager to associate the job applicant with deviance. On the other hand, being dishonest may have future implications, since any inaccuracies or critical information that an applicant elects not to provide may lead others to question their integrity and suitability for employment if/ when discovered (Adler, 1993). These challenges are heightened if employers conduct cross-referencing, a process whereby various screening tools are used simultaneously for comparison and to uncover various negative aspects of an individual's history (Bonanni et al., 2011). Indeed, simply googling a person's name can potentially reveal any past action that is culturally read as a transgression. In general, it is more and more difficult for former prisoners to conceal their criminal records in light of the many technological advancements that easily grant employers access to this information (Atkin & Armstrong, 2013).

Former prisoners are further marginalized if they have one or more socially stigmatized characteristics. Gausel and Thørrisen (2014) propose that former prisoners might experience *multiple stigmas* where they face social stigmatization based on multiple stigmatized associations. For instance, former prisoners who are also members of racial minorities typically face further challenges in securing employment (Holzer et al., 2006; Pager, Western, and Sugie, 2009). Based on an experimental audit of employer responses to job applications for entry-level postings in Milwaukee, Wisconsin (USA), Pager and Quillian (2005) found that Black individuals with a criminal record were significantly less likely to be considered for employment than White individuals with a criminal record. Given the social stigmas attached to former prisoners in the United States, employers that actively attempt to avoid hiring former prisoners may be more apt to discriminate against men from "high-incarceration demographic groups" irrespective of their actual criminal record history (or absence thereof). Said another way, demographic groups with documented higher rates of incarceration (e.g., Aboriginal, Black, and Hispanic persons) are discriminated against by employers even if they have not been incarcerated or committed a crime (Pager & Shepherd, 2008).

## EMPLOYMENT PROSPECTS

Researchers suggest that employers' apprehensions towards hiring former prisoners are typically tied to a plethora of perceived risks for the organizational environment, including a concern for the genuineness of a former prisoner's search for employment, the safety of their workforce, the integrity of their products/services, a loss of potential and/or loyal customers, as well as an overall perception that former prisoners' lack of social skills may be disruptive in a work environment (Giguere & Dundes, 2002; Gill, 1997; Graffam et al., 2008; Harris & Keller, 2005). Although much progress in changing these perceptions is yet to be made, research findings suggest that some advancement has occurred. For example, Pager and Quillian (2005) studied employers located in high-crime areas (Dallas and Houston, Texas, USA) and found that while employers who were hiring for entry-level positions indicated that they would be willing to hire individuals with a criminal record, few actually did so in practice. These findings suggest that former prisoners were likely to encounter employers who were simply not receptive or open to employing them (Albright & Denq, 1996; Pager & Quillian, 2005). In comparison, based on a diverse sample of employers (representing unskilled to skilled employment) across nine states in the USA, Swanson and colleagues (2012) found that 63 percent of the employers surveyed had willingly hired an individual with a criminal history in the past. While the difference in findings may signify changing attitudes, it may also reflect the notion that "the magnitude of stigma depends on expectations and the crime rate" (Rasmusen, 1996.) Thus, we expect employers in high-crime areas to stigmatize former prisoners more so than employers in areas with lower crime rates.

Notably, some offending backgrounds (i.e., sex offence, murder) are thought to pose more significant risks for employers, and thus can affect applicants' perceived suitability for some occupations. As a result, conviction offence can be highly influential on hiring decisions (Atkin & Armstrong, 2013). For example, in a study of employers' willingness to hire former prisoners in Texas, Atkin and Armstrong (2013) found that most employers were generally willing to hire former prisoners; however, this willingness varied depending on the applicants' conviction(s). Similarly, Waldfogel (1994) found that individuals who were college-educated and had committed fraud, or breached a trust in any other way, were less likely to be employed following their first conviction than others who did not reveal/possess these attributes. This may be due to the perceptually overarching breach of trust that links each of these conditions. Individuals who have committed fraud have defied systems in place, and society may not expect college-educated individuals to commit crimes (e.g., Moretti, 2005). Thus, engaging in crime under either of these circumstances may be seen as a personal breach of trust in and of itself. Having demonstrated dishonesty in the past, employers may be reluctant to trust these individuals to perform at work and abide by the rules.

Employers have also considered violence and the exploitation of an individual's vulnerability as the kind of criminal behaviour that could potentially posit a risk to the safety and well-being of their workforce and customers. For example, in a study conducted by Albright and Denq (1996), employers were reluctant to hire former prisoners who had been incarcerated for a violent offence or convicted of a crime against children. In another study that drew on semi-structured in-depth interviews with 16 formerly incarcerated Chinese young men post-release, Chui and Cheng (2013) found that although some employers did not reject applications from former prisoners outright, they used various techniques to terminate the former prisoners' employment once they discovered their history. For instance, the authors discovered that an employer could suddenly, without directly stating that the job was being terminated due to their criminal history, contend that an individual was not suitable for the job or that their performance at work was poor.

Some employers have further expressed fears that they would be found liable for negligent hiring if they willingly hired an individual who had a criminal record and then engaged in a criminal act (Adler, 1993; Connerley, Arvey, & Bernardy, 2001) or became harmful to others while at work (Gill,

1997; Wang & Kleiner, 2000). In the United States and Canada, employers may be held responsible for their employee's behaviours if the employer knew or ought to have known that the employee was "likely" to behave in a particular manner (Lam & Harcourt, 2003). A criminal record, in its stigmatizing essence, is thought to be indicative of likely behaviour that accords to the offence, and this leaves employers uneasy about hiring former prisoners (Lam & Harcourt, 2003). While a significant concern for employers has been the perceived risk that employing former prisoners poses for employees and consumers, workplace violence research has found that workers are more apt to experience assault from a stranger or within personal relationships (e.g., partner/spouse and family members) than from their co-workers (Duhart, 2001; Tjaden & Thoennes, 2001). In fact, no research to date has found there to be an increased likelihood of victimization for an organization, a co-worker, or a client who has been exposed to an individual with a history of criminal offences (e.g., Harris & Keller, 2005).

Some employers have specified that government incentives could entice them to hire more individuals who have been released from prison (Albright & Denq, 1996). Yet, it is typically difficult for former prisoners to find permanent, unsubsidized employment post-release because they lack the necessary skills and abilities (Waldfogel, 1994). These skills may include education, level of numeracy and literacy, as well as occupational and interpersonal experience and skills (Graffam, Shinkfield, Lavelle, & McPherson, 2004; Fletcher, 2001; Nally, Lockwood, & Ho, 2011; Nelson, Deess, & Allen, 2011; Waldfogel, 1994). These barriers make it especially challenging for individuals to obtain legitimate employment since a majority of jobs today require candidates to have at least a high school diploma, alongside relevant skills and experience (Holzer, 1996).

Based on a study of the perspectives held by employers in Dallas and Houston, Texas, USA, Albright and Denq (1996) found that former prisoners with a college diploma or with vocational training (e.g., in the trades) were more likely to be hired by employers. Relatedly, based on the employment experiences of 740 males post-release in Illinois, Texas, and Ohio, USA, Visher et al. (2011) found that consistent work experience prior to incarceration, and connecting with employers before release improved employment outcomes after release. Together, these studies reveal that although the nature of the employment landscape has changed over time, the consistent determinant for individual success post-release seems to be at least in part determined by the relevant training, experience, and expertise obtained by the individual prior to their release.

## SOCIAL BENEFITS AND POLICY IMPLICATIONS

According to Graffam and colleagues (2008), employing former prisoners is often associated with several community and social justice benefits such as: less crime, greater public safety, and reduced costs for the government and taxpayers and improved community attitudes toward former prisoners. Similarly, Ruddell and Winfree (2006) propose that enabling individuals with a criminal history to transition smoothly into society may, by reducing their propensity to commit crime again, enhance public safety. Overall, research suggests that communities should provide resources to enable former prisoners to successfully transition back into their communities as valuable, productive, and contributing members of society (Andress et al., 2004). Yet, there is a disconnect between the expectations that former prisoners reintegrate successfully into society and the policies that impede their ability to do so (Demleitner, 2002). In general, former prisoners are treated as inferior to other members of society, and are discriminated against in the employment context. The attempt to navigate the challenges involved may result in a lack of confidence and trust in building and maintaining working relationships with others, as well as feelings of isolation and lack of social acceptance. In the face of these obstacles, former prisoners require material, psychological, and social support; otherwise they may have an especially difficult experience reintegrating into society (Griffiths et al., 2007).

In the workplace, support may be found in mentorship opportunities, employee resource groups, coaching, personal counselling, and supportive supervisor(s) and/or colleagues (e.g., Huffman, Watrous-Rodriguez, & King, 2008). Employers have consistently advocated for diversity management initiatives to be implemented and supported by top management for the benefit of the overall workforce (Riccucci, 2002). Diversity management initiatives essentially advocate for the rights of marginalized groups as well as promote the idea of a workforce that is representative of the general population. However, the alienation experienced by former prisoners is not fully recognized (Blessett & Pryor, 2013). There are undoubtedly several positive implications of employment for successful reintegration post-release. The widespread lack of implemented legal protections for former prisoners in the workplace (Lam & Harcourt, 2003) and the numerous barriers to employment post-release underscores the need to highlight the experiences of this population and to consider better facilitation of post-release employment opportunities in order to encourage desistance from crime.

With respect to policy implications, some researchers have argued that criminal justice policies are designed to emphasize punishment and separation from society rather than to facilitate rehabilitation (Dhami &

Cruise, 2013; Kenemore & Roldan, 2005). While the suspension of certain rights and privileges for former and current prisoners vary across local and national contexts, individuals often suffer from the invisible consequences of imprisonment (Dhami & Cruise, 2013), such as those related to employment presented throughout this chapter. Thus, despite the expectations former prisoners have of reintegrating successfully, policies impede their ability to do so (Demleitner, 2002). By shedding light on the employment experiences of former prisoners, we encourage more inclusive, anti-discriminatory social and organizational policies for former prisoners.

## CONCLUSION

As individuals reintegrate into society post-release, an important aspect of their long-term success is desistance from crime. Individuals who desist from crime are personally successful in that they can provide for themselves and their families in a legitimate and meaningful way. A community that supports desistance from crime will derive positive benefits, including increased safety and perhaps improved compliance with social systems and procedures.

Recognizing that desistance from crime can occur for varying time spans upon release, it is important for social systems to encourage and support permanent desistance from crime. As we unpack the numerous barriers and obstacles that former prisoners face as they strive to desist from crime, it becomes clear that there are several areas where we can grow as a society in supporting former prisoner reintegration. First and foremost, the overarching stigma attached to the former prisoner identity is an undeniable hindrance that can be detrimental to successful reintegration as it can limit the receptiveness of employers and can also be internalized causing individuals to rule themselves out from possible opportunities. In light of this, we may consider how we might overcome the detrimental effects of stigma—as a society. One place to start would be to consider how this stigma has influenced those social and structural systems that we expect former prisoners to return and reintegrate into, and by becoming educated, as a society, about the realities of incarceration and about the effects a lack of social support post-release can have.

Although we may not be able to definitively articulate *when* or *why* desistance occurs, it is clear that employment is a key feature of the desistance process. As we explore desistance from crime and the various obstacles that individuals face in their quest to desist from crime, we might consider whether we can truly understand the nature of the challenge of integrating into a society from which one has been completely detached for a period of time, now facing greater obstacles due to the nature of one's absence. Not only is social support important for the individuals who have been absent from society; a society that is educated about former prisoners may be more inclusive, which may contribute to more realistic expectations of successful reintegration. Structurally, several systems and procedures exist that continue to promote a punitive approach to criminal justice, where a person is understood to be "punished" for their crimes by serving time in prison, and by being disconnected from society thereafter. Instead, justice systems may be more effective in promoting successful reintegration and, in turn, desistance from crime by moving towards more restorative than retributive criminal justice philosophies. Coinciding with this, structural systems within society may better support this endeavour by contributing to, creating, and supporting employment contexts where individuals are simply given a second chance.

## NOTES

1  See also Moffitt's (1993) work on adolescent-limited and life-course-persistent anti-social behaviour.
2  See also Smart and Wegner's (1999) work on women with an eating disorder.

## REFERENCES

Adler, S. (1993). Verifying a job candidate's background: The state of practice in a vital human resources activity. *Review of Business, 15*(2), 3–8.

Albright, S., & Denq, F. (1996). Employer attitudes toward hiring ex-offenders. *The Prison Journal, 76*(2), 118–137.

Alvarez, R. D., & Loureiro, M. L. (2012). Stigma, ex-convicts and labour markets. *German Economic Review, 13*(4), 470–486.

Andress, D., Wildes, T., Rechtine, D., & Moritsugu, K. P. (2004). Jails, prisons, and your community's health. *Journal of Law, Medicine and Ethics, 32*(4), 50–51.

Atkin, C. A., & Armstrong, G. S. (2013). Does the concentration of parolees in a community impact employer attitudes toward the hiring of ex-offenders. *Criminal Justice Policy Review, 24*(1), 71–93.

Blessett, B., & Pryor, M. (2013). The invisible job seeker: The absence of ex-offenders in discussions of diversity management. *Public Administration Quarterly, 37*(3), 433–455.

Bonanni, C., Drysdale, D., Hughes, A., & Doyle, P. (2011). Employee background verification: The cross-referencing effect. *International Business & Economics Research Journal, 5*(11), 1–7.

Bottoms, A., & Shapland, J. (2011). Steps toward desistance among male young adult recidivists. In S. Farrall, M. Hough, S. Maruna, & R. Sparks (Eds.), *Escape routes: Contemporary perspectives on life after punishment* (pp. 43–80). Abingdon, UK: Routledge.

Bottoms, A., Shapland, J., Costello, A., Holmes, D., & Muir, G. (2004). Towards desistance: Theoretical underpinnings for an empirical study. *Howard Journal of Criminal Justice, 43*(4), 368–389.

Cavoukian, A. (2007). What is involved if you are asked to provide a police background check? Toronto, ON: Office of the Information and Privacy Commissioner/Ontario.

Chui, W. H., & Cheng, K. K.-Y. (2013). The mark of an ex-prisoner: Perceived discrimination and self-stigma of young men after prison in Hong Kong. *Deviant Behavior, 34*(8), 671–684.

Clay, J. M., & Stephens, E. C. (1995). Liability for negligent hiring: The importance of background checks. *Cornell Hotel and Restaurant Administration Quarterly, 36*(5), 74–81.

Connerley, M., Arvey, R., & Bernardy, C. (2001). Criminal background checks for prospective and current employees: Current practices among municipal agencies. *Public Personnel Management, 30*(2), 173–183.

Correctional Service Canada. (2003). *Evaluation of the Employment and Employability Program* (Performance Assurance Sector No. 394-2-017). Ottawa, ON: Correctional Service Canada. Retrieved from http://www.csc-scc.gc.ca/text/pa/ev-eep-394-2-017/action_report_eep_evaluation_e.pdf

Corrigan, P. W. (2005). Dealing with stigma through personal disclosure. In P. W. Corrigan (Ed.), *On the stigma of mental illness: Practical strategies for research and social change* (pp. 257–280). Washington, DC: American Psychological Association.

Corrigan, P. W., Larson, J. E., & Kuwabara, S. A. (2010). Social psychology of the stigma of mental illness: Public and self-stigma models. In J. E. Maddux & J. P. Tangney (Eds.), *Social psychological foundations of clinical psychology* (pp. 51–68). New York, NY: Guilford Press.

Davis, C., Bahr, S. J., & Ward, C. (2012). The process of offender reintegration: Perceptions of what helps prisoners reenter society. *Criminology and Criminal Justice, 13*(4), 446–469.

Decker, S. H., Spohn, C., Ortiz, N. R., & Hedberg, E. (2014). *Criminal stigma, race, gender, and employment: An expanded assessment of the consequences of imprisonment for employment* (No. 2010-MU-MU-004). Final report to the National Institute of Justice. Retrieved from http://thecrimereport.s3.amazon aws.com/2/fb/e/2362/criminal_stigma_race_crime_and_unemployment.pdf

Demleitner, N. V. (2002). "Collateral damage": No re-entry for drug offenders. *Villanova Law Review, 47*, 1027–1054.

Devaney, T. (2011, July 4). Feds recommend ex-cons for hard-to-fill jobs. *Washington Times*. Retrieved from http://www.washingtontimes.com/news/2011/jul/4/ex-cons-recommended-for-hard-to-fill-jobs/

Dhami, M. K., & Cruise, P. A. (2013). Prisoner disenfranchisement: Prisoner and public views of an invisible punishment. *Analyses of Social Issues and Public Policy, 13*(1), 211–227.

Dominguez Alvarez, R., & Loureiro, M. L. (2012). Stigma, Ex-convicts and Labour Markets. *German Economic Review, 13*, 470–486.Duhart, D. T. (2001). *Violence in the workplace 1993–99* (Special Report: National Crime Victimization survey No. NCJ 190076). Retrieved from http://www.bjs.gov/content/pub/pdf/vw99.pdf

Dwyer, C. D. (2013). "Sometimes I wish I was an 'ex' ex-prisoner": Identity processes in the collective action participation of former prisoners in Northern

Ireland. *Contemporary Justice Review: Issues in Criminal, Social, and Restorative Justice, 16*(4), 425–444.

Finn, P. (1998). Job placement for offenders in relation to recidivism. *Journal of Offender Rehabilitation, 28*(1), 89–106.

Fletcher, D. R. (2001). Ex-offenders, the labour market and the new public administration. *Public Administration, 79*(4), 871–891.

Gardiner, T. (2012, May 4). Prisoners can be honest and motivated workers, Ken Clarke tells business as he urges the High Street to give ex-offenders jobs. *Daily Mail Online.* Retrieved from http://www.dailymail.co.uk/news/article-2139390/Prisoners-honest-motivated-workers-Ken-Clarke-tells-business-urges-High-Street-ex-offenders-jobs.html

Gausel, N., & Thørrisen, M. M. (2014). A theoretical model of multiple stigma: Ostracized for being an inmate with intellectual disabilities. *Journal of Scandinavian Studies in Criminology and Crime Prevention, 15*(1), 89–95.

Giguere, R., & Dundes, L. (2002). Help wanted: A survey of employer concerns about hiring ex-convicts. *Criminal Justice Policy Review, 13*(4), 396–408.

Gill, M. (1997). Employing ex-offenders: A risk or an opportunity? *Howard Journal of Criminal Justice, 36*(4), 337–351.

Giordano, P. C., Cernkovich, S. A., & Rudolph, J. L. (2002). Gender, crime, and desistance: Toward a theory of cognitive transformation. *American Journal of Sociology, 107*(4), 990–1064.

Goffman, E. (1963). *Stigma: Notes on the management of spoiled identity.* Englewood Cliffs, NJ: Prentice-Hall.

Graffam, J., Shinkfield, A. J., & Hardcastle, L. (2008). The perceived employability of ex-prisoners and offenders. *International Journal of Offender Therapy and Comparative Criminology, 52*(6), 673–685.

Graffam, J., Shinkfield, A., Lavelle, B., & McPherson, W. (2004). Variables affecting successful reintegration as perceived by offenders and professionals. *Journal of Offender Rehabilitation, 40*(1), 147–171.

Griffiths, C. T., Dandurand, Y., & Murdoch, D. (2007). *The social reintegration of offenders and crime prevention* (Research Report No. 2007-2). Ottawa, ON: National Crime Prevention Centre.

Hammett, T., Roberts, C., & Kennedy, S. (2001). Health-related issues in prisoner reentry. *Crime & Delinquency, 47*(3), 390–409.

Harding, D. J. (2003). Jean Valjean's dilemma: The management of ex-convict identity in the search for employment. *Deviant Behavior, 24*(6), 571–595.

Harris, P. M., & Keller, K. S. (2005). Ex-offenders need not apply: The criminal background check in hiring decisions. *Journal of Contemporary Criminal Justice, 21*(1), 6–30.

Harrison, B., & Schehr, R. C. (2004). Offenders and post-release jobs: Variables influencing success and failure. *Journal of Offender Rehabilitation, 39*(3), 35–68.

Holzer, H. J. (1996). *What employers want: Job prospects for less-educated workers.* New York, NY: Russell Sage Foundation.

Holzer, H. J., Raphael, S., & Stoll, M. A. (2003). Employment barriers facing ex-offenders. *The Urban Institute Reentry Roundtable Discussion Paper.*

Holzer, H. J., Raphael, S., & Stoll, M. A. (2004). The effect of an applicant's criminal history on employer hiring decisions and screening practices: Evidence from Los Angeles. National Poverty Center Working Paper Series #04-15.

Holzer, H. J., Raphael, S., & Stoll, M. A. (2006). Perceived Criminality, Criminal Background Checks, and the Racial Hiring Practices of Employers. *Journal of Law and Economics, 49*, 451–480.

Holzer, H. J., Raphael, S., & Stoll, M. A. (2007). The effect of an applicant's criminal history on employer hiring decisions and screening practices: Evidence from Los Angeles. In S. Bushway, M. A. Stoll, & D. F. Weiman (Eds.), *Barriers to reentry? The labor market for released prisoners in post-industrial America* (pp. 117–150). New York, NY: Russell Sage Foundation.

Homant, R. J. (1984). Employment of ex-offenders: The role of prisonization and self-esteem. *Journal of Offender Counseling Services Rehabilitation, 8*(3), 5–23.

Hoskins, Z. (2014). Ex-offender restrictions. *Journal of Applied Philosophy, 31*(1), 33–48.

Huffman, A. H., Watrous-Rodriguez, K. M., & King, E. B. (2008). Supporting a diverse workforce: What type of support is most meaningful for lesbian and gay employees? *Human Resource Management, 47*(2), 237–253.

James, S. A., LaCroix, A. Z., Kleinbaum, D. G., & Strogatz, D. S. (1984). John Henryism and blood pressure differences among black men. II. The role of occupational stressors. *Journal of Behavioral Medicine, 7*(3), 259–275.

Jolson, M. A. (1975). Are ex-offenders successful employees? *California Management Review, 17*(3), 65–73.

Kenemore, T., & Roldan, I. (2005). Staying straight: Lessons from ex-offenders. *Clinical Social Work Journal, 34*(1), 5–21.

Lam, H., & Harcourt, M. (2003). The use of criminal record in employment decisions: The rights of ex-offenders, employers and the public. *Journal of Business Ethics, 47*(3), 237–252.

Laub, J. H., & Sampson, R. J. (2001). Understanding desistance from crime. *Crime and Justice, 28*, 1–69.

LeBel, T. P. (2012). Invisible stripes? Formerly incarcerated persons' perceptions of stigma. *Deviant Behavior, 33*(2), 89–107.

LeBel, T. P., Burnett, R., Maruna, S., & Bushway, S. (2008). The "Chicken and Egg" of Subjective and Social Factors in Desistance from Crime. *European Journal of Criminology, 5*(2), 131–159.

Lemert, Edwin M. 1951. *Social pathology: Systematic approaches to the study of sociopathic behavior.* New York, NY: McGraw-Hill.

Lichtenberger, E. (2006). Where do ex-offenders find jobs? An industrial profile of the employers of ex-offenders in Virginia. *Journal of Correctional Education, 57*(4), 297–311.

Lin, N. (2001). *Social capital: A theory of social structure and action.* New York, NY: Cambridge University Press.

Link, B. G., Cullen, F. T., Frank, J., & Wozniak, J. F. (1987). The social rejection of former mental patients: Understanding why labels matter. *American Journal of Sociology, 92*(6), 1461–1500.

Link, B. G., & Phelan, J. C. (2001). Conceptualizing stigma. *Annual Review of Sociology, 27*, 363–385.

Luther, J. B., Reichert, E. S., Holloway, E. D., Roth, A. M., & Aalsma, M. C. (2011). An exploration of community reentry needs and services for prisoners: A focus on care to limit return to high-risk behavior. *AIDS Patient Care and STDs, 25*(8), 475–481.

Luyckx, K., Schwartz, S. J., Goossens, L., & Pollock, S. (2008). Employment, sense of coherence, and identity formation: Contextual and psychological processes on the pathway to sense of adulthood. *Journal of Adolescent Research, 23*(5), 566–591.

Maruna, S. (2001). *Making good: How ex-convicts reform and rebuild their lives.* Washington, DC: American Psychological Association.

Maruna, S. (2011). A signaling perspective on employment-based re-entry: Elements of successful desistance signaling. *Criminology and Public Policy, 11*(1), 73–86.

Maruna, S., Lebel, T. P., Mitchell, N., & Naples, M. (2004). Pygmalion in the reintegration process: Desistance from crime through the looking glass. *Psychology, Crime & Law, 10*(3), 271–281.

Maruna, S., LeBel, T. P., Naples, M., & Mitchell, N. (2009). Looking-glass identity transformation: Pygmalion and Golem in the rehabilitation process. In B. Veysey, J. Christian, and D. Martinez (Eds.), *How offenders transform their lives* (pp. 30–55). Cullompton, UK: Willan Publishing.

Maton, K. (2012). Good practice guide for social enterprises: Ex-offenders & employment. London, UK: Social Enterprise West Midlands (SEWM CIC). Retrieved from http://www.socialenterprisewm.org.uk/wp-content/uploads/2012/07/Good-Practice-Ex-offenders-and-Employment-K-Maton-SEWM-CIC-June-2012.pdf

McNeill, F., Farrall, S., Lightowler, C., & Maruna, S. (2012, April 15). How and why people stop offending: Discovering desistance. Institute for Research and Innovation in Social Sciences. Retrieved from http://www.iriss.org.uk/sites/default/files/iriss-insight-15.pdf

Moffitt, T. E. (1993). Adolescent-limited and life-course-persistent antisocial behaviour: A developmental taxonomy. *Psychological Review, 100*, 674–701.

Moore, K., Stuewig, J., & Tangney, J. (2013). Jail inmates' perceived and anticipated stigma: Implications for post-release functioning. *Self and Identity, 12*, 527–547.

Moretti, E. (2005, October). *Does education reduce participation in criminal activities?* Presented at the Symposium on the Social Costs of Inadequate Education, Columbia University, New York, NY. Retrieved from http://devweb.tc.columbia.edu/manager/symposium/Files/74_Moretti_Symp.pdf

Nagin, D., & Waldfogel, J. (1998). The effect of conviction on income through the life cycle. *International Review of Law and Economics, 18*(1), 25–40.

Nally, J. M., Lockwood, S. R., & Ho, T. (2011). Employment of ex-offenders during the recession. *Journal of Correctional Education, 62*(2), 47–61.

Nelson, M., Deess, P., & Allen, C. (2011). The first month out: Post-incarceration experiences in New York City. *Federal Sentencing Reporter, 24*(1), 72–75.

Nolan, A., Wilton, G., Cousineau, C., & Stewart, L. (2014). *Outcomes for offender employment programs: Assessing CORCAN participation* (Research Report No. R-283). Ottawa, ON: Correctional Service Canada.

Pachankis, J. E. (2007). The psychological implications of concealing a stigma: A cognitive-affective-behavioral model. *Psychological Bulletin, 133*, 328–345.

Pager, D. (2003). The mark of a criminal record. *American Journal of Sociology, 108*(5), 937–975.

Pager, D. (2007). *Marked: Race, crime and finding work in an era of mass incarceration.* Chicago, IL: University of Chicago Press.

Pager, D., & Quillian, L. (2005). Walking the talk? What employers say versus what they do. *American Sociological Review, 70*(3), 355–380.

Pager, D., & Shepherd, H. (2008). The sociology of discrimination: Racial discrimination in employment, housing, credit, and consumer markets. *Annual Review of Sociology, 34*, 181–209.

Pager, D., Western, B., & Sugie, N. (2009). Sequencing disadvantage: Barriers to employment facing young black and white men with criminal records. *Annals of the American Academy of Political and Social Science, 623*(1), 195–213.

Petersilia, J. (2007). Employ behavioral contracting for "earned discharge" parole. *Criminology & Public Policy, 6*, 807–814.

Purser, G. (2012). "Still doin' time:" Clamoring for work in the day labor industry. *WorkingUSA: The Journal of Labor & Society, 15*, 397–415.

Raphael, S. (2011). Incarceration and prisoner reentry in the United States. *Annals of the American Academy of Political and Social Science, 635*(1), 192–215.

Rasmusen, E. (1996). Stigma and self-fulfilling expectations of criminality. *Journal of Law and Economics, 39*, 519–544.

Riccucci, N. (2002). *Managing diversity in public sector workforces.* Boulder, CO: Westview Press.

Richards, S. C., & Jones, R. S. (2004). Beating the perceptual incarceration machine: Overcoming structural impediments to re-entry. In S. Maruna & R. Immarigeon (Eds.), *After crime and punishment: Pathways to offender reintegration* (pp. 201–232). Portland, OR: Willan Publishing.

Rosen, L. S. (2002). Background screening and safe hiring: An introduction. *Occupational Health & Safety, 71*(4), 16–20.

Rosenfeld, R., Petersilia, J., & Visher, C. (2008). The first days after release can make a difference. *Corrections Today, 70*(3), 86–87.

Ruddell, R., & Winfree, L. T. (2006). Setting aside criminal convictions in Canada: A successful approach to offender reintegration. *Prison Journal, 86*(4), 452–469.

Sampson, R. J., & Laub, J. (1992). Crime and deviance in the life course. *Annual Review of Sociology, 18*, 63–84.

Sampson, R. J., & Laub, J. (1993). *Crime in the making: Pathways and turning points through life.* Cambridge, MA: Harvard University Press.

Sampson, R. J., & Laub, J. (1995). Understanding variability in lives through time: Contributions of life-course criminology. *Studies in Crime and Crime Prevention, 4*, 143–158.

Scanlon, W. (2001). Ex-convicts: A workplace diversity issue. *Employee Assistance Quarterly, 16*(4), 35–51.

Scott, T.-L. (2010). Offender perceptions on the value of employment. *Journal of Correctional Education, 61*(1), 46–67.

Skardhamar, T., & Savolainen, J. (2014). Changes in criminal offending around the time of job entry: A study of employment and desistance. *Criminology, 52*(2), 263–291.

Smart, L., & Wegner, D. M. (1999). Covering up what can't be seen: Concealable stigma and mental control. *Journal of Personality and Social Psychology, 77*(3), 474–486.

Swanson, S. J., Langfitt-Reese, S., & Bond, G. R. (2012). Employer attitudes about criminal histories. *Psychiatric Rehabilitation Journal, 35*(5), 385–390.

Tjaden, P. G., & Thoennes, N. (2001). Coworker violence and gender: Findings from the National Violence Against Women Survey. *American Journal of Preventive Medicine, 20*(2), 85–89.

Travis, J. (2005). *But they all come back: Facing the challenges of prisoner reentry.* Washington, DC: Urban Institute Press.

Travis, J., Solomon, A. L., & Waul, M. (2001). From prison to home: The dimensions and consequences of prisoner reentry. Washington, DC: Urban Institute.

Tripodi, S. J., Kim, J. S., & Bender, K. (2010). Is employment associated with reduced recidivism? The complex relationship between employment and crime. *International Journal of Offender Therapy and Comparative Criminology, 54*(5), 706–720.

Uggen, C. (1999). Ex-offenders and the conformist alternative: A job quality model of work and crime. *Social Problems, 46,* 127–151.

Uggen, C. (2000). Work as a turning point in the life course of criminals: A duration model of age, employment, and recidivism. *American Sociological Review, 65*(4), 529–546.

Vernick, S. H., & Reardon, R. C. (2001). Career development programs in corrections. *Journal of Career Development, 27*(4), 265–277.

Visher, C. A., Debus-Sherrill, S. A., & Yahner, J. (2011). Employment after prison: A longitudinal study of former prisoners. *Justice Quarterly, 28*(5), 698–718.

Visher, C. A., & Travis, J. (2003). Transitions from prison to community: Understanding individual pathways. *Annual Review of Sociology, 29*(1), 89–113.

Visher, C. A., Winterfield, L., & Coggeshall, M. B. (2005). Ex-offender employment programs and recidivism: A meta-analysis. *Journal of Experimental Criminology, 1*(3), 295–315.

Vogel, D. L., Bitman, R. L., Hammer, J. H., & Wade, N. G. (2013). Is stigma internalized? The longitudinal impact of public stigma on self-stigma. *Journal of Counseling Psychology, 60*(2), 311–316.

Waldfogel, J. (1994). The effect of criminal conviction on income and the trust "reposed in the workmen." *Journal of Human Resources, 29*(1), 62–81.

Wang, J.-M., & Kleiner, B. H. (2000). Effective employment screening practices. *Management Research News, 23*(5/6), 73–81.

Western, B. (2002). The impact of incarceration on wage mobility and inequality. *American Sociological Review, 67*(4), 526–546.

Western, B. (2007). Mass imprisonment and economic inequality. *Social Research, 74*(2), 509–532.

Western, B., Kling, J. R., & Weiman, D. F. (2001). The labor market consequences of incarceration. *Crime and Delinquency, 47,* 410–427.

Western, B., & Pettit, B. (2005). Black–White wage inequality, employment rates, and incarceration. *American Journal of Sociology, 111,* 553–578.

# CHAPTER 3

# Employment and Criminal Offenders with Mental Illness

Krystle Martin

## INTRODUCTION

**F**or the majority of individuals, employment is a necessary means to earn an income and provide the necessities of life. Beyond fulfilling our basic needs, however, it has been said that "working is important, and indeed can be essential, for psychological health" (Blustein, 2008, p. 230). More specifically, employment can promote a connection to the community and fuel a sense of accomplishment. Alternatively, the loss of employment and periods of unemployment may lead to mental health struggles (e.g., Blustein, 2008; Drydakis, 2015; Fergusson, McLeod, & Horwood, 2014). Individuals incarcerated in a correctional facility experience a potentially severe disruption in their vocational pursuits and are likely to experience challenges re-entering the workforce. Identified as one of the "central eight" risk factors for recidivism (Bonta & Andrews, 2007), employment instability reduces former prisoners' chances for successful reintegration into society (Rakis, 2005) and therefore could negatively impact society by increasing the chance of reoffending (Graffam, Shinkfield, Lavelle, & Hardcastle, 2004). Conversely, finding and maintaining a job once released into the community has been demonstrated to have numerous benefits, such as helping former prisoners structure their time, gain financial security, increase their self-worth, and improve their interpersonal skills (e.g., Bonta & Andrews, 2007; Hoare & Machin, 2006).

In this chapter, I integrate two bodies of literature: one focused on the criminal justice system and prisoners identified as having mental illness; and the second stemming from mental health agencies supporting psychiatric patients with criminal records living in the community. Both of these bodies of literature will be taken into account to shed light on the nuances shaping employment reintegration for former prisoners with mental illness. While the context at the time of exploration slightly differs (individuals in the corrections versus the mental health system), researchers contributing to these two areas are essentially studying the same population. Next, I discuss this population's barriers for participating in the workforce, including education, psychiatric symptoms, stigma, and hiring policies/legislation, followed by current clinical interventions from the perspectives of both staff and clients. Finally, I make some suggestions for adapting current programs and approaches.

## EMPLOYMENT AND THE FORMER PRISONER

Unfortunately, former prisoners often struggle to find employment and are are also likely to have been unemployed prior to incarceration. Based on the results of one study, 65 percent of federal prisoners were unemployed at the time of arrest (Boe, Sinclair, & Vuong, 2002). Furthermore, Correctional Service Canada (CSC) reports that eight out of ten new admissions into federal penitentiaries between 1995 and 2005 had not obtained a high school diploma and up to 20 percent had less than a grade eight education (Boe, 2005). This lack of employment history combined with poor educational attainment prior to incarceration places offenders at a great disadvantage compared to other people entering the workforce. Beyond these factors, former prisoners face barriers to obtaining employment due to biased hiring practices (e.g., Holzer, Raphael, & Stoll, 2004) and policies that restrict employers from hiring individuals with criminal records.

The presence of mental illness can be an additional barrier for former prisoners to obtaining employment. CSC reported that approximately 13 percent of men and 29 percent of women in federal institutions were identified as having a mental health problem at admission (Dupuis, MacKay, & Nicol, 2013). Furthermore, across Canada, an estimated 4,500 offenders with serious mental illness are under the care of review boards as a result of being found not criminally responsible on account of mental disorder (A. Broughm, personal communication, September 24, 2015). Similarly, in a survey of psychiatric clients seeking help from supported employment agencies, almost half had had some interaction with the criminal justice system, with 36 percent having at least one criminal conviction (Theriot & Segal, 2005).

Working is beneficial for former prisoners—particularly those with mental illness—in terms of supporting psychiatric recovery and desistance from crime. For example, Delaney (2011) examined recidivism rates of 866 substance-abusing mentally ill offenders who were being supervised in the community. Results indicated that employed, substance-abusing, mentally ill offenders were significantly less likely to reoffend in the (mean 24-month) follow-up period. Similarly, in a study comparing the clinical outcomes of psychiatric patients who were employed with those who were unemployed over an 18-month period, researchers found that the patients who worked had better global functioning, fewer general mental health symptoms, and less social disability (i.e., regarding family, social, citizen, and occupation subscales) than those who did not work (Burns et al., 2009). Improvements in quality of life, personal fulfillment, and psychiatric well-being were also found in other studies of individuals with mental illness who were employed (e.g., Bond et al., 2001; Nordt, Muller, Rossler, & Lauber, 2007).

## EMPLOYMENT BARRIERS FOR FORMER PRISONERS WITH MENTAL ILLNESS

### Educational/Vocational Experience

Individuals with mental illness are at higher risk for poor employment and/ or educational experiences as a result of their illness(es) and the related disruptions in their vocational pursuits (e.g., Breslau, Lane, Sampson, & Kessler, 2008; Gibb, Fergusson, & Horwood, 2010; Holmes, Silvestri, & Kostakos, 2011). This is also true for former offenders with mental illness, particularly in cases where they have been found not criminally responsible on account of mental disorder. This is exemplified by an American study by the Bureau of Justice Statistics (2003) where offenders with mental illness were found to have poorer education and employment histories compared to those without mental illness. For example, 38 to 47 percent of state and federal prisoners with mental illness were unemployed prior to arrest compared to 28 to 33 percent of state and federal prisoners without mental illness. Sneed and colleagues (2006) found even higher rates of unemployment in a study of offenders with mental illness who were being diverted through a mental health court: of the 94 offenders assessed, nearly 30 percent had not graduated high school and 74.5 percent reported being unemployed. The authors were dismayed to note that while employment information was dispersed among the offenders in the program, not a single referral to a supported employment service agency was made, and after a 12-month follow-up period 89.7 percent of the participants indicated that their employment status had not changed (Sneed, Koch, Estes, & Quinn, 2006).

Not only do offenders with mental illness enter the correctional system more disadvantaged than their peers without mental illness with regard to vocation, they also continue to struggle in their vocational pursuits while incarcerated. In a study of over 3,400 prisoners in several Iowa correctional facilities, it was reported that prisoners with mental illness were 27 percent less likely to complete vocational programming compared to other prisoners (Skinner, 2010). This is troubling given that prisoners who completed these programs had improved re-entry outcomes: completion of vocational training increased their odds of gaining full-time employment by 19 percent and prisoners who later were fully employed had lower recidivism rates (Skinner, 2010). Furthermore, former offenders with mental illness have more difficulty finding employment compared to those without mental illness challenges. Mallik-Kane and Visher (2008) examined the re-entry experience of over 1000 offenders in Ohio and Texas and concluded that the "rates of employment [for offenders with mental health conditions] were significantly lower than the rates reported by other returning prisoners" (p. 38). This was true at both the 2–3 month and the 8–10 month follow-up interview. Notably, most other former offenders reported that they had found employment at or exceeding their pre-incarceration level by the later follow-up period, while former offenders with mental illness had not yet returned to their pre-incarceration employment level. Similarly, in the United States, the Bureau of Justice Statistics released a report in 2006 revealing that, post-release, only 50 percent of probationers with mental illness, compared to 75 percent of probationers without mental illness, indicated that they were employed. In another study with a longer follow-up period, Silver, Cohen, and Spodak (1989) compared the employment outcomes of former prisoners at five years post-release into the community. They reported that former prisoners without mental illness were approximately three times more likely to be employed than the former prisoner group with mental illness (Silver et al., 1989).

## Psychiatric Factors and Psychosocial Functioning
Former offenders with mental illness may struggle to obtain and sustain employment as a direct result of their illness. For example, psychiatric symptoms may interfere with time management, motivation, interpersonal skills, and attentional abilities, which negatively affect job performance (Corrigan, Rao, & Lam, 1999). Additionally, the cyclical and recurrent nature of some mental disorders may affect vocational functioning and increase absenteeism (Tschopp, Perkins, Wood, Leczycki, & Oyer, 2011). Aside from symptoms, individuals with mental illness may also experience side effects from their psychiatric medications such as sedation, sialorrhea (drooling),

nausea, or sensitivity to the sun, all of which can further impair their ability to effectively manage employment. Psychiatric patients in the community with criminal justice involvement who present at community mental health agencies seemingly have worse psychosocial functioning than those without criminal justice involvement. For example, in a study by Theriot and Segal (2005), psychiatric patients with criminal convictions were more likely to be homeless and drug-dependent than those without a history of criminal justice involvement. These individuals also presented with greater psychiatric disability, as rated by the Brief Psychiatric Rating Scale, and less personal empowerment. Taken together, psychiatric symptoms may interfere with employment, but when a person is also struggling with a history of criminal justice involvement, this seems to lead to poorer psychosocial outcomes. Therefore, psychiatric patients with criminal justice involvement may experience greater challenges in successfully joining the paid workforce and maintaining employment because their mental health needs are greater than those of other psychiatric patients living in the community.

Reintegration into the community after a period of incarceration can be a stressful transition for former offenders (e.g., Durcan, 2012). This is especially true for former offenders with mental illness who require additional support to manage their psychiatric health. Furthermore, there is strong evidence pointing to stress as a trigger for, and exacerbator of, psychiatric symptoms (e.g., Moghaddam, 2002). For example, former prisoners with mental illness are expected to connect with psychiatric services and manage their medication regimens, in addition to managing other life tasks, such as finding affordable and stable housing and reconnecting with friends and family. In instances where post-release support for these issues is lacking, such conditions have been shown to predict a worsening of psychiatric symptoms for offenders with mental illness that can lead to reoffending and a subsequent return to the criminal justice system (e.g., Lovell, Gagliardi, & Peterson, 2002). It is therefore expected that former offenders with mental illness may have greater difficulty than those without in obtaining employment when released into the community due to the stress of reintegration and its effect on their mental health status.

Individuals with mental illness and criminal justice involvement also report that certain aspects of their work can increase their stress levels (Tschopp et al., 2011). Perceived stigma from co-workers may contribute to workplace stress. For example, reports of co-workers being rude and thus instigating interpersonal conflict were documented in interviews with employees with mental illness and criminal justice involvement (Tschopp et al., 2011). Individuals may also experience negative comments from others and feel socially marginalized (Stuart, 2006) or stress as they manage their symptoms at work and make decisions about disclosing their mental health status. Yet another source of stress for this population stems from the precarious nature of the employment to which they are often relegated (Marmot et al., 2008). Individuals with mental illness are more likely to obtain temporary, part-time, and/or minimum-wage jobs than stable positions (Cook, 2007) and so, based on this and the presented research, it is reasonable to expect that former offenders with mental illness would also find themselves more likely to obtain these types of jobs. These positions rarely offer benefits or reliable income, and are particularly vulnerable to the fluctuations of the economy.

### Stigma

Another factor that acts as a barrier to employment is the stigma related to mental illness, which fuels discriminatory practices by employers (e.g., Krupa, Kirsh, Cockburn, & Gewurtz, 2009; Stuart, 2006). The Canadian Mental Health Association (2015) purports that "of all persons with disabilities, those with a serious mental illness face the highest degree of stigmatization in the workplace, and the greatest barriers to employment" (para. 1). This barrier is then exacerbated by the presence of a criminal record, which alone impedes successful employment goals (e.g., Pager, 2003). Batastini, Bolanos, and Morgan (2014) examined the attitudes of employers toward hiring applicants who were involved in the criminal justice system and/or had a mental illness. Employers were provided with a vignette describing a potential applicant with or without mental illness and with or without a criminal record, and asked how acceptable the applicant was for employment, as well as the likelihood they would hire the applicant. Analyses determined that employers rated the least acceptable job applicants as those with both mental illness and a criminal record (Batastini et al., 2014). Employer responses regarding the respective hireability of applicants with mental illness with and without a criminal record were undifferentiated. However, employers anticipated that individuals with mental illness and/or a criminal record would perform poorly at their job (Batastini et al., 2014). When the authors provided employers with a psychoeducational component[1] explaining the individual and community-level benefits of employment, employers were more likely to rate the potential applicants as acceptable and to consider hiring them; however, this was due to their adjusting their preexisting thoughts about a criminal record, and not mental illness, since psychoeducation did not alter the attitude of the hypothetical employers when the potential applicant only had mental illness (Batastini et al., 2014).

The results of Batastini et al.'s (2014) study highlight the general stigma former offenders face when applying for jobs, as well as the challenges faced by former offenders who also struggle with mental illness. In another study by Perkins and colleagues (2009), the authors interviewed a random sampling of adult residents in the state of Indiana. They found that people felt less social distance and therefore directed less stigma toward individuals with schizophrenia if the person was employed. This was true even when the person was described as having a criminal record. The rated social distance was almost identical for persons with schizophrenia who had a history of a felony offence but were working, as they were for unemployed persons with schizophrenia with only a misdemeanor offence (Perkins, Raines, Tschopp, & Warner, 2009). The presence of employment mitigated the fact that the person had committed a more serious criminal act.

As a result of psychiatric factors, accommodations may be required for a former offender with mental illness to be successful in the workplace. Even employers who may be open to the idea of providing accommodations, however, may be resistant or have difficulty when putting these into practice (Shankar et al., 2014). For example, in a qualitative review of barriers to hiring and accommodating workers with mental disorders, Shankar and colleagues (2014) found that employers were more supportive of providing accommodations when they had worked with employees with mental illness in the past and/or had positive experiences working with employment placement providers. Conversely, employers who expressed negative views of employees with mental illness indicated that they would require more information about mental illness before making hiring decisions. Therefore, if managers do not feel like they have the necessary information about potential employees with mental illness, and are also experiencing productivity pressures, lacking support services, and/or are lacking positive relationships with placement providers, these may act as barriers to providing accommodations. Furthermore, most employers attributed mental illness to personal factors outside the workplace, which the authors argued may impede their ability to recognize the importance of the workplace for individuals with mental illness and reduce the likelihood of taking steps to accommodate these workers (Shankar et al., 2014).

## Hiring Policies and Legislation

Many employers today request criminal record checks as a component of the job application process and this practice appears to be increasingly common (e.g., Ontario Association of Chiefs of Police, 2014). This practice immediately hinders former offenders, both with and without mental illness, and acts as a significant barrier to obtaining employment. There has been a "Ban the Box" movement—mostly within the United States and driven by civil rights groups supporting former offenders—that discourages employers from asking about a criminal record on job applications. As also discussed later in chapters 4 and 6, this campaign strives to ensure former offenders are welcomed back into society and workplaces, and also institutes fair hiring practices. To date, 45 cities and counties in the United States—including large metropolitan cities such as Boston and New York—have removed the box inquiring about a criminal record from the public job applications (Legal Services for Prisoners with Children, 2015).

The movement has not gained as much traction in Canada. Until recently in some provinces, the Canadian Police Information Centre (CPIC) report that employers could request their applicants include noncriminal mental health encounters with police, such as suicide attempts or psychological crises. Employers and volunteer agencies requesting background checks on applicants were permitted access to such information, which led to discrimination and exclusion in some cases for individuals dually marked by mental illness and criminal justice involvement. Due to pressures from the Canadian Civil Liberties Association, the Ontario Human Rights Commission and the Information and Privacy Commissioner of Ontario, police departments in Ontario put an end to releasing mental-health-related information to potential employers in the spring of 2015. Additional changes have occurred in Ontario that include legislation compelling police departments to review these records every two years (instead of every five) to expunge mental-health records that are no longer relevant on a more regular basis. Consequently, the CPIC's reports on individuals with mental illness are now less stigmatizing and less likely to negatively affect securing employment. In British Columbia, the Information and Privacy Commissioner recently reviewed the province's use of police information and made similar recommendations that the government should stop including mental health information in police checks (Denham, 2014). It is not routine practice for police agencies in other provinces (e.g., Newfoundland, Saskatchewan, and Prince Edward Island) to release mental-health-related information for criminal record checks (see Denham, 2014).

The factors outlined above—low educational attainment, psychiatric symptoms, stress, stigma, discriminatory hiring policies—all serve to make reintegration into the community more difficult for former offenders with mental illness, considering that they act as barriers to obtaining and maintaining employment. In response to the enormity of the challenges faced by these individuals to enter the workforce, efforts have been made by governments and non-profit organizations to provide resources and support—supported employment being one such approach.

## EMPLOYMENT/VOCATIONAL INTERVENTIONS FOR PRISONERS WITH MENTAL ILLNESS

### Supported Employment

Supported employment is a person-centred approach intended to provide people with disabilities assistance in finding and maintaining meaningful employment. Supported employment emerged from vocational rehabilitation programs with psychiatric patients and is an effective strategy to assist individuals with mental illness in their efforts to participate in society and make a living (Whitley, Kostick, & Bush, 2009). Based on the individual placement and support model, the key principles of supported employment include: (1) the search for competitive employment (rather than temporary positions or those that do not offer at least minimum wage compensation); (2) consumer choice/preference regardless of readiness; (3) rapid search instead of including lengthy pre-employment assessments; (4) unlimited support rather than time-limited; (5) mental health support; and (6) benefits planning (Marshall et al., 2014). In a review of nine randomized control studies, Bond (2004) reported that, whereas only 20 percent of people with psychiatric illness obtained employment in the control groups, upwards of 40 to 60 percent of people in the supported employment groups did so. These results are similar to those from a multi-state, multi-site study that reported 34 percent of control subjects and 55 percent of supported employment participants as having achieved competitive employment (Cook et al., 2005). There are very few studies, however, that have investigated the employment outcomes of supported employment programs with psychiatric patients who have criminal justice involvement. Findings from the study by Cook et al. (2005) suggested that supported employment participants were more successful than controls even when they had recent criminal justice involvement. Similarly, in a retrospective chart review of over 150 individuals who received supported employment, there were no differences in the employment outcomes between individuals with or without criminal justice involvement (Frounfelker et al., 2011). The authors concluded that the supported employment program was beneficial for psychiatric patients who also had histories of criminal justice involvement.

Further evidence for the advantages of this model of employment intervention for people with mental illness and criminal justice involvement is provided by a randomized control trial by Bond and colleagues (2015). Individuals with mental illness were randomly assigned to either individual placement and support (essentially supported employment) or a job club approach[2] and followed for one year. When interviewed 12 months after intake, 31 percent of participants in the individual placement and support group reported having secured competitive employment, while only 7 percent in the job club had similar success (Bond et al., 2015). While evidence for the supported employment approach for individuals with mental illness is well documented (see Marshall et al., 2014), the studies outlined here provide strong evidence that this employment approach is also appropriate and successful for individuals with both mental illness and criminal justice involvement. Despite this, there is evidence indicating that it takes longer for individuals with both mental illness and criminal justice involvement (compared to individuals with mental illness alone) to become engaged with supported employment programming, waiting up to twice as long for formal supported employment services (Frounfelker, Glover, Teachout, Wilkniss, & Whitley, 2010).

*Supported Employment: Employment Specialists' Perspectives.* Employment specialists help clients who use supported employment services find, maintain, and/or improve employment opportunities based on their clients' vocational goals. When asked about assisting psychiatric patients with criminal justice involvement, employment specialists admitted that this was one of the "hardest ... challenges" of their jobs, especially when clients had histories of sexual offences (Whitley, Kostick, & Bush, 2009, p. 1639). Using semi-structured interviews, Whitley and colleagues (2009) investigated the experiences of employment specialists who worked with psychiatric patients both with and without criminal justice involvement. The respondents commonly noted that they felt their ability to offer support was limited by employers' willingness to hire individuals with criminal records or hiring regulations preventing the hiring of individuals with criminal records (Whitley et al., 2009). Consequently, they were forced to look for entry-level jobs and use an incremental approach to finding employment (i.e., find less preferred jobs in order to obtain a job at all) which deviates from the traditional individual placement and support model that attempts to locate client-preferred positions. Employment specialists felt this deviation was justified due to the obstacles faced by clients with criminal justice involvement. Traditional methods of individual placement and support therefore needed to be adapted to meet the needs of this population.

Another strategy that was used universally with clients with criminal justice involvement was to focus on strengths, such as particular skills or the length of time since incarceration. While this approach is part of the individual placement and support model and not uniquely helpful to this particular population (see Rapp, 1997), the participants in this study indicated that they were more conscious of searching out and emphasizing the strengths of clients with both mental illness and criminal justice involvement compared to those with mental illness alone (Whitley et al., 2009). The last strategy used with clients with criminal justice involvement compared to those without was to direct these clients toward "mom and pop" businesses as a way to sidestep the policies or laws more stringently enforced at some larger companies. This approach was the only action that was distinctly applied to clients with both mental illness and criminal justice involvement. Participants acknowledged that this approach often meant deviating from the individual placement and support model in that client preferences were not strictly adhered to, but indicated that this compromise was reasonable and the only way to manage the policy restrictions larger companies often maintained. The participants believed that this strategy increased their success in finding clients employment.

In a similar study, employment specialists were asked the following questions:

> How do individuals with mental illness as well as an offense history impact employment service provision?
>
> What barriers do employment service providers face when providing supported employment services for individuals with both mental illness and offense history?
>
> Which strategies have been effective in producing successful employment outcomes for these individuals? (Tschopp, Perkins, Hart-Katuin, Born, & Holt, 2007, p. 176)

Four main themes emerged from the grounded theory methodology, two of which relate to employment reintegration: "(1) barriers to successful employment outcomes; and (2) contributors to successful employment outcomes," (Tschopp et al., 2007, p. 177). Under the "barriers" theme, employment specialists noted that some clients with criminal justice involvement did not immediately disclose their criminal history to the employment specialist. Also, employment specialists indicated that their clients' expectations about workload and wages for legitimate jobs seemed unrealistic, perhaps given their history of illicit employment (Tschopp et al., 2007). As a result, consumers of supported employment may express frustration and/or reluctance to engage in employment that requires them to work harder, longer, and for less pay than their illegal pursuits in their past. Lastly, these clients often held antisocial attitudes and/or expressed limited remorse for their offences, which made placement in jobs a challenge. Evidence suggests that employers are more likely to hire former offenders when they are able to discuss their criminal past honestly while outlining the steps they have taken to improve their lives (e.g., Swanson, Langfitt-Reese, & Bond, 2012). Antisocial attitudes and lack of remorse expressed may limit applicants' ability to effectively communicate this to potential employers and thereby act as a barrier to successful job placement.

In addition to consumer-based barriers, environmental barriers were also highlighted. Employment specialists described difficulty managing the stigma that accompanied individuals' mental illness and criminal justice involvement. They reported feeling taxed to educate employers about mental illness, and particularly its link to violence, in their already overstretched/restricted time. Another environmental barrier described by employment specialist participants was the lack of family and community support for their clients. Former offenders with mental illness often experience extreme social isolation (Griffiths, Dandurand, & Murdoch, 2007). A consequence of incarceration and unemployment is a reduction in one's social network, which is then compounded by the stigma and discrimination often faced by individuals with mental illness and/or criminal justice involvement. Both employment specialists and consumers have reported that without this social support, individuals are less likely to actively seek employment and meet their goals (Frounfelker et al., 2010).

The second theme identified in the study highlighted "contributors" to vocational success. Participants noted that when clients were able to show accountability for their actions and were actively taking steps to change their lives, the process of finding employment became easier and led to consumer success. Characteristics exhibited by the service providers were also important for successful vocational outcomes. These included being non-judgmental, expressing optimism, and being persistent (Tschopp et al., 2007). In this way, employment specialists could model positive attitudes and traits that, if adopted by clients, could serve to boost outcomes. An important environmental contributor to success that was highlighted was encouraging and supporting community connections to family, probation officers, and community agencies. In response to their findings, the authors suggested that employment agencies should employ staff that have strong counselling and relationship-building skills (Tschopp et al. 2007). With two significant sources of stigma faced by these clients—mental illness and criminal justice involvement—advocacy and awareness-building are two important tasks that should be part of employment specialists' roles. This conveys to the consumers that they have a right to employment despite their histories. It can also educate employers about the realities of mental illness, rehabilitation, and recovery.

Based on these findings, Whitley et al. (2009) concluded that employment specialists require more guidance to work competently with people who have criminal justice involvement. When considering adapting typical supported employment programs to be used in populations of psychiatric patients with criminal justice involvement, efforts should be made to accommodate the unique conditions of this population (Osher & Steadman, 2007; Whitley et al., 2009). In describing how to adapt the individual placement and support model of supported employment, Bond (2013) emphasizes that vocational supports would be most beneficial when working closely with mental health treatment teams. This coordination could be facilitated by IPS teams who specialize in this population. Similarly, employment specialists should be mindful of when it may be necessary to refer clients to additional resources to attend to mental health issues (Tschopp et al. 2007). Employment specialists should coach individuals with mental illness and criminal justice involvement on how to address their criminal justice involvement with employers based on feedback that employers have provided. For example, in a study examining employers attitudes when considering hiring people with past criminal justice involvement , the results suggested that employers were more likely to hire individuals who were forthcoming about their criminal record, arrived at interviews prepared to discuss their criminal justice involvement, and could talk about the steps they had taken to improve their lives (Swanson et al., 2012). This finding corroborates reports of employment specialists who note better vocational outcomes when clients are repeatedly coached on being honest about their criminal justice involvement and how to put a positive spin on their past (Tschopp et al., 2007). Knowing the hiring preferences of employers can guide employment rehabilitation specialists in their work with former offenders who have mental illness.

Based on this information, Swanson and colleagues (2012) outline three main strategies employment specialists should use:

a) help clients make face-to-face contact with employers;
b) help clients prepare to talk about skills and strengths related to the job for which they are applying; and
c) help clients practise the way they will talk about prior convictions and efforts to avoid legal problems in the future. (p. 389)

Face-to-face contact is important because individuals who honestly report their criminal justice involvement on application forms may often be screened out early in the application review process; however, research suggests that employers are more likely to hire individuals, including those who have a criminal record, following a positive interaction; they make case-by-case decisions even if they have a criminal record (Swanson et al., 2012; Tschopp et al., 2007). Employers are interested in hearing what former offenders have learned from their criminal justice involvement and what they are doing to prevent future problems with the law. Employment rehabilitation specialists can practise interviews with former offenders with mental illness to shape their responses to be in line with these employer preferences. Since employers reported hiring individuals with criminal justice involvement as a result of their possessing the necessary skills for the position, former offenders with mental illness can be coached to effectively discuss their own skills and experience in relation to the respective job (Swanson et al., 2012).

*Supported Employment: Clients' Perspectives.* Baron, Draine, and Salzer (2013) examined the first-hand experiences of former offenders with mental illness by employing unstructured interviews in which they asked individuals to describe their job search experiences following their most recent release from jail. Their results indicated that none of the 17 participants had secured long-term employment (Baron et al., 2013). Moreover, the participants demonstrated little surprise or frustration with this result; they seemed resigned to their circumstance and felt it was an ordinary part of their lives (Baron et al., 2013). Most of the respondents were looking for entry-level positions and had little ambition to reach for better jobs. Beyond ambition, however, it seemed that the participants felt that these other positions were unrealistic and unobtainable. The respondents "set their job sights quite low," and involvement in employment support had not changed this view. Any progress they had made as a result of being involved in employment training or support programming was seen as "agonizingly slow" (Baron et al., 2013, p. 5).

Respondents also identified their psychiatric illness as a barrier to being hired and to maintaining employment; they felt that employers viewed their psychiatric problems as limiting their ability to work. Some respondents identified their criminal justice involvement as the main barrier to obtaining gainful employment. These latter respondents noted that there was little systematic focus on their employment futures and that little assistance was offered to them while they were in prison. Another common theme that arose was that these individuals had few other social connections in their communities to assist them in finding employment. For example, they had limited contact with family members who might otherwise have been able to help them or provide them with a larger social network through which to find employment. The results of this study suggest that former offenders with mental illness are painfully aware of their limited employment opportunities and seem to have adopted a learned helplessness approach in response.

A similar study was conducted by Tschopp, Perkins, Wood, Leckzycki, and Oyer (2011) who interviewed 14 beneficiaries of a supported employment program who had mental illness and had had criminal justice involvement. The authors were interested in understanding the barriers—both internal and external—to finding and maintaining gainful employment, as well as the factors that helped consumers to be successful in this realm. Participants described how their mental illness contributed to their criminal behaviour, but how unemployment and poverty did as well. They expressed concerns about employers' misperceptions of mental illness and criminal justice involvement and how they felt these were barriers to finding employment. Factors that helped them in their job search were positive attitudes and emotional support from employment specialists, learning practical skills such as role-playing interviewing, and coaching on how to disclose and explain their criminal justice involvement to potential employers (Tschopp et al. 2011).

## Adaptations Needed for Programs Offered to Individuals with Mental Illness and Criminal Justice Involvement

It is clear from the evidence presented above regarding the importance of employment for former offenders with mental illness that effort should be made to provide vocational training and support for this population. However, given that offenders with mental illness may struggle with typical vocational programming provided in correctional institutions (see Skinner, 2010), development of programming aimed specifically at this population is recommended. Correctional programs could incorporate schemes for managing psychiatric symptoms and discussing mental health, and hire staff who are dually informed about the criminogenic and mental health needs of the populations under their supervision. In fact, providing mental health care for prisoners at an equivalent level of care offered to individuals in the community was a specific recommendation of the World Health Organization (2007) in a paper on legislation change needed for mental health and human rights released nearly a decade ago. When such dual knowledge is present among correctional staff, there are clear benefits. For example, when offender programming is adapted to be used with prisoners who have mental illness, there is evidence to suggest that these programs are successful. One such adaptation was made for the Reasoning & Rehabilitation program, a cognitive-behavioural program aimed at increasing pro-social attitudes and behaviours in offenders, and frequently offered within Canadian correctional centres. Termed Reasoning and Rehabilitation 2 for Mentally Disordered Offenders (R&R2M), this adapted group was delivered to medium- and high-security prisoners, after which data on pre- and post-measures of violence, problem-solving, coping, and disruptive behaviour were collected (Young, Chick, & Gudjonsson, 2010). Results indicated that the program was successful in reducing attitudes supportive of violent behaviour, as well as disruptive behaviour, as measured by a nurse informant (Young et al., 2010). Without this knowledge, correctional staff usually respond to mental health symptoms presented by prisoners with force and security measures such as segregation (Sorenson, 2010). Unfortunately, these security measures often lead to an exacerbation of mental health symptoms (Sapers & Zinger, 2012). It is crucial that prisoners' mental health needs are addressed to ensure they are adequately equipped to participate in vocational training and/or educational programming during incarceration and once released into the community. In relation to mental health programs offered in the community for psychiatric patients, it also holds that broader training is required for staff in order to effectively attend not only to their patients' mental health, but also to meet the special needs arising out of their involvement in the criminal justice system. For example, Osher and Steadman (2007) discussed how to adapt best practices for psychiatric patients who have criminal justice involvement. They noted that attention should be given to criminogenic thinking patterns in this population as this may help to target behaviours that interfere with the job search process. In addition, they argue that the stress of being in custody may make community adjustment more difficult (Osher & Steadman, 2007).

Adaptations to best practices of community programming for psychiatric patients should also consider that many of these individuals are mandated to attend treatment and comply with medication orders once they have been released from prison. If these conditions are mandated, former prisoners may perceive programming as coercive since participation may be linked to early release and conditions of re-entry (Osher & Steadman, 2007). Awareness of these factors may assist staff in community agencies in understanding the context of individuals with mental illness and criminal involvement in order to work more effectively with this population, thereby leading to better employment outcomes. Any adaptations should therefore address issues of coercion, whether these are real or perceived. Broadly speaking, vocational programming offered by the criminal justice system should take into consideration the mental health needs of offenders; and similarly, programs offered by psychiatric agencies should be aware of the unique needs of patients with criminal justice involvement.

## CONCLUSION

In conclusion, we know that employment plays an integral part in many of our lives. Furthermore, it is an essential component of reintegration for former offenders, especially for those with mental illness. Employment helps to reconnect this marginalized population with their communities, enhances recovery, and is linked to reductions in recidivism. However, finding a job is difficult for offenders, especially when compounded by psychiatric conditions. External barriers to employment include such things as employer stigma, restrictive hiring practices, and lack of community support. Barriers inherent with the job seeker may include poor educational attainment, lack of motivation, hopelessness, and psychiatric symptoms. Offenders with mental illness have typically struggled in school prior to being incarcerated and they also have more difficulty completing vocational programs offered in correctional institutions compared to offenders without mental illness. Both of these factors then limit their vocational success once released.

While there are supported-employment agencies in the community that assist these individuals, employment specialists have reported that psychiatric clients with criminal justice involvement are often the most difficult populations to support in this process. Consequently, adaptations to current programming to specifically attend to the particular needs of individuals with both mental illness and criminal justice involvement are recommended. In the absence of these modified approaches, programs may actually do harm by perpetuating inadequate outcomes of people with multiple disabilities such as psychiatric illness and criminal backgrounds, and contributing to the sense of learned helplessness many people in this population develop. Just as law enforcers (e.g., police officers and lawyers) should be made aware of disability (i.e., mental illness) upon making an arrest in order to appropriately respond to offenders with mental illness, experts argue that educational and vocational needs should be assessed as soon as an offender is incarcerated to ensure that future employability and employment opportunities are prioritized throughout offenders' treatment (Foster, 1999). Correctional programming aimed at boosting vocational achievement should also address the learning needs of offenders with mental illness.

Similarly, supported employment programs in the community should be able to competently serve this population with comprehensive skill, knowledge, and experience. Beyond supporting the individual, however, efforts to provide information and education to employers should be made to combat current discriminatory practices resulting from stigma for both mental illness and criminal justice involvement. Advocacy at the political level also needs to occur. For example, advocates in Ontario, Canada, have successfully argued for the removal of mental-health-related information from police record checks. This could perhaps go further to make it easier to expunge criminal records or reduce employers' reliance on background checks for certain jobs. As researchers have demonstrated, stigma toward individuals with mental-illness is reduced once individuals are employed, efforts to establish a work history in a mental-illness-friendly environment should be a priority (Perkins et al., 2009). This could perhaps be accomplished by mental health agencies and the social services sectors of the government providing work opportunities for this population. Investing in employment opportunities may also help to promote social inclusion and break the cycle of reinstitutionalization for individuals with mental illness and criminal justice involvement. With governments taking a leadership role, it is hoped that private industry will follow. Additionally, more research about the particular needs of this population—individuals with *both* mental illness and criminal justice involvement—is needed, with greater effort made to combine the seemingly disparate silos of research that come from out of the correctional and psychiatric arenas.

## NOTES

1 The psychoeducational component included "an academic journal article describing the benefits of employment to the employee and to the community in general with the hope of generating a better understanding about the role of work in reducing negative outcomes" (Batastini et al., 2014, p. 527).
2 Job clubs are small groups of people who come together to discuss job searching and support each other in this endeavour. Members may also receive support from trained staff and are encouraged to engage employers in the community on their own. The approach often invites members to attend programming at a resource centre to learn skills to find and maintain a job (e.g., resumé building, interviewing tips, etc.). Bond and colleagues (2015) based their job club on the program described in Azrin, N. H. & Philip, R. A. (1979, pp. 144–155).

## REFERENCES

Azrin, N. H., & Philip, R. A. (1979). The job club method for the job handicapped: A comparative outcome study. *Rehabilitation Counseling Bulletin, 23*, 144–155.

Baron, R. C., Draine, J., & Salzer, M. S. (2013). "I'm not sure that I can figure out how to do that": Pursuit of work among people with mental illnesses leaving jail. *American Journal of Psychiatric Rehabilitation, 16*(2), 115–135.

Batastini, A. B., Bolanos, A. D., & Morgan, R. D. (2014). Attitudes toward hiring applicants with mental illness and criminal justice involvement: The impact of education and experience. *International Journal of Law and Psychiatry, 37*(5), 524–533.

Blustein, D. L. (2008). The role of work in psychological health and well-being: A conceptual, historical, and public policy perspective. *American Psychologist, 63*(4), 228–240.

Boe, R. (2005). Unemployment risk trends and the implications for Canadian federal offenders. *Forum on Corrections Research, 17*(1), 3. Correctional Service Canada.

Boe, R., Sinclair, R., & Vuong, B. (2002). *Profiles of the federal offender population by security level, 1997 and 2001.* Draft report prepared for the Correctional Service Canada.

Bond, G. R. (2004). Supported employment: Evidence for an evidence-based practice. *Psychiatric Rehabilitation Journal, 27*, 345–359.

Bond, G. R. (2013). *Supported employment for justice-involved people with mental illness.* Delmar, NY: National GAINS Center for Evidence-Based Programs in the Justice System.

Bond, G. R., Resnick, S. G., Drake, R. E., Xie, H., McHugo, G. J., & Bebout, R. R. (2001). Does competitive employment improve nonvocational outcomes for people with severe mental illness? *Journal of Consulting and Clinical Psychology, 69*(3), 489–501.

Bond, G. R., Kim, J. S., Becker, D. R., Swanson, S. J., Drake, R. E., Krzos, I. M., Fraser, V. V., O'Neill, S., & Froundfelker, R. L. (2015). A controlled trial of supported employment for people with severe mental illness and justice involvement. *Psychiatric Services, 66*, 1027–1034.

Bonta, J., & Andrews, D. (2007). Risk, need, responsivity model for offender assessment and rehabilitation. *Rehabilitation, 6*, 1–22.

Breslau, J., Lane, M., Sampson, N., & Kessler, R. C. (2008). Mental disorders and subsequent educational attainment in a US national sample. *Journal of Psychiatric Research, 42*(9), 708–716.

Bureau of Justice Statistics. (2003). *Education and correctional populations.* Washington, DC: US Department of Justice.

Bureau of Justice Statistics. (2006). *Mental health problems of prison and jail inmates.* Washington, DC: US Department of Justice.

Burns, T., Catty, J., White, S., Becker, T., Koletsi, M., Fioritti, A., ... Lauber, C. (2009). The impact of supported employment and working on clinical and social functioning: Results of an international study of individual placement and support. *Schizophrenia Bulletin, 35*(5), 949–958.

Canadian Mental Health Association. (2015). *Employment.* Retrieved from https://www.cmha.ca/mental-health/find-help/employment/

Cook, J. A. (2007). *Executive summary of findings from the employment intervention demonstration program.* Chicago: Employment Intervention Demonstration Program of the University of Illinois at Chicago.

Cook, J. A., Leff, H. S., Blyler, C. R., Gold, P. B., Goldberg, R. W., Mueser, K. T., ... & Dudek, K. (2005). Results of a multisite randomized trial of supported employment interventions for individuals with severe mental illness. *Archives of General Psychiatry, 62*(5), 505–512.

Corrigan, P. W., Rao, D., & Lam, C. (1999). Psychiatric rehabilitation. In F. Chan & M. J. Leahy (Eds.), *Health Care and Disability: Case Management* (pp. 527–563). Lake Zurich, IL: Vocational Consultants Press.

Delaney, R. B. (2011). A retrospective study on the relationship among social controls and individual factors as indicators in predicting desistance or persistence in the substance abusing mentally ill supervised offender population.

Dissertation Abstracts International: Section B: The Sciences and Engineering 71(10-B): 6464.

Denham, E. (2014, April 15). *Use of police information checks in British Columbia.* Office of the Information and Privacy Commissioner for British Columbia.

Drydakis, N. (2015). The effect of unemployment on self-reported health and mental health in Greece from 2008 to 2013: A longitudinal study before and during the financial crisis. *Social Science & Medicine, 128,* 43–51.

Dupuis, T., MacKay, R., & Nicol, J. (2013). *Current issues in mental health in Canada: Mental health and the criminal justice system.* Ottawa, Canada: Parliamentary Information and Research Service.

Durcan, G. (2012). Beyond the gate: Supporting the employment aspirations of offenders with mental health conditions. *Mental Health & Social Inclusion, 16*(4), 188–193.

Fergusson, D. M., McLeod, G. F., & Horwood, L. J. (2014). Unemployment and psychosocial outcomes at age 30: A fixed-effects regression analysis. *Australian and New Zealand Journal of Psychiatry, 48*(8), 735–742.

Foster, T. (1999). When will they ever work? The importance of employment. *Journal of Forensic Psychiatry, 10*(2), 245–248.

Frounfelker R. L., Glover, C., Teachout, A., Wilkniss, S., & Whitley, R. (2010). Access to supported employment for consumers with criminal justice involvement. *Psychiatric Rehabilitation Journal, 34*(1), 49.

Frounfelker, R., Teachout, A., Bond, G. R., & Drake, R. E. (2011). Criminal justice involvement of individuals with severe mental illness and supported employment outcomes. *Community Mental Health Journal, 47*(6), 737–741.

Gibb, S. J., Fergusson, D. M., & Horwood, L. J. (2010) Burden of psychiatric disorder in young adulthood and life outcomes at age 30. *British Journal of Psychiatry, 197*(2), 122–127.

Graffam, J., Shinkfield, A., Lavelle, B., & Hardcastle, L. (2004). Attitudes of employers, corrective services workers, employment support workers, and prisoners and offenders towards employing ex-prisoners and ex-offenders. *Criminology Research Council, 2,* 1–65.

Griffiths, C. T., Dandurand, Y., & Murdoch, D. (2007). *The social reintegration of offenders and crime prevention.* National Crime Prevention Centre.

Hoare, N. P., & Machin, M. M. (2006) Maintaining wellbeing during unemployment. *Australian Journal of Career Development, 15,* 19–27.

Holmes, A., Silvestri, R., Kostakos, M. (2011). *The Impact of Mental Health Problems in the Community College Student Population.* Higher Education Quality Council of Ontario.

Holzer, H. J., Raphael, S. & Stoll, M. A. (2004). Will employers hire ex-offenders? Employer preferences, background checks, and their determinants. In M. Pattillo, D. Weiman, & B. Western (Eds.), *Imprisoning America: The social effects of mass incarceration* (pp. 205–246). New York: Russell Sage Foundation.

Krupa, T., Kirsh, B., Cockburn, L., & Gewurtz, R. (2009). Understanding the stigma of mental illness in employment. *Work, 33*(4), 413–425.

Legal Services for Prisoners with Children. (2015). *Ban the Box.* Retrieved from http://www.prisonerswithchildren.org/our-projects/allofus-or-none/ban-the-box-campaign/

Lovell, D., Gagliardi, G. J., & Peterson, P. D. (2002). Recidivism and use of services among persons with mental illness after release from prison. *Psychiatric Services, 53*(10), 1290–1296.

Mallik-Kane, K., & Visher, C. A. (2008). *Health and prisoner reentry: How physical, mental, and substance abuse conditions shape the process of reintegration.* Washington, DC: Urban Institute.

Marmot, M., Friel, S., Bell, R., Houweling, T. A., Taylor, S., & Commission on Social Determinants of Health. (2008). Closing the gap in a generation: Health equity through action on the social determinants of health. *The Lancet, 372*(9650), 1661–1669.

Marshall, T., Goldberg, R. W., Braude, L., Dougherty, R. H., Daniels, A. S., Ghose, S. S., ... Delphin-Rittmon, M. E. (2014). Supported employment: Assessing the evidence. *Psychiatric Services, 65*(1), 16–23.

Moghaddam, B. (2002). Stress activation of glutamate neurotransmission in the prefrontal cortex: Implications for dopamine-associated psychiatric disorders. *Biological Psychiatry, 51*(10), 775–787.

Nordt, C., Muller, B., Rossler, W., & Lauber, C. (2007). Predictors and course of vocational status, income, and quality of life in people with severe mental illness: A naturalistic study. *Social Science and Medicine, 65*(7), 1420–1429.

Ontario Association of Chiefs of Police. (2014). *Guideline for police record checks.* Retrieved from http://www.oacp.on.ca/Userfiles/Files/NewAndEvents/Public ResourceDocuments/GUIDELINES%20FOR%20POLICE%20RECORD%20 CHECKS%20%20_%20June%202014_FINAL.pdf

Osher, F. C., & Steadman, H. J. (2007). Adapting evidence-based practices for persons with mental illness involved with the criminal justice system. *Psychiatric Services, 58*, 1472–1478.

Pager, D. (2003). The mark of a criminal record. *American Journal of Sociology, 108*(5), 937–975.

Perkins, D. V., Raines, J. A., Tschopp, M. K., & Warner, T. C. (2009). Gainful employment reduces stigma toward people recovering from schizophrenia. *Community Mental Health Journal, 45*(3), 158–162.

Rakis, J. (2005). Improving the employment rates of ex-prisoners under parole. *Federal Probation, 69*, 7–12.

Rapp, C. (1997). *The strengths model: Case management for people suffering from severe and persistent mental illness.* New York, NY: Oxford University Press.

Sapers, H., & Zinger, I. (2012). *Annual report of the Office of the Correctional Investigator 2011–2012.* Ottawa, ON: Correctional Investigator of Canada. Retrieved from http://www.oci-bec.gc.ca/cnt/rpt/annrpt/annrpt20112012-eng.aspx

Shankar, J., Liu, L., Nicholas, D., Warren, S., Lai, D., Tan, S., ... Sear, A. (2014). Employers' perspectives on hiring and accommodating workers with mental illness. *SAGE Open, 4*(3), 1–13.

Silver, S. B., Cohen, M. I., Spodak, M. K. (1989). Follow-up after release of insanity acquittees, mentally disordered offenders, and convicted felons. *Bulletin of the American Academy of Psychiatry & the Law, 17*(4), 387–400.

Skinner, B. A. (2010). *To what extent does prisoners' mental illness undermine programming effectiveness?* (Unpublished thesis). University of Iowa.

Sneed, Z., Koch, D. S., Estes, H., & Quinn, J. (2006). Employment and psychosocial outcomes for offenders with mental illness. *International Journal of Psychosocial Rehabilitation, 10*(2), 103–112.

Sorenson, K. (2010). *Mental health and drug and alcohol addiction in the federal correctional system: Report of the Standing Committee on Public Safety and National Security.* Ottawa, ON: Standing Committee on Public Safety and National Security.

Stuart, H. (2006). Mental illness and employment discrimination. *Current Opinion in Psychiatry, 19*(5), 522–526.

Swanson, S. J., Langfitt-Reese, S., & Bond, G. R. (2012). Employer attitudes about criminal histories. *Psychiatric Rehabilitation Journal, 35*(5), 385–390.

Theriot, M. T., & Segal, S. P. (2005). Involvement with the criminal justice system among new clients at outpatient mental health agencies. *Psychiatric Services, 2,* 179–185.

Tschopp, M. K., Perkins, D. V., Hart-Katuin, C., Born, D. L., & Holt, S. L. (2007). Employment barriers and strategies for individuals with psychiatric disabilities and criminal histories. *Journal of Vocational Rehabilitation, 26,* 175–187.

Tschopp, M. K., Perkins, D. V., Wood, H., Leczycki, A., & Oyer, L. (2011). Employment considerations for individuals with psychiatric disabilities and criminal histories: Consumer perspectives. *Journal of Vocational Rehabilitation, 35*(2), 129–141.

Whitley, R., Kostick, K. M., & Bush, P. W. (2009). Supported employment specialist strategies to assist clients with severe mental illness and criminal justice issues. *Psychiatric Services, 60*(12), 1637–1641.

World Health Organization. (2007). *Mental health and prisons.* Retrieved from http://www.who.int/mental_health/policy/development/MH&PrisonsFactsheet.pdf

Young, S. J., Chick, K., & Gudjonsson, G. (2010). A preliminary evaluation of reasoning and rehabilitation 2 in mentally disordered offenders (R&R2M) across two secure forensic settings in the United Kingdom. *Journal of Forensic Psychiatry and Psychology, 21*(3), 336–349.

# Section II
Criminal Histories, Employment Prospects, and Moving Forward

# CHAPTER 4

# Job Search, Suspended
## Changes to Canada's Pardon Program and the Impact on Finding Employment

Samantha McAleese

## INTRODUCTION

> *What is the point of "challenging criminal thinking" or providing prisoners with suitable job training if upon their release they will be prohibited from finding legitimate employment because of their criminal records?*
> (Maruna, 2014, p. 126)

T he task of finding stable and meaningful employment is challenging for many Canadians, especially given the increasing competitiveness and "growing problem of surging inequality" in today's job market (Jackson, 2010, p. 50). The job hunt is even more complicated for the approximately 3.8 million Canadians with a criminal record (Public Safety Canada, 2013, p. 107), particularly as more and more employers "are incorporating police record checks into their hiring and management practices" (Canadian Civil Liberties Association, 2014, p. 5). Whether the decision to ban the hiring of criminalized persons comes from sweeping corporate policies or the personal views of a small business owner, it is a decision that has a negative impact since securing employment is often identified as an important milestone of re-entry (Munn & Bruckert, 2013; Pager, 2007; Petersilia, 2005).

Pager (2007) uses the phrase "the credentialing of stigma" to describe the work-related exclusion experienced by criminalized persons in the community (p. 4), and Jacobs (2015) refers to the criminal record as a "negative curriculum vitae or résumé" (p. 2). Indeed, employers are increasingly concerned about the assumed risks associated with hiring people with a criminal record (Albright & Denq, 1996; Backman, 2011) even though "over time knowledge that one committed an offence becomes less of a predictor of whether offending will take place again in the future" (Murphy, Sprott, & Doob, 2015, p. 210). Considering the long-term impact a criminal record has on access to a variety of social domains—including employment, education, vocational training opportunities, and stable housing—it is important that individuals who have successfully desisted from crime are able to eventually rid themselves of the associated stigma (Kilgour, 2013; Travis, 2002).

In their article on the benefits of sealing or expunging criminal convictions, Ruddell and Winfree (2006) applauded Canada's pardon system as a sensible and logical approach to reintegration. They stated that allowing someone with a criminal record to apply to the Parole Board of Canada (PBC) to have that record sealed after living crime-free in the community for several years was a socially responsible way to acknowledge successful desistance, and the 96 percent success rate of the Canadian pardon system supported this claim (PBC, 2014). Unfortunately, this pardon system has recently been replaced with a more expensive, restrictive, and punitive record suspension program. The resulting changes have been criticized by criminologists, practitioners, and criminalized persons alike. Given that, I begin this chapter by outlining the changes made to the pardon program and addressing the impact of these changes on criminalized persons seeking employment. Next, and in light of the fact that many criminalized persons experience exclusion or anticipate discrimination by others in the community (Munn, 2012), I draw attention to the active resistance to the stigma associated with a criminal record. I discuss both individual and community resistance, emphasizing how it relates to improving employment opportunities for criminalized persons. I conclude this section with an overview of the "Ban the Box" campaign, a social movement in the United States that asks employers to refrain from eliminating everyone with a criminal record from the hiring process by removing any questions about previous involvement with the criminal justice system from job applications (Ban the Box, 2015a). Finally, to better situate Canada's new record suspension program, I provide an overview of international practices of criminal records management and expungement processes.

## CRIMINAL RECORDS MANAGEMENT IN CANADA

*Originally enacted in 1970, the Criminal Records Act (CRA) provided that an individual was eligible to submit an application for a pardon, after fulfilling the requirements of his/her sentence, if he/she had been of "good conduct" for a prescribed length of time.... A pardon under the CRA enabled an offender who had demonstrated that he/she had successfully reintegrated into society to reduce the legal, economic and social limitations associated with possessing a criminal record.* (Wallace-Capretta, 2000, p. 3)

The intent of Canada's pardon program was to formally acknowledge successful desistance from crime and allow individuals to move forward with their lives without harbouring the mark of a criminal record. The pardon system, however, never completely erased a criminal conviction from the Canadian Police Information Centre (CPIC),[1] but rather sealed the record to ensure the information would not appear on a criminal record check. Initially the application process was free of charge, but several amendments were introduced in the 1990s to increase efficiency, including the addition of a $50 application fee to supplement resources at the Parole Board of Canada. Despite a noticeable drop in pardon applications after these amendments, the pardon program remained successful—as demonstrated through the high grant rates and a very small number of revocations (PBC, 2014).

In 2000, Suzanne Wallace-Capretta from the Department of the Solicitor General Canada examined Canada's pardon program. Her report included three quantitative studies that detail who received pardons, which applicants were denied, and what kind of circumstances led to pardons being revoked. Findings indicated that persons convicted of violent and/or sexual offences, as well as people with multiple convictions for such crimes, were less likely to be granted a pardon compared to people convicted of property and/or non-violent crimes (Wallace-Capretta, 2000, p. 10). Those who had pardons revoked were often male, unemployed, and had a history of violent offences. Wallace-Capretta (2000) further points out that revocation of pardons were not necessarily due to the commission of a new violent offence, but often instead to "liquor and traffic violations along with property offences" (p. 16). The third study focused on applicants with a history of sexual offending, recognizing the vast public concerns about having persons convicted of sexual harm in the community and the fact that they too were eligible to apply for pardons. Analysis showed that those convicted of sexual harm make up only 2 percent of pardon recipients in Canada. This number, combined with a low recidivism rate among persons with a history of sexual harm on their criminal records, does not warrant prohibiting such people from applying for a pardon (Wallace-Capretta, 2000). All in all, this report demonstrates that the pardon program in Canada was a success—a point reiterated by Ruddell and Winfree (2006). In writing about the benefits, for criminalized persons as well as for the community, of setting aside criminal convictions, the authors describe the impact of mass imprisonment on communities across the United States and then point to Canada's pardon program as a successful model for supporting re-entry and desistance.

Despite these positive endorsements, the pardon program has undergone significant changes, as a result of a general shift in Canadian criminal justice policy. In 2010, Bill C-23A, the *Limiting Pardons for Serious Crimes Act*, extended the required wait periods[2] for persons convicted of violent offences and child sexual offences from five to ten years. That same year, the application fee was increased from $50 to $150 and then, in February 2012, the fee jumped from $150 to $631, as the result of a decision made in complete opposition to feedback from a public consultation[3] (Parole Board of Canada, 2011). In March 2012, more changes to the pardon program were brought in under Bill C-10—the *Safe Streets and Communities Act* (2012):

- The word *pardon* was replaced with the term *record suspension*.
- The wait periods before eligibility were extended again, from three years to five years for summary offences, and from five years to ten years for all indictable offences.
- Certain individuals were excluded from applying for a pardon altogether, including those with more than four indictable offences on their record and persons convicted of having engaged in sexual harm.

All of these changes were said to be made in the name of increasing public safety and providing additional protection to victims (Sullivan, 2014), even though the pardon program was not a threat to either of those needs (Ruddell & Winfree, 2006).

The tough-on-crime approach embodied in the *Safe Streets and Communities Act* was a cornerstone of Stephen Harper's Conservative government and just one example of their risk-averse rhetoric. Changes to the pardon system in particular sought to "quell the general public's fear of crime" by monitoring people with criminal records long after the completion of their sentence (Kilgour, 2013, p. 146). This "fear of crime," or more specifically, the fear of dangerous individuals living in our communities, was largely generated by the media, and also by the punitive turn in politics leading politicians to strive not to appear "soft on crime" (Pratt, 2007). The cases of Graham

James and Karla Homolka have been used repeatedly to justify the unwarranted changes to Canada's pardon program.

Graham James, a former Canadian hockey coach who was charged with sexually assaulting several of his players, was granted a pardon in 2010 (Emonds, 2013). Initial media reports on this issue claimed that James benefited from a "routine pardon" and this revelation sparked a political will to make changes to Canada's pardon system (Cheadle & Bronskill, 2011). Despite the false portrayal of the pardon program—which was never an automatic process in Canada, and instead required a lengthy application followed by a rigorous investigation and confirmation of several years of crime-free activity in the community—the *Safe Streets and Communities Act* received Royal Assent in March 2012 and the new record suspension program came into effect. The media was quick to report on these changes, and Graham James continues to be used as an example by both politicians and media contributors when justifying tougher sentences for people convicted of sexual harm (Brodbeck, 2012; Leblanc, 2013).

Another name that has been repeated in the media to justify changes to the pardon system is that of Karla Homolka.[4] In April 2010, it was reported that "the government [was] moving 'very quickly' to draft new legislation to prevent heinous offenders—like infamous killer Karla Homolka—from easily being pardoned for their crimes" (Weese, 2010, para. 1). Once again, the media did not accurately describe the process for granting someone a pardon, and made the public (and politicians) believe that it was openly available and automatic for everyone with a criminal record regardless of the severity of the offence history. The government was able to fast-track changes through parliament to ensure that Homolka would be excluded from ever applying for a pardon, as it would "bring the administration of justice into disrepute" (Jeffords, 2013, para. 116). This achievement received great praise in the media by Tim Danson, the lawyer who represented the families of the victims: "Certainly, we have to applaud the politicians—that doesn't happen very often—that they did act, reached a consensus so that she cannot apply for a pardon in a few weeks" (as cited in CTV.ca News Staff, 2010, para. 4).

Karla Homolka is often "presented as a rare and sensational figure of dangerousness, which has only served to confuse and incite fear" among the general public (Kilty & Frigon, 2006, p. 57). When the media uses Homolka, and others like her, to promote stories on the failings of the justice system, it opens the floor for politicians who capitalize on the creation of new, more punitive policies—such as the changes to the pardon program. This impulsive approach to policy-making is unfortunately becoming "the norm" as media sensationalism combined with a general fear of dangerous and risky people encourages politicians to act fast in order to gain votes (Pratt, 2013, p. 106).

Although using the presence of a criminal record as a predictor of future involvement in activities defined as crime is supported by many criminological studies on re-entry and desistance (e.g., Blumstein & Nakamura, 2009), there is much to be said for the value of forgiveness and for providing criminalized and formerly incarcerated persons with opportunities for growth and redemption in the community (Henry & Jacobs, 2007; Maruna, 2001). In this context, the capacity to seal criminal records would be the most advantageous for those interested in promoting the successful re-entry and employment of criminalized persons. Instead, however, criminalized persons living in Canada must now endure longer periods of discrimination and exclusion before becoming eligible for a record suspension while others will never be eligible under this new regime. The $631 application fee also heavily restricts those with little to no income from applying to have their criminal record sealed. Unfortunately, this meets the description of many criminalized and formerly incarcerated persons in Canada and other countries (Stacey, 2015; Visher & Travis, 2011).

Requirements of the record suspension program function in opposition to statements within the mission and operating principles of the Parole Board of Canada (PBC) that pertain to safe, effective, and timely re-entry and respecting the needs and rights of all persons in the community (PBC, 2000). Given the reported 96 percent success rate of the pardon program, the 2010 and 2012 changes were seemingly a needless reaction to the unique and sensationalized cases of Graham James and Karla Homolka by politicians and policy-makers. The in-depth and increasingly exhaustive screening process required of applicants ensured the integrity of the program. Therefore, the introduction of longer wait periods before eligibility and the exclusion of certain individuals from the program altogether were completely unnecessary.

Limiting access to pardons arguably "makes society less safe by not only failing to encourage and promote rehabilitation but by positively discouraging it" (Maruna, 2014, p. 135). The invisible and ongoing punishment associated with a criminal record creates a social and economic divide between people with a criminal record and those without (Travis, 2002) and "is akin to double jeopardy" (Pager, 2007, p. 58). Canada's pardon program offered criminalized and formerly incarcerated persons a concrete and obtainable incentive to remain crime free in the community, but the restrictions associated with the new record suspension program fail to improve the experience of re-entry. In fact, more recent (and more critical) media reports have featured stories of individual hardship that help illustrate the negative impact of the new criminal records management regime (Cheadle, 2013; Crawford, 2013). For example, CBC News profiled three individuals—an aspiring social worker from British Columbia, a father of two from Ontario, and a business owner from Calgary—demonstrating both the widespread and long lasting impact of a criminal record and the new rules which make it harder to move on from past mistakes (Ireland, 2016).

The controversial legal and policy changes to the *Criminal Records Act* were part of a broader "tough on crime" agenda that was promoted by Canada's former Conservative federal government, gaining momentum in 2006 and coming to an end in 2015 when the Conservative Party was succeeded by the Liberal Party.[5] Previous researchers have suggested that Canada resisted the punitive turn evidenced in other Western democracies, such as the United States and the United Kingdom, and maintained well-funded social supports and a low incarceration rate (Christie, 2004; Doob & Webster, 2006; Meyer & O'Malley, 2005; Pratt, 2007). However, the 2012 *Safe Streets and Communities Act*, along with other legislation and increased government spending on police, courts, and prisons (despite falling crime rates; Easton, Furness, & Brantingham, 2014), indicated a shift in Canada that continues to warrant attention. As resources are transferred from prison re-entry programs (e.g., vocational training, see Sapers, 2014) to prison expansion (Piché, 2014), more people will require support as they re-enter the community, including support in resisting the stigma associated with a criminal record.

## STIGMA

> *Based on their criminal conviction, judgment has been passed not only on the actions of former prisoners but also on their character.* (Munn & Bruckert, 2013, p. 98)

The increasing exclusion of people with criminal records from the workforce is largely driven by stigma[6] and generalizations about the "bad" people who commit crimes. Unfortunately for criminalized persons, labels such as ex-convict, ex-offender, or ex-prisoner become their primary identifiers in social interactions and the generalizations associated with these labels often leads to social exclusion and discrimination (Munn & Bruckert, 2013). Beyond this stigma, employers have become increasingly concerned with "the notions of risk management and harm prevention" (Backman, 2011, p. 39). In consequence, keeping people with criminal records off the payroll has become best practice. Pager (2007) surveyed employers in Milwaukee, Wisconsin, to understand more about their decision-making processes. She discovered that most employers will not hire someone with a criminal record, regardless of the nature or severity of the record. These employers associate criminality with a poor work ethic and dishonesty. They also found that having a criminal record trumps any professional qualifications or work/ training experience the job candidate holds. This stigma (Goffman, 1963) bars criminalized persons from more prestigious, stable, full-time, higher-wage jobs and pushes them to accept work in precarious, low-pay work environments, like restaurants, maintenance and service, construction, and general labour positions (Albright & Denq, 1996; Freeman, 2008; Pager, 2007). In making these hiring decisions, employers may believe they are contributing to community safety, but the lack of viable job opportunities for criminalized persons actually "makes reoffending more likely" (Naylor, 2011, p. 79) and interferes with successful desistance.

Aside from this *interpersonal stigma,* referring to the distancing between "normals" and "others" that occurs between individual social actors (Goffman, 1963; Bruckert & Hannem, 2012), that encourages the active discrimination of criminalized persons, there is also a more structural form of stigma. Hannem (2012) defines *structural stigma* as a bureaucratic strategy that helps institutions separate and manage individuals based on their perceived "risk." While people are sometimes able to negotiate and resist various forms of interpersonal stigma in everyday life, stigma that moves beyond the individual into taking the form of institutional risk-management tools is much harder to navigate. Recent changes to the pardon program in Canada, along with an increase in requests for criminal background checks by employers, landlords, and educational institutions, represent forms of structural stigma that restrict criminalized individuals from becoming fully integrated into society.

## Resistance to Stigma

*Resistance, then, can be found in the individual and collective voices of those who are usually silenced.* (Hannem, 2012, p. 26)

While former prisoners and criminalized persons face multiple forms of stigma and discrimination during community re-entry, they still need to find work—whether this is to appease their parole conditions, to put food on the table, or because they enjoy working and wish to identify themselves as employees (Jackson, 2010). People with criminal records, then, must actively resist stigma and find a way into a workforce that is reluctant to have them. The anticipation of stigma can be a source of anxiety for those who are targeted (Munn, 2012). Yet, many criminalized and formerly incarcerated persons successfully overcome this anxiety to re-settle in the community (Davis, Bahr, & Ward, 2012; Munn & Bruckert, 2013).

At the micro level, stigma is resisted through personal contact between the employer and the job seeker. Face-to-face interviews are the perfect opportunity for people with criminal records to provide information and credentials that nullify the "stereotyped expectations" and assumptions of the employer (Pager, 2007, p. 103). Researchers looking at stigma and identity management have shown that people in general "do not simply accept the dominant discourses regarding those who are criminalized" and instead use their own value and belief systems to make decisions about other individuals (Munn, 2012, p. 154). During a job interview, people can rely on their own confidence, skill sets, and previous work experience to convince the employer that they are the best fit for the job—more valuable information than that available in criminal record checks (Uggen, Vuolo, Lageson, Ruhland, & Witham, 2014).

Unfortunately, the ability to convince an employer that someone with a criminal record has good character traits and is reliable means very little when corporate policies are in place that dictate blanket bans on hiring people with criminal records. Resistance to more structural forms of stigma is somewhat more complicated, but there are promising efforts underway in the United States that could easily be translated into the Canadian context.

In February 2015, *The New York Times* published a story that profiled Michael Mirsky, a man living in New Jersey who had been unemployed for more than 30 years as a result of his criminal record. After detailing the hardship endured by Mr. Mirsky since his conviction, the writer provides readers with information about a national campaign entitled "Ban the Box" (Appelbaum, 2015). The campaign was initiated by the group "All of Us or None"[7] in 2004, and to date "over 45 cities and counties, including New York City, Boston, Philadelphia, Atlanta, Chicago, Detroit, Seattle, and San Francisco have removed the question regarding conviction history from their employment applications" (Ban the Box, 2015a). The grassroots movement is continuing to expand across the country and is having a positive effect on the successful re-entry of criminalized and formerly incarcerated persons in communities across the country.

Working in the community with criminalized and formerly incarcerated individuals, I too see the importance of engaging in public education efforts that ignite conversations about the impact of stigma. Although sharing stories of personal discrimination and hardship can be daunting, we must create safe spaces for such dialogue. There is a promising level of support among members of the community for policies that are less punitive and more accepting of individuals, both youth (e.g., Piquero, Cullen, Unnever, Piquero, & Gordon, 2010) and adult (e.g., Webster & Doob, 2015), who have made mistakes in their past. We should therefore make a stronger effort to harness this community acceptance and engage in collaborative and collective resistance (Hannem & Bruckert, 2012) to the unnecessary discrimination and exclusion of criminalized persons.

Canada is not the only country to experience a punitive shift in crime policy, nor is it the only nation to exclude criminalized persons from certain workplaces based on the stigma associated with a criminal record. The following section will review international practices of criminal records management in order to better situate Canadian policies in this area.

## INTERNATIONAL PRACTICES OF CRIMINAL RECORDS MANAGEMENT

In 2011, Martine Herzog-Evans edited a special volume of the *European Journal of Probation* focused specifically on Shadd Maruna's (2011) concept of "judicial rehabilitation"—the process of sealing criminal records after criminalized persons demonstrate personal efforts at rehabilitation and reintegration in the community. This volume provides an accessible summary of criminal records management procedures in several countries including Australia, France, England, the Netherlands, Germany, and Spain. This section of my chapter draws from this review, and allows for a comparison of international practices to better situate and evaluate Canada's new record suspension program.

### Australia

In Australia, as in many other jurisdictions, the criminal justice system's goals are to deter people from committing crime, to ensure retribution for those who do engage in criminal behaviour, to offer protection to the community, and to rehabilitate criminalized persons (Naylor, 2011). Unfortunately, the rehabilitation component of this plan is rarely achieved and criminalized persons remain characterized as a risk to public safety. Naylor (2011) notes that, similarly to in Canada, the media in Australia plays a role in the public naming and shaming of criminals and this style of reporting decreases public confidence in the ability of the criminal justice system to successfully rehabilitate and reintegrate prisoners.

Criminal records in Australia are maintained by an agency called Crim-Trac, and the policies under the common law system allow for any employer to request information stored in CrimTrac when making hiring decisions (Naylor, 2011). In order to reconcile the negative stigma associated with a criminal record, Australian judiciaries "have emphasized that the mere existence of a criminal record does not mean that a person is not of 'good character'" (Naylor, 2011, p. 85), and efforts at rehabilitation and reintegration need to be acknowledged by the community—including employers. Privacy laws help ensure information about a criminal record cannot be shared without consent and anti-discrimination laws prohibit exclusion based merely on the presence of a criminal record, although most complaints under this legislation have gone unaddressed.

In terms of pardoning or expunging criminal records, many jurisdictions across Australia have implemented a system wherein convictions become "spent" after a set period of time (Naylor, 2011). Under this program, minor convictions are considered "spent" after ten years, whereas exemptions are made for persons considered to be high-risk, for instance those with a history of violent and/or sexual offending or those applying to work with vulnerable populations such as children or the elderly might not be eligible under the spent record system. There is no formal application process put in place and therefore no guarantee that the record will actually be sealed.

### France

Both reintegration and privacy are respected concepts in France, and these fundamental values influence how criminal records are managed and disseminated. Criminal records are maintained by the National Judicial Record and all citizens of France are able to view their records on a secure online system (Herzog-Evans, 2011). While employers may also have access to this information, this access is limited in light of the potential impact on "employment and consequently ... desistance/resocialization" (Herzog-Evans, 2011, p. 8). Once again, however, for jobs that involve working with vulnerable populations and/or that place employees in a position of trust, criminal records are widely accessed during the hiring process, specifically to screen out individuals with a history of sexual offending.

In terms of expungement processes, there are several options available in the French legal system. First, the *Hundred Years Rule* allows for criminal records to be cleared once an individual has reached 100 years of age and the *Forty Years Rule* allows for criminal records to be cleared 40 years after the last recorded conviction. While these two rules function on the "right to be forgotten" principle[8] that is a cornerstone in the French legal system (Herzog-Evans, 2011, p. 10), neither support successful reintegration because wait times for the record to be sealed are too lengthy.

Other expungement options include *legal rehabilitation* and *relèvement.* Legal rehabilitation allows people with less serious offences to have their records cleared after three, ten, or 20 years after the offence, an option similar in format to what we see in Australia. *Relèvement* is a more formal process that takes place in a court setting and requires an examination and investigation of the applicant's personal situation (Herzog-Evans, 2011). The *relèvement* is very similar to Canada's pardon system, but it is more restrictive in the sense that it clears the individual with a criminal record to apply only for jobs from which they were previously prohibited due to the nature of their offence(s) (Herzog-Evans, 2011).

Although France seems to operate a far less punitive system than either Canada or Australia, the focus on mitigating risk—especially when it comes to people convicted of sexual harm—remains.

## England

The criminal records management and expungement processes in England are fairly straightforward. Criminal records are kept in the Police National Computer, and the Criminal Records Bureau is responsible for processing criminal background checks. The *Rehabilitation of Offenders Act* (1974) allows for conviction records to become "spent" after a fixed period of time, but, consistent with Canadian practice, records are never deleted from the system—only sealed. The fixed periods include five years for those who received fines or community sentences, seven years for a sentence less than six months, and ten years if the sentence was between six and 30 months (Padfield, 2011). If someone received a sentence longer than 30 months, their conviction can never be "spent." While the intent of this act was to encourage desistance and facilitate re-entry, other policies and practices in England now lean "towards much greater disclosure of criminal records" (Padfield, 2011, p. 37). Legislation around re-entry is developed on skewed notions of risk, public safety, and employer hiring practices have become part of this risk-averse trend.

## Netherlands

Aspects of the criminal justice system in the Netherlands are inspired by the Risk–Need–Responsivity model and other concepts stemming from the work of Canadian psychologists Don Andrews and James Bonta (e.g., Andrews & Bonta, 2010; Bonta & Andrews, 2007). Reintegration and re-socialization remains "an important aim of the implementation of sanctions in the Netherlands" (Boone, 2011, p. 64), although exceptions are made for people with a history of violent and/or sexual harm on their criminal record.

Criminal records are stored in the Judicial Documentation System and managed by the Minister of Justice. As per the law in the Netherlands, requests for records are delivered orally to individuals. If further information is required before an offer of employment can be made, applicants can produce a *Conduct Certificate*—a document produced by the Minister of Justice which indicates that the person with a criminal record is cleared to work in the specified job (Boone, 2011). This certificate is a formal recognition of rehabilitation and desistance and "restores a former prisoner's rights" to employment (Boone, 2011, p. 72).

There is nothing similar to the Canadian pardon system in the Netherlands—despite several attempts to introduce such processes. Instead, conviction information is maintained in the Judicial Documentation System for 30 years after sentence completion; data on sexual offences are stored until 20 years after the individual's death (Boone, 2011). For minor offences, the record remains in the system "until five years after the irrevocable settlement of the case" (Boone, 2011, p. 71) although this time is extended if the person served time in prison or was required to complete a community service order.[9]

## Germany

In Germany, once again the focus is on reintegration, with harsher regulations for persons convicted of sexual harm. Specifically, all employers working with children or other vulnerable populations are required to check their employees for any past criminal activity. Criminal records are stored on the Federal Crime Register and can be removed if the individual has reached 90 years of age, if three years have passed since their death, or if they were found not criminally responsible for their crime. In such cases the record will be removed ten or 20 years after their offence, depending on the seriousness of the crime (Morgenstern, 2011).

Similar to the Netherlands, Germany also issues *Certificates of Conduct*. These certificates list all conviction information and can be requested by either public or private employers as a condition of employment. Offences committed as a youth and/or minor offences where "a day fine below 90 units or a prison sentence below three months" was issued are *not* included on the Certificate of Conduct (Morgenstern, 2011, p. 26). Other conviction information can also be removed from the Certificate of Conduct after set periods of time. If the sentence received was less than one year, then the record can be removed after three years; for other convictions (i.e., longer than a year), the wait period is five years before the conviction information is removed. Individuals with a history of sexual offending must wait ten years before the conviction is removed (Morgenstern, 2011).

## Spain

Spanish authorities maintain their criminal records in the National Conviction Register, which is not considered public "and very few public agencies and no private agencies at all have access to it" (Larrauri, 2011, p. 51). Only a small number of jobs (e.g., typically in the police service or public administration) in Spain require a criminal background check and employers that do must adhere to strict legal regulations (Laurrauri, 2011). Criminal records are sealed (not erased) anywhere between six months and five years after sentence completion, depending on the severity of the sentence. This is an automatic process, requiring neither an application nor a court hearing. All in all, criminal records seem to "play only a minor role in Spanish society" (Larrauri, 2011, p. 60) and therefore both legal and academic discussions around criminal records management and expungement processes are quite minimal.

## Discussion of International Practices of Criminal Records Management

In comparing international practices of criminal records management and expungement processes, we can see how different jurisdictions value individual privacy and how they balance the risks and needs of criminalized persons with community safety upon re-entry. For example, while many of the countries discussed in this section—especially Spain—seem to recognize the collateral consequences of criminal records and therefore make efforts to limit public availability of them, jurisdictions such as the United States do not place such limits on this information (Jacobs & Larrauri, 2012). In the United States, criminal records are widely accessible to the public and to employers through a variety of channels including courthouse records, private information firms, and online searches. This open access policy to criminal records does not serve to support successful re-entry, but instead promotes an ongoing punitive response to those who break the law. While people with criminal records in Canada do not face the same level of social exclusion and disenfranchisement as those in the United States (Uggen, Behrens, & Manza, 2005), there is certainly a noticeable shift in the use of criminal records by Canadian employers (CCLA, 2014).

It is difficult to compare the effectiveness of each country's approach to criminal record management and expungement without further empirical study, but some analysis can be conducted by drawing from the literature on stigma and desistance. For example, Maruna (2011) states that good re-entry processes (or "rituals") help reduce, and sometimes eliminate, the stigma of a criminal record, therefore providing a formal "end" to punishment. By allowing people to "wipe the slate clean" through a "de-labelling" process (Maruna,

2011, p. 23) we can restore social solidarity and reduce unnecessary instances of discrimination. In other words, when the focus of the re-entry process is on change and progress rather than on continually assessing risk, we can help create an environment where criminalized and formerly incarcerated persons are better able to contribute to the community in which they live. With these caveats in mind, we can look to countries like Australia, England, and Spain where automatic "spent" processes are in place for dealing with certain criminal records. A "spent" record acts as a clear end to the punishment and criminalization process and allows the individual to move forward in life free of the negative label.

Alternatively, countries like Germany and France appear far more reluctant to completely expunge criminal records. With policies like the *Hundred Years Rule* (Herzog-Evans, 2011) and *Certificates of Conduct* that list all conviction information (Morgenstern, 2011), it is difficult for people to define themselves without referring to their past involvement with the criminal justice system. As stated previously, both countries see value in the social reintegration of criminalized and formerly incarcerated persons, still there seems to be a greater concern with assessing and managing risk as a way to achieve public safety.

Canada's former pardon system seemed to strike a balance between privacy rights and community safety, in that people who received pardons were protected from discrimination under the *Canadian Human Rights Act* (1985) and the community was protected by the guidelines provided to the Parole Board of Canada when processing pardon applications. The new record suspension program is far more risk-averse and seems to fall in line with a widespread punitive turn in criminal justice policies and practices, such as an increase in the use of mandatory minimum sentencing and the elimination of accelerated parole reviews (Webster & Doob, 2015). Aside from changes to the *Criminal Records Act*, other decisions made under Canada's previous Conservative majority government affect the ability of criminalized persons to move on with their lives. For example, cuts to programs such as *Lifeline*[10] and *Circles of Support and Accountability*[11] reduce institutional and community-based supports available to prisoners and formerly incarcerated persons. These program cuts combined with a reduction in the use of gradual, supported release and escorted temporary absences from prison indicates a general disregard for safe and successful re-entry and both worsens and lengthens the punishment and discrimination faced by criminalized persons in the community.

## CONCLUSION

> *Equality is, at the very least, freedom from adverse discrimination. But what constitutes adverse discrimination changes with time, with information, with experience, and with insight. What we tolerated as a society 100, 50, or even 10 years ago is no longer necessarily tolerable. Equality is thus a process—a process of constant and flexible examination, of vigilant introspection, and of aggressive open-mindedness.* (Abella, 1984, p. 1)

Recent critical literature on labour and employment continues to address various personal characteristics that affect access to the workforce in Canada, including: gender, race, Aboriginal identity, culture, ability, age, and immigration status (Agócs, 2014; Anand, 2014, Cornish, Faraday, & Borowy, 2014). Criminalization is not identified as one of these factors even though 13 percent of Canadians have a criminal record (CCLA, 2014, p. 61). At the same time, however, Canada has also experienced a shift in penal policy that has amplified barriers to successful re-entry and prolonged the punishment of former prisoners who have completed their sentence. A growing concern for managing personal and professional risk has influenced the way those who are marginalized and stigmatized in our communities, especially individuals with a criminal record, are treated. Those responsible for the changes made to Canada's pardon program failed to consider the long-term impact of the new record suspension program on desistance and re-entry (Kilgour, 2013), and therefore future research on prisoner reintegration and employment should consider exploring consequences.

The international literature on criminal records management and expungement offers several suggestions for reforms to these processes, including increasing the use of certificates of conduct/rehabilitation (Maruna, 2014) or relying more on the automatic "spent" processes utilized in England, Australia, and Spain. Outside of these criminal justice system-based approaches, the best solutions to remedy the stigma and discrimination experienced by criminalized and formerly incarcerated individuals lie in the community. Grassroots movements such as the "Ban the Box" campaign and community vocational and job-training programs connect with employers to overcome the stigma, help support safe and successful reintegration, and improve the availability of job opportunities to people with criminal records.

My own work in the community allowed me to witness first-hand the impact of the changes to Canada's pardon system and the struggles caused by the new record suspension regime and an increasingly risk-averse workforce. In speaking with criminalized persons about their struggle to find work I often heard things like "I can't even get a job at Wal-Mart" or "The interview was going really well until they asked me if I had a criminal record." This constant rejection by employers is very discouraging and damaging to the process of reintegration. The cost of a record suspension now amounts to deadlock for many applicants: they cannot typically afford the $631 user fee without employment, but cannot secure employment without the record suspension. Ultimately, if finding meaningful and stable employment is held up as one of the most important factors of successful re-entry, then policies and practices should not be developed that interfere directly with this goal.

The purpose of this chapter has been to draw attention to the issues around criminal records management and expungement practices in general and, more specifically, to encourage contributions to the Canadian literature on this topic. New empirical research is required in order to better understand the impact of the recent legislative changes to Canada's pardon program on re-entry and reintegration, and future studies should make an effort to learn more about the employment opportunities (or lack thereof) available to people with criminal records.

## NOTES

1  The Canadian Police Information Centre (CPIC) is Canada's criminal record-keeping system and it is maintained and managed by the Royal Canadian Mounted Police (RCMP). CPIC contains information from all police services across the country and allows departments to share and update records as needed (CPIC, 2015).

2  The wait period before being eligible to apply for a pardon begins at sentence completion. All fines and restitution must also be paid before the wait period begins.

3  Out of the 1,086 responses received during the consultation process 1,074 were not in favour of the fee increase and only 12 showed support. A total of 16 complaints were submitted and were to be reviewed by an Independent Advisory Panel.

4  Karla Homolka is the former wife of convicted serial killer Paul Bernardo (known in the Canadian media as the Scarborough Rapist). While Homolka herself was convicted of manslaughter and played a role in the accidental death of her own sister, she was also a victim of Bernardo's abusive and dangerous behaviour (Kilty & Frigon, 2006).

5  In January 2016, the Liberal government's Public Safety Minister, Ralph Goodale, announced that his department would consider reversing the 2010 and 2012 changes made to the *Criminal Records Act*. Minister Goodale said that the new record suspension program is "punitive" and the changes under the previous Conservative government do not promote public safety (Crawford, 2016).

6  In his often-cited book *Stigma: Notes on the Management of Spoiled Identity*, Goffman (1963) defines stigma as "an undesired differentness" (p. 5), which serves as justification for excluding and discriminating against specific individuals or groups of people.

7  "'All of Us or None' is a grassroots civil rights organizing initiative, started in 2003 by formerly-incarcerated people and [their] families" (Ban the Box, 2015b).

8  The right to be forgotten principle (*le droit à l'oubli*) is upheld as a basic human right in France and across Europe. This principle protects one's public reputation and personal dignity "against compromising intrusions by others" and is often directly applied to individuals with past criminal records (Walker, 2012, p. 270).

9   A community service order is a sentencing option that requires an individual to dedicate time to volunteer in their local community as a way to repair any harm done.
10  The Lifeline program was available for more than 20 years to Canadian prisoners serving life sentences in federal institutions. The program supported lifers inside of the prisons and eased the transition to community for those released on parole (Graham, 1992).
11  Circles of Support and Accountability (CoSA) is a community-based reintegration program that supports individuals convicted of sexual harm and "are usually kept in prison to the end of their sentences and don't receive parole" (CoSA Canada, 2015). The program has been proven effective at improving public safety through a number of studies and is now being replicated in other countries, including South Korea.

## REFERENCES

Abella, R. S. (1984). *Equality in employment: A Royal Commission.* Ottawa, ON: Minister of Supply and Services Canada.

Agócs, C. (2014). Introduction: Perspectives on employment equity in Canada. In C. Agócs (Ed.), *Employment equity in Canada: The legacy of the Abella Report* (pp. 3–28). Toronto, ON: University of Toronto Press.

Albright, S., & Denq, F. (1996). Employer attitudes toward hiring ex-offenders. *The Prison Journal, 76*(2), 118–137.

Anand, R. (2014). Real change? Reflections on employment equity's last thirty years. In C. Agócs (Ed.), *Employment equity in Canada: The legacy of the Abella Report* (pp. 51–70). Toronto, ON: University of Toronto Press.

Andrews, D. A., & Bonta, J. (2010). Rehabilitating criminal justice policy and practice. *Psychology, Public Policy, and Law, 16*(1), 39–55.

Appelbaum, B. (2015, February 28). Out of trouble, but criminal records keep men out of work. *New York Times.* Retrieved from http://www.nytimes.com/2015/03/01/business/out-of-trouble-but-criminal-records-keep-men-out-of-work.html

Backman, C. (2011). Vocabularies of motive among employers conducting criminal background checks. *Acta Sociologica, 54*(1), 27–44.

Ban the Box. (2015a). *About.* Retrieved from http://bantheboxcampaign.org/?p=20#.VgHzevlViko

Ban the Box. (2015b). *Who we are.* Retrieved from http://bantheboxcampaign.org/?p=23#.VgH6HvlViko

Blumstein, A., & Nakamura, K. (2009). Redemption in the presence of widespread criminal background checks. *Criminology, 47*(2), 327–359.

Bonta, J. L., & Andrews, D. A. (2007). *Risk–need–responsivity model for offender assessment and rehabilitation.* Ottawa, ON: Public Safety Canada.

Boone, M. (2011). Judicial rehabilitation in the Netherlands: Balancing between safety and privacy. *European Journal of Probation, 3*(1), 63–78.

Brodbeck, T. (2012, April 7). No chance of pardon for Graham James. *Toronto Sun.* Retrieved from http://www.torontosun.com/2012/04/07/law-means-no-pardon-for-james

Bruckert, C., & Hannem, S. (2012). Introduction. In S. Hannem & C. Bruckert (Eds.), *Stigma revisited: Implications of the mark* (pp. 1–15). Ottawa, ON: University of Ottawa.

Canadian Civil Liberties Association. (2014). *False promises, hidden costs: The case for reframing employment and volunteer police record check practices in Canada*. Retrieved from http://www.ccla.org/recordchecks/falsepromises Canadian Police Information Centre (CPIC). (2015). *About*. Retrieved from http://www.cpic-cipc.ca/about-ausujet/index-eng.htm

Cheadle, B. (2013, April 2). Former convicts reluctant to go public for forum on pardons. *CTV News*. Retrieved from http://www.ctvnews.ca/canada/former-convicts-reluctant-to-go-public-for-forum-on-pardons-1.1221313_

Cheadle, B., & Bronskill, J. (2011, December 7). Accuser who uncovered James Pardon sparked changes to system. *The Star*. Retrieved from http://www.thestar.com/sports/hockey/2011/12/07/accuser_who_uncovered_james_pardon_sparked_changes_to_system.html

Christie, N. (2004). *Suitable amount of crime*. London, UK: Routledge.

Cornish, M., Faraday, F., & Borowy, J. (2014). Securing employment equity by enforcing human rights laws. In C. Agócs (Ed.), *Employment equity in Canada: The legacy of the Abella Report* (pp. 217–241). Toronto, ON: University of Toronto Press.

CoSA Canada. (2015). *Home*. Retrieved from http://cosacanada.com/

Crawford, A. (2013, November 21). Requests for pardons drop in wake of changes. *CBC News*. Retrieved from http://www.cbc.ca/m/touch/politics/story/1.2434526_

Crawford, A. (2016, January 20). Public Safety Minister vows to overhaul "punitive" criminal pardons system. *CBC News*. Retrieved from http://www.cbc.ca/beta/news/politics/liberal-criminal-justice-pardons-1.3412533

CTV.ca News Staff. (2010, June 17). MPs pass bill to block pardon for Karla Homolka. *CTV News*. Retrieved from http://www.ctvnews.ca/mps-pass-bill-to-block-pardon-for-karla-homolka-1.523631

Davis, C., Bahr, S. J., & Ward, C. (2012). The process of offender reintegration: Perceptions of what helps prisoners reenter society. *Criminology and Criminal Justice, 13*, 446–469.

Doob, A. N., & Webster, C. M. (2006). Countering punitiveness: Understanding stability in Canada's imprisonment rate. *Law & Society Review, 40*, 325–368.

Easton, S., Furness, H., & Brantingham, P. (2014). The cost of crime in Canada. *Fraser Institute*. Retrieved from http://www.fraserinstitute.org/research-news/display.aspx?id=21876

Emonds, S. (2013, February 15). Sex offender Graham James' sentence increased to five years. *Globe and Mail*. Retrieved from http://www.theglobeandmail.com/news/national/sex-offender-graham-james-sentence-increased-to-five-years/article8715245/

Freeman, R. (2008). Incarceration, criminal background checks, and employment in a low(er) crime society. *Criminology & Public Policy, 7*(3), 405–412.

Goffman, E. (1963). *Stigma: Notes on the management of spoiled identity*. Englewood Cliffs, NJ: Prentice-Hall.

Graham, S. (1992). The Life Line Project. *FORUM on Corrections Research, 4*(2). Retrieved from http://www.csc-scc.gc.ca/research/forum/e042/e042m-eng.shtml

Hannem, S. (2012) Theorizing stigma and the politics of resistance: Symbolic and structural stigma in everyday life. In S. Hannem & C. Bruckert (Eds.), *Stigma revisited: Implications of the mark* (pp. 10–28). Ottawa, ON: University of Ottawa Press.

Hannem, S., & Bruckert, C. (2012). Concluding thoughts: Academic activism: A call to action. In S. Hannem & C. Bruckert (Eds.), *Stigma revisited: Implications of the mark* (pp. 176–182). Ottawa, ON: University of Ottawa Press.

Henry, J. S., & Jacobs, J. B. (2007). Ban the box to promote ex-offender employment. *Criminology & Public Policy, 6*, 755–762.

Herzog-Evans, M. (2011). Judicial rehabilitation in France: Helping with the desisting process and acknowledging achieved desistance. *European Journal of Probation, 3*(1), 4–19.

Ireland, N. (2016, January 24). Pardons system's harsher rules blocks ex-criminals from jobs, housing. *CBC News.* Retrieved from http://www.cbc.ca/news/canada/criminal-justice-pardons-impact-1.3416380

Jackson, A. (2010). *Work and labour in Canada: Critical issues* (2nd ed.). Toronto, ON: Canadian Scholars' Press.

Jacobs, J. B. (2015). *The eternal criminal record.* Cambridge, MA: Harvard University Press.

Jacobs, J. B. & Larrauri, E. (2012). Are criminal convictions a public matter? The USA and Spain. *Punishment & Society, 14*(1), 3–28.

Jeffords, S. (2013, September 26). Karla Homolka has tried to dodge the public eye. *Toronto Sun.* Retrieved from http://www.torontosun.com/2013/09/26/karla-homolka-has-tried-to-dodge-public-eye

Kilgour, L. (2013). Tracing the lifecycle of Canadian criminal records: A critical examination in relation to public policy and user access and comprehension. *Records Management Journal, 23*(2), 136–148.

Kilty, J. M., & Frigon, S. (2006). Karla Homolka—From a woman in danger to a dangerous woman: Chronicling the shifts. *Women & Criminal Justice, 17*(4), 37–61.

Larrauri, E. (2011). Conviction records in Spain: Obstacles to reintegration of offenders? *European Journal of Probation, 3*(1), 50–62.

LeBel, T. P. (2008). Perceptions of and responses to stigma. *Sociology Compass, 2*(2), 409–432.

LeBlanc, D. (2013, February 4). Tories to announce tougher sentences for child predators. *Globe and Mail.* Retrieved from http://www.theglobeandmail.com/news/politics/tories-to-announce-tougher-sentences-for-child-predators/article8158009/

Maruna, S. (2001) *Making good: How ex-convicts reform and rebuild their lives.* Washington, DC: American Psychological Association.

Maruna, S. (2011). Judicial rehabilitation and the "Clean bill of health" in criminal justice. *European Journal of Probation, 3*(1), 97–117.

Maruna, S. (2014). Reintegration as a right and the rites of reintegration: A comparative review of de-stigmatization practices. In P. Cordella & J. A. Humphrey (Eds.), *Effective interventions in the lives of criminal offenders* (pp. 121–138). New York, NY: Springer.

Meyer, J., & O'Malley, P. (2005) Missing the punitive turn? Canadian criminal justice, "balance" and penal modernism. In J. Pratt, D. Brown, S. Hallsworth, M. Brown & W. Morrison (Eds.), *The new punitiveness: Trends, theories, perspectives* (pp. 201–217). London, UK: Willan Publishing.

Morgenstern, C. (2011). Judicial rehabilitation in Germany—The use of criminal records and the removal of recorded convictions. *European Journal of Probation, 3*(1), 20–35.

Munn, M. (2012). The mark of criminality: Rejections and reversals, disclosure and distance: Stigma and the ex-prisoner. In S. Hannem & C. Bruckert (Eds.), *Stigma revisited: Implications of the mark* (pp. 147–169). Ottawa, ON: University of Ottawa Press.

Munn, M. & Bruckert, C. (2013). *On the outside: From lengthy imprisonment to lasting freedom.* Vancouver, BC: UBC Press.

Murphy, Y., Sprott, J. B., & Doob, A. (2015) Pardoning people who once offended. *Criminal Law Quarterly, 62*(1), 209–225.

Naylor, B. (2011). Criminal records and rehabilitation in Australia. *European Journal of Probation, 3*(1), 79–96.

Padfield, N. (2011). Judicial rehabilitation? A view from England. *European Journal of Probation, 3*(1), 36–49.

Pager, D. (2007). *Marked: Race, crime, and finding work in an era of mass incarceration*, Chicago, IL: University of Chicago Press.

Parole Board of Canada. (2000). *Mission statement of the Parole Board of Canada.* Retrieved from http://pbcclcc.gc.ca/about/miss-eng.shtml

Parole Board of Canada. (2011). *Consultation report: Proposed increase to the pardon application user fee.* Retrieved from http://pbc-clcc.gc.ca/infocntr/factsh/pdf/Consult-rprt-prdn-use-fee-eng.pdf

Parole Board of Canada. (2014). *PBC quick stats.* Retrieved from http://pbc-clcc.gc.ca/infocntr/factsh/parole_stats-eng.shtml

Petersilia, J. (2005). *Hard time: Ex-offenders returning home after prison.* Lanham, MD: American Correctional Association.

Piché, J. (2014). A contradictory and finishing state: Explaining recent prison capacity expansion in Canada's provinces and territories. *Champ penal/Penal Field,* XI. Retrieved from https://champpenal.revues.org/8797

Piquero, A. R., Cullen, F. T., Unnever, J. D., Piquero, N. L., & Gordon, J. A. (2010). Never too late: Public optimism about juvenile rehabilitation. *Punishment & Society, 12*(1), 187–207.

Pratt, J. (2007). *Penal populism.* London, UK: Routledge.

Pratt, J. (2013). Punishment and "the civilizing process." In J. Simon & R. Sparks (Eds.), *The SAGE handbook of punishment and society* (pp. 90–113). London, UK: Sage Publications.

Public Safety Canada. (2013). *Corrections and conditional release statistical overview.* Ottawa, ON: Public Works and Government Services Canada. Retrieved from http://www.publicsafety.gc.ca/cnt/rsrcs/pblctns/crrctns-cndtnl-rls-2013/crrctns-cndtnl-rls-2013-eng.pdf.

Ruddell, R., & Winfree, L. T. (2006). Setting aside criminal convictions in Canada: A successful approach to offender reintegration. *Prison Journal, 86*(4), 452–469.

Sapers, H. (2014). *Annual report of the Office of the Correctional Investigator, 2013–2014.* Ottawa, ON: Minister of Public Works and Government Services Canada.

Stacey, C. (2015). Looking beyond re-offending: Criminal records and poverty. *CriminalJustice Matters, 99*(1), pp. 4–5.

Sullivan, S. (2014, July 2). Jobs and justice: How the pardon crackdown made Canada less safe. *iPolitics*. Retrieved from http://ipolitics.ca/2014/07/02/jobs-and-justice-how-the-pardon-crackdown-made-canada-less-safe/

Thacher, D. (2008) The rise of criminal background screening in rental housing. *Law and Social Inquiry, 33*(1), 5–30.

Travis, J. (2002). Invisible punishment: An instrument of social exclusion. In M. Mauer & M. Chesney-Lind (Eds.), *Invisible punishment: The collateral consequences of mass imprisonment* (pp. 15–36). New York, NY: New Press.

Uggen, C., Behrens, A., & Manza, J. (2005). Criminal disenfranchisement. *Annual Review of Law and Social Science, 1*(1), 307–322.

Uggen, C., Vuolo, M., Lageson, S., Ruhland, E., & Whitham, H. K. (2014). The edge of stigma: An experimental audit of the effects of low-level criminal records on employment. *Criminology, 52*(4), 627–654.

Visher, C. A., & Travis, J. (2011). Life on the outside: Returning home after incarceration. *Prison Journal, 91*(3), 102S–119S.

Walker, R. K. (2012). The right to be forgotten. *Hastings Law Journal, 64*(1), 257–286.

Wallace-Capretta, S. (2000). *Pardoned offenders in Canada: A statistical analysis.* Ottawa, ON: Solicitor General Canada.

Webster, C. M., & Doob, A. N. (2015). US punitiveness "Canadian Style"? Cultural values and Canadian punishment policy. *Punishment & Society, 17*(3), 299–321.

Weese, B. (2010, April 19). Killer Karla Homolka eligible for a pardon this year. *Toronto Sun*. Retrieved from http://www.torontosun.com/news/canada/2010/04/19/13637726-qmi.html

## Statutes Cited

Canadian Charter of Rights and Freedoms. Part I of the *Constitution Act, 1982*, being Schedule B to the *Canada Act* 1982 (UK), 1982, c 11

*Canadian Human Rights Act*, RSC 1985, c H-6

*Criminal Records Act*, RSC 1985, c 47

*Employment Equity Act*, SC 1995, c 44

*Limiting Pardons for Serious Crimes Act*, SC 2010, c 5

*Rehabilitation of Offenders Act* 1974, c 53, Parliament of the United Kingdom

*Safe Streets and Communities Act*, SC 2012, c 1

# CHAPTER 5

# Vulnerabilities and Barriers in Post-Release Employment Reintegration as Indicated by Parolees

Rose Ricciardelli and Taylor Mooney

R esearchers have long connected employment after prison with desistance from crime, although the language used tends to remain within the framework of recidivism and the "need" to protect the public from "offenders" (Myers, 1983; Tripodi, Kim, & Bender, 2009). After prison, men and women are vulnerable. They are entering society anew—after months, years, or even decades of incarceration—and with that transition comes uncertainty and a multitude of concerns that can be easily understood as diverse vulnerabilities. Not surprisingly, being selected for an occupational position can be a source of esteem for a parolee or probationer, just as not being chosen can be a letdown. The financial stability provided by employment is likely to reduce the possibility of a person reoffending—said another way, having income increases the likelihood of successful desistance from crime (Albright & Denq, 1996). Employment, then, provides individuals with social and economic value and a network of social supports—employees are contributing members of society and participants in the labour force (Berk, Lenihan, & Rossi, 1980; Uggen, 2000). Yet, the movement from prison to community living is laced with challenges, and finding employment, particularly gainful employment, is difficult.

To lend insight into the challenges that former prisoners must navigate as they strive to reintegrate into society and acquire employment, we draw on preliminary results from a longitudinal study of 24 men and women released from federal prison into a large metropolitan city in Ontario, Canada. These men and women were followed across multiple semi-structured, in-depth interviews. This chapter provides an overview of the diverse challenges they describe as most concerning or that permeate their thoughts, and hence our conversations, when interviewing. Specifically, we focus on their concerns of (1) not having any previous job experience; (2) having a criminal record; (3) navigating their parole and residency conditions; and (4) their readiness to return to employment in contrast to the timing pressures imposed by their case management team (e.g., parole officers) during employment reintegration. We frame our discussion with theories of stigma and bare life (Agamben, 1995; Goffman, 1963).

## THE STIGMA OF INCARCERATION: EMPLOYMENT AND REINTEGRATION

For decades, the self-esteem and financial stability provided by employment have been documented as likely to reduce the probability that individuals would reoffend (Albright & Denq, 1996). Desistance theorists also argue that being invested in society, be it through employment, marriage, or other commitments, helps formerly criminally active individuals cease participation in said activities (Graffam, Shinkfield, Lavelle, & McPherson, 2004; Maruna & Toch, 2005; Visher, Kachnakowski, La Vigne, & Travis, 2004). Employment is considered one of several "protective factors" that assist in deterring future criminal activity (Draine, Salzer, Culhane, & Hadley, 2002; Lipsey & Derzon, 1998; Lösel & Farrington, 2012; Resnick, Ireland, & Borowsky, 2004). It provides people with a position imbued with greater social value in that they are seen as contributing members of society; employment also provides a greater network of social support, which is yet another "protective factor" that former prisoners too often are without (Maruna & Toch, 2005; Visher et al., 2004).

In addition to the benefits mentioned above, individuals also reap the benefit of devoting time to work. Western society is often more than ready to label former prisoners as lifelong criminals, but employment is known to provide direct competition for time spent on illegal activity (Berk et al., 1980). The label former prisoners often bear is rooted in a stigma, defined as the negative interpretation of a person rooted in an ideology shaped by stereotypes (see Ricciardelli & Moir, 2013). This ideology is applied to a trait or attribute that the individual is believed to hold (Goffman, 1963). Goffman (1963) identified three types of stigma, one of which is the stigma of character traits, where one is perceived as having "blemishes of individual character," and is the most commonly imputed to former prisoners (p. 4). Former prisoners become viewed as being of "weak will, domineering or unnatural passions, treacherous and rigid beliefs, and dishonesty, these being inferred from a known record of, for example, mental disorder, *imprisonment*, addiction ..."

(Goffman, 1963, p. 4; emphasis ours). Stigmatized individuals are viewed negatively, as dangerous, inferior, and less than human, once—as in the case of a former prisoner—the stigmatizing attribute (i.e., their perceived criminality) becomes known. In this sense, once the individual's criminal history is revealed they are discredited, as prior they were only "discreditable" (Goffman, 1963); others are then free to view them as "of a less desirable kind—in the extreme, a person who is quite thoroughly bad, or dangerous, or weak. He is thus reduced in our mind from a whole and usual person to a tainted, discounted one" (Goffman, 1963, p. 3).

This leads to lessening an individual's social worth or credibility based on the "branding" effect, or label, of the stigma (Goffman, 1963). Stigma affects how individuals are viewed by others and can evolve into a "master status"—or the attribute that defines a person's identity—and nullifies any positive association tied to the positive attributes they possess (Goffman, 1963). Goffman (1963) described the emergence of a "virtual social identity" (p. 4), in that stigma incites others to view the stigmatized individual in a certain way. Thus, the assumption-based expectations that people have about others' social identities leads them to disregard their "actual social identity."

Arguably, Agamben's (1995) concept of the homo sacer, a person deprived of their human rights, expands the understanding of stigma and the implication of virtual social identities. This person is treated as being outside the law, and can have great violence and injustice imposed upon them without consequence (Agamben, 1995). The homo sacer, despite existing within the community, is viewed as being outside the community and in a "state of exception" (Agamben, 1995, p. 17). They are viewed by individuals within the community as being inherently other—in essence, stigmatized—and as not deserving of the rights and freedoms afforded to the rest of society. The homo sacer is someone who is considered to have violated some societally held ideal (Agamben, 1995; see also Ricciardelli & Spencer, 2014), thus making them "impure" or "dirty" (Spencer, 2009, p. 222). They can be interpreted as inclusively excluded—a part of society, but not deserving of the same rights and freedoms as everyone else. A homo sacer is not completely free of society, but is instead included in society by the nature of their exclusion: "What has been banned is delivered over to its own separateness and, at the same time, consigned to the mercy of the one who abandons it—at once excluded and included, removed and at the same time captured" (Agamben, 1995, p. 65). Because the individual is actively excluded by society, the homo sacer feels the effects of the law, and so is paradoxically included by their exclusion.

Bearing a stigma when seeking employment, particularly the harsh stigma tied to select forms of criminality where one can become homo sacer, largely ensures that the former prisoner is negatively affected by their perceptions of others' judgments—they bear invisible strips as they wait to be discredited (Goffman, 1963). Balancing impression management with deciding if they should disclose, to whom, where, when, and so on (see Goffman, 1963), leaves former prisoners navigating interactions wherein they do not face immediate prejudice against themselves, but instead "must face unwitting acceptance of himself by individuals who are prejudiced against persons of the kind he can be revealed to be" (p. 42). Goffman refers to this process as "passing" (p. 42). "Passing" is stressful; in essence, it is a process of waiting to be outed and labelled. Yet, despite the challenges associated with passing, Goffman indicates that all who have the opportunity to do so will, due to the "great rewards in being considered normal" (p. 74). Acquiring and maintaining regular employment is considered a way to ease a variety of tensions that accompany post-incarceration reintegration by acting as an organizing and stabilizing agent (Curtis & Schulman, 1984). Employment is a normalizing agent—and thus a central means to assist with successful re-entry post-incarceration.

## Gainful Employment?

Stable employment, characterized as maintaining full-time work over a period of time or remaining employed despite job changes, beyond providing improved economic and health outcomes, aids in developing an individual's level of social functioning and self-worth, and positively affects processes of community re-entry (Parsons & Warner-Robbins, 2002; Richie, 2001). Former prisoners, however, are more likely to obtain menial employment that is low-paying, low-skilled, seasonal or part-time, and precarious (Western, 2002; Freeman, 1992). To put what this means into context, Sharp (1992) found that in Texas, USA, where the minimum wage was $4.25 per hour, 42 percent of employed former prisoners were earning less than $6.00 per hour. More recently, Western (2002) found, through analyzing the American National Longitudinal Study of Youth (1979–1998), strong evidence to suggest that former prisoners' wages were reduced by 10 to 20 percent as a result of incarceration, and that incarceration reduces the rate of wage growth by roughly 30 percent.

Former prisoners with higher levels of education tend to experience lower rates of recidivism, and researchers have also shown those who worked white collar jobs prior to their incarceration were more likely to be employed and less likely to reoffend post-release (Albright & Denq, 1996). Upon analyzing the demography of a sample of 210 people convicted of white-collar crimes, which are arguably less stigmatized than property and violent crimes,

Wheeler, Weisburd, Bode, and Waring (1988) found that the sample had higher educational attainment and more steady employment histories than those convicted of common crimes. More recently, Lochner (2004) used the American National Longitudinal Survey of Youth to suggest a strong negative correlation between education and both property and violent crimes. Besides level of education, former prisoners in the United States are more likely to lack key employment and basic life skills, have low levels of literacy and numeracy, and have poor social competencies (Fletcher, 2001; Harlow, 2003; Nelson, Deess, & Allen, 1999; Rahill-Beuler & Kretzer, 1997). As well, there is low likelihood that former prisoners will have formal employment qualifications or stable, well-paid, or skilled employment histories (Graffam et al., 2004; Hollin & Palmer, 1995; Varghese, Hardin, & Bauer, 2009; Varghese, Hardin, Bauer, & Morgan, 2010; Webster, Hedderman, Turnbull, & May, 2001).

Individuals, however, are more likely to find employment post-release if they have a strong work history (Visher et al., 2008). Incarceration, particularly when experienced during youth, denies prisoners employment opportunities by impeding participation in apprenticeships or training programs (Nagin & Waldfogel, 1995). Moreover, being incarcerated disrupts positive employment development and experiences for prisoners, and decreases opportunities for prisoners to develop a work history and attain related skills (Austin & Hardyman, 2004). Time spent incarcerated also interrupts an individual's ability to form the social connections that lead to employment, and tends to erode their existing social networks (Graffam et al., 2004; Wilson & Vito, 1988)—another consequence of the stigma of incarceration and criminality. Social isolation is often described as a "core experience" of many former prisoners (Baldry, McDonnell, Maplestone, & Peeters, 2002). Beyond the negative effects on self tied to social isolation or alienation, such experiences are especially problematic in that former prisoners, like other members of society, are most likely to find employment through existing contacts—which they tend to lack (Visher et al., 2008).

Former prisoners are also more likely than the general population to contend with health issues, including substance dependence and psychiatric or neurological impairments, and are vulnerable to more broad health issues including poor diet, lack of exercise, and smoking (Graffam et al., 2004). Releasees often have no savings or financial support upon release (Petersilia, 2000) and thus must also deal with the financial barriers of finding clothing and equipment for work, as well as accommodations, while simultaneously seeking employment (Wilson & Vito, 1988). The lack of financial resources evident among most releasees tends to relegate former prisoners to isolated,

low-income communities with a lack of employment opportunities, which
serves to only further complicate their search for employment (Harrison &
Schehr, 2004). Even if an individual is able to successfully submit a resumé
and is deemed a potential candidate for a job, how can they be called back
for an interview if they have no phone number or place of residence?

## Needs: Can Employment Be Attainable?

A review of extant literature on employment reintegration reveals former
prisoners face a variety of competing needs that tend to compound and mul-
tiply (Graffam et al., 2004; Solomon, Gouvis & Waul, 2001; Mukamel, 2001).
Beyond structural barriers to employment, releasees are more likely to have
additional needs to manage, such as maintaining sobriety, finding housing,
reuniting with family and working for custody of or visitation with their children, and rebuilding positive social support networks (Graffam et al., 2004).
Such needs are each tied to diverse interactions and life events that must be
navigated and actualized in order to have these rather significant needs met.
Moreover, the actions required to begin the process of meeting these different
needs may be in competition. For example, the stress of family reunification
may have a negative rather than positive effect on a person's ability to remain
sober, while custody hearings may impair the ability to adhere to a work
schedule and thus lead to job loss.

Focusing on employment needs, former prisoners face legal restrictions
in their search for employment (Mukamel, 2001). The simple fact that, in
many cases, a potential employee is asked to disclose if they have a criminal
record begins the process of discriminating against the hiring of a former
prisoner. Although it is not illegal to fail to disclose having a criminal record,
it is dishonest and therefore not a recommended way to start a new life or
new job post-release. If the question is answered truthfully, it is likely that the
applicant will be viewed as unqualified for the job (Albright & Denq, 1996;
Pager, 2003). Yet if answered untruthfully, the former prisoner must live with
the fact that he/she has been deceptive, and in fear that the falsehood will be
discovered (Dale, 1976; see also Goffman, 1963). The criminal background
checks required by some employers—in Canada performed by the Canadian
Police Information Centre—can also be compromising for the former prisoner (Albright & Denq, 1996; Dale, 1976). This is further complicated by the
fact that official records of arrest and conviction histories can be erroneous
and outdated, potentially providing a more negative image of the former
prisoner than necessary (Mukamel, 2001).

In the United States, employment restrictions often bar individuals with
criminal records from working in fields with vulnerable populations, such

as health or childcare, as well as from careers in law enforcement (Harrison & Schehr, 2004). Further, the criminal history of a former prisoner can legally bar them from seeking employment in select occupations by imposing employment caveats in the parolee's parole conditions (Kerley & Copes, 2004). For example, a former prisoner who engaged in fraud while working at a bank could be barred from working in banking in the future. It should be noted as well that employers tend to have a preference for job applicants that do not have a criminal history or record, and often possess attitudes towards former prisoners informed by stereotypes and stigma (Mukamel, 2001). The reasoning behind this aversion includes fear of incurring liability if they hire a former prisoner who later commits a new crime, referred to as negligent hiring (Mukamel, 2001). This is exemplified by Albright & Denq's (1996) study of 300 employers in the Dallas and Houston areas, which indicates that only 12 percent of employers were "inclined" to hire someone with a criminal record. Other studies show that between 50 and 70 percent of employers are willing to hire a person with a criminal record (Atkinson, Fenster, & Blumberg, 1976; Whiting & Winters, 1981). Scholars suggest that this variance in employers' attitudes may be attributed to wider labour market patterns, indicating that employers' attitudes may be more favourable toward hiring former prisoners during times of low unemployment (Henry, 2000; Shapiro, 2000).

In the United States, to further complicate the needs of former prisoners, certain states ban the provision of public assistance for this population, making it more difficult for former prisoners to sustain themselves while looking for work (Mukamel, 2001). The situation in Canada is slightly different, yet not ideal by any means. Former prisoners living in homeless shelters or halfway houses are provided with a daily parole allowance of $4.00 per day. Although they do qualify for some forms of social assistance, access is limited and qualifying is a rather trying and humbling process. Simultaneously to managing the challenges associated with financial and housing needs, releasees must contend with a variety of arduous responsibilities imposed by their parole conditions, such as random drug screenings, day centre and program reporting, curfews, programming participation, case management meetings, and regular reporting to their parole officer (Buck, 2000). These responsibilities often strain former prisoners and may only allow for part-time work (Graffam et al., 2004). Restrictive parole conditions may also induce pressure on the releasee to find employment before they are ready (e.g., mentally, physically, emotionally) and, depending on the location of the work, may necessitate special permissions from their parole officer to cross-geographic boundaries set by their parole (Buck, 2000).

## Current Study

Recognizing the challenges underlying the transition from prison to community living experienced by men and women after incarceration, particularly as they strive to attain employment, we seek to understand the realities and concerns associated with their reintegration journey. We put forth emergent themes from a preliminary analysis of a sample of 24 men and women on parole who participated in longitudinal semi-structured, in-depth interviews, over a three-year period. Specifically, we shed light on what they perceived as most challenging during their employment reintegration, the details and the issues that permeated their thoughts, and thus our conversation when interviewing. We asked: (1) What is perceived as the greatest barrier to acquiring employment post-release? (2) How do limitations of their parole conditions impact their employment reintegration experiences? and, (3) Do they feel ready for employment? What makes them nervous or anxious about the endeavour? Our intent is to shed light on how stigma and negative perception play into their reintegration experiences, as well as to give an accurate account of their needs.

## METHODS

The participants of the study were parolees released into a city in Ontario, Canada, who were referred by their parole officer to a day reporting centre program. Participation at each stage was voluntary and all potential participants were told about the study by the day reporting centre case workers. Prior to commencing the data collection, parolees understood that their participation or non-participation would not affect their relationships with the centre, their case management team, or the program itself. Only one participant did not participate in the interviews. Participants were interviewed either in person or by phone, in an attempt to be accommodating. Although all were first interviewed when they were referred to the day reporting centre program, follow-up interviews varied due to attrition, parole breaches, and the accessibility of the interviewees. Generally, follow-ups occurred around six months after their first interview and, if possible, after 12 months and, finally, at the end of the study.

The study's primary investigator conducted all but the final interviews. These final interviews were conducted by a research assistant and were done so as to (1) provide an opportunity for the interviewers to request clarification or new explanations of incidents, (2) help train the research assistant, and (3) ensure these final interviews were all conducted in person at the original day reporting centre. Of note, most interviewees either followed up with the primary investigator after their end of study interview and/or made remarks directly to her through the digital voice recorder during their interview. Thus, the rapport established was evinced. Although an interview guide was constructed, it was quickly abandoned when conversation flowed. Consent and ethics approval were both obtained and the interviews were each at least an hour in duration.

## Data Analyses

Employing a semi-grounded approach, interviews underwent deep thematic analysis. Consistent with grounded theory, we began with a question, rather than a theory (Corbin & Straus, 1990); however, our study was only semi-grounded because although rooted in an open question (i.e., what barriers do former prisoners face upon employment reintegration?), the research was conducted with knowledge that former prisoners face barriers during employment reintegration. Indeed, our prior knowledge—applied, empirical, and theoretical—cannot be abandoned when researching (see Ricciardelli, 2014; Ricciardelli & White, 2011). Our approach allowed themes to unfold organically, and prioritizes the voices and concerns of the participants who, as former prisoners, are often overlooked and silenced in society, by consciously avoiding imposing the authors' ideas upon the data. We therefore proceeded with the knowledge that these individuals do face barriers, but allowed respondents to identify which specific issues affected them. Respondents were then afforded agency as they determined how the struggles they face were represented and, as such, we were able to reveal their unique perspectives and voice issues that would otherwise not have been easily identified by an outsider.

Thematic analysis was used to organize and categorize data (Glaser, 1992) and reveal nuances, and to interpret and make connections across participant experiences (Boyatzis, 1998; Daly et al., 1997). To this end, we attentively read each transcript multiple times and used a form of pattern recognition to identify emergent themes, which became the coding categories (Rice & Ezzy, 1999).

First, basic open coding by means of NVivo software was used as we looked for the barriers to employment and difficulties participants faced as they pursued work. In this initial code, four broad themes emerged: personal issues, legal complications, administrative issues, and interpersonal issues. Within each broad theme was a variety of subthemes, including but not limited to: skill erosion, the criminal record, lack of experience, lack of education, lack of social network, stigma, and post-prison readjustment. Next, axial coding was used to disaggregate and then link and analyze these emergent subthemes to create a cohesive and organized image of the challenges releasees faced during employment reintegration. The result was a different broad organization of subthemes: lack of employment experience; looking for work with a criminal record; conditions of parole and residency; and readjusting/timing.

## The Participants

Six cohorts of participants were followed over a period of three years, from 2012 to 2014. The first consisted of nine men on parole, between the ages of 22 and 45, with a mean age of 32 and a median age of 31. The second cohort included three participants, two male and one female between 25 and 53 years of age, with a mean average age of 41.5 and a median of 47. The third cohort consisted of four male participants, between the ages 21 and 47, with an average age of 32 and median age of 30.

The fourth cohort was three male participants, between the ages of 25 and 37, with an average age of 29 and median age of 26. The fifth cohort of three male participants between the ages of 30 and 38, had an average age of 32.5 and median age of 30, while the sixth cohort included two participants, one male and one female, aged 21 and 36 years respectively.

Of these participants, 23 were Canadian Citizens. Ethnic/racial identity was self-reported as: White (n=7), Black (n=13), East Indian (n=1), Hispanic (n=2), Hispanic/Black/Aboriginal (n=1). A total of 13 participants had children who they identified as their own (with the exception of one who had step-children, all were biological children). Only one participant entered prison married and was still married post-incarceration; another was newly engaged and two were in serious relationships. Three parolees had entered prison in long-term common-law partnerships, one of whom was no longer in the relationship after incarceration (while the other two still were). Two participants were divorced, whereof one had remarried; and 11 were single before and after incarceration.

The participants' educational profiles were quite diverse as well. Twenty-three participants had gained their GED (i.e., graduate equivalency diploma)—most were earned while in prison; one had less than high school; one had some college experience; and another two participants held a university degree; while two had some university experience. All but one (i.e., 23) of the participants identified as in need of income; one said he was "good for money." Among the residential/living arrangements of the participants, 15 lived in a halfway house, one in an Aboriginal healing shelter, four with a family member, two were staying in a homeless shelter, one had moved out of a homeless shelter and into an apartment, and another was living in a room in a home that he described as being in a very "bad" area.

Eleven men had served previous provincial sentences, and ten had formerly been charged as youths and spent time in youth detention centres. Only two of the men/women in our sample were released from a second or third federal sentence; thus 22 participants were on parole after their first time in federal prison—most were released on statutory release rather than parole. The parolees' sentences had ranged from two years to life, but participants served from 16 months in prison to over 22 years (based on information provided—one participant was unclear about his time served, and the issue was not pressed). Two participants had received a Long Term Offender designation and all others were actively on parole. The range of criminal convictions included: criminality related to domestic violence, drug-related convictions (both possession and trafficking), property offence convictions (e.g., theft, breaking and entering), cybercrimes, violent offence convictions (e.g., assault, robbery, forcible confinement, possession of firearms), sex-related convictions, attempted murder, manslaughter, and first and second degree murder(s). All of the men and women in our sample had served time in reception, nine had served in a maximum secure facility, 20 in a medium secure, and 12 in a minimum secure prison. At the time of interview, one participant's parole had been revoked and he had returned to prison as a result. He was released anew at the conclusion of the study.

Overall, of the 24 participants, four parolees returned to prison during the course of the evaluation, including one person who had secured full-time employment, while another had been suspended. Post-evaluation, another parolee has returned to prison. More positively, seven have acquired and remained in full-time gainful employment positions (two in "management" positions), one is in a part-time position, and two, who were previously employed, are now in school full time; six participants remain unemployed.

## RESULTS

Our participants reported encountering many of the same barriers and having needs consistent with those indicated in the literature during their experiences of post-release employment reintegration. Men and women releasees all struggled with the effects of the stigma of their incarceration and criminal record as they sought employment. To this end, we first outline how releasees' lack of previous job experience and their criminal record have affected their attempts to reintegrate into the workforce. Next, the experiences of parolees navigating their parole and residency conditions are presented. Finally, the disconnection between parolees' readiness to return to employment upon release in relation to the timing pressures often imposed by their parole officers, and the vulnerabilities and stresses that accompany those pressures, are revealed.

## Lack of Employment Experience

Many respondents in our study had never been legally employed before their incarceration (in many cases because they entered prison in their youth), had never had the opportunity for legitimate employment, or had earned income through illegal means. As a result, they were uncertain both about how to approach finding work and about their ability to maintain work if found. Participants described approaching the interview process and compiling a resumé, critical components to securing employment, as particularly stressful. When asked which aspect of looking for work he was finding most difficult, a male releasee replied: "Just the fact that I had never done an interview. How to talk, present myself, the right words to say." His words, echoing others, show that uncertainty about the interview process and of what constitutes acceptable, let alone optimal, self-presentation during an interview are both barriers to employment. For this reason, participants indicated that opportunities to participate in mock interviews or pre-employment training workshops in the community were particularly helpful in bolstering their confidence and preparedness to look for work.

Compiling resumés was also described as stressful, both due to the gap in work experience that comes with incarceration and the lack of experience preparing a resumé. Participants also had little experience with technologies, some had never even used the Internet or email, phones, understood what "data" was or that it was now possible to search and apply for jobs online. To illustrate just how overwhelming and complex technology could be for some, for example, one man whom the main interlocutor asked to send her an email actually sought assistance from a day reporting centre staff member to print out a typed message through a word processing program on the computer and then proceeded to hand it to her. Regarding the construction of resumés, respondents described being concerned about their disjointed job experience, specifically the fact that they had not worked in free society when incarcerated: "a lot of guys don't know how to do one or don't know what to put on it because they were incarcerated." To deal with this "gap," many interviewees created resumés that suggested they engage in a form of "passing" as described by Goffman (1963). Specifically, they elected to describe their less traditional (illegal) employment experiences or lack of experience in more socially acceptable terms. For example, some parolees explained that they lied to cover up their resumé gap: "I basically [write it as though I] continued working while I was incarcerated." Another type of "white lie" used by respondents was to tie their resumé "gaps" to family or health justifications, which are more socially acceptable, and/or to tie them to privacy norms, thereby making them uncheckable: "I came up with the fact that I had to take time off due to family reasons and I know that's a bit of a white lie." In a similar vein, another respondent, who had never held employment outside of the institution, described using his institutional work experiences on his resumé, but presenting them in such a way that it suggests the experiences occurred in free society:

> If I had more job interviews I don't know how that would've gone, but my resumé doesn't reflect the fact that everything happened in prison. When I write things down I say that I managed the accounting cycle for four businesses, maintained computers for an adult education college. The people who wrote my letters understood my position and the reference letters don't reflect I was in prison as well. And I've contacted the references ahead of time to let them know that I was going for an interview and they'll answer the phone and not say that it's the prison and say that it's the college, as it's CSC.

In essence, this interviewee is "passing" and his references helped support his attempts to pass, a situation made possible by his stigma not being immediately apparent. As such, he may not face immediate prejudice but instead "must face unwitting acceptance of himself by individuals who are prejudiced against persons of the kind he can be revealed to be" (Goffman, 1963, p. 42). In hoping to pass as "normal," the secretly stigmatized person "conceals information about his real social identity, receiving and accepting treatment based on false suppositions concerning himself" (Goffman, 1963, p. 42). Of course, even the stresses of passing are to be preferred over those of being stigmatized or, as would be the case given the criminality of many men and women in our sample, of being a homo sacer (Agamben, 1995). In this case the rewards of having employment experience when seeking a job—passing as a former employee—are clearly desirable.

Participants noted that poor employment and educational histories were not adequately addressed by institutionally provided programming and that they benefited greatly from workshops on resumé building. It was noted that these workshops would have been particularly helpful if offered in prison: "I think this type of [pre-employment readiness] program would help a lot in all types of institutions. Even if it was one week a month. That way if someone is getting released the next month, they get that week to get some training just before they get out. That way everything is fresh." In this same regard, participants described the quality of institutionally-provided education and employment programming as rather poor or, said another way, as in desperate need of improvement. Many noted that educational opportunities were often limited to the GED:

> [Before], they would make it work so you could get money from the community. Now the emphasis is that you need to read and write in English and get a high school diploma and beyond that we [the institution] don't care. Even high school stuff now is online, and they don't care. Not the individual teachers, but CSC as an organization. "We don't need you to access this and the requirements are that so tough luck, go away."

As evinced in this respondent's words and further articulated by others, institutionally provided post-secondary courses may be available, but only to individuals facing a long period of incarceration. Some explained this may be due to the time it takes to acquire the required books for the courses or other administrative details on the part of the prison staff or institutions. In essence, respondents suggested this would allow the institution to advertise itself as providing a certain amount of programming at diverse levels, despite it not being widely available or easily accessible. Indeed, programs were described as "kind of for their [CSC's] own purpose, to say that they had given someone programming. That's kind of negative but I got that feeling." In this sense, it became apparent that participants felt they were considered unworthy of true efforts being made for their education or programming even by the institutional structures, administration and staff by whom they were confined—they felt their stigma and its implications on their self-worth even before returning to society.

Given technology was mentioned a number of times as being something that people needed to adjust to and learn upon release, it is not surprising that when asked what types of programming would be practical to offer, a respondent said:

> Things like computer skills. Doesn't even need to be Internet access but they don't teach it. Just to teach them Word, PowerPoint, Excel. Those are all things that you could teach them so they would have a basic understanding. A lot of guys I know inside wanted to start their own business but they had no skills of how to do that. So why not teach them those types of things?

The releasee explained that the lack of basic computer skills hampers the ability of parolees to navigate the realities of employment or even applying for jobs post-release. It became apparent in conversation with parolees that basic computer literacy and knowledge of online means of correspondence were new to many and this lack of knowledge was a source of discomfort and anxiety. For example, interviewees explain:

> Well that's what I'm thinking, just the little things. You had to learn about email and you had to learn about cellphone technology and what's going on with the outside.

> I wanted to brush up on some skills and there was a lot of things that were new to me. So that was very helpful; learning about the computer was very helpful to me because time has changed. The Internet and how to make a resumé, and all of that.

The excerpts taken from the transcripts of former prisoners evinced the importance of providing programming to acclimatize individuals to technological changes. In addition to computer skills, resumé building, and interview skills, respondents indicated that guidance on how to navigate the fact that they had a criminal past would be beneficial to address the realities they face upon release. Here men and women spoke of the need for coaching that prepares individuals for community reintegration, including strategies for discussing, or not discussing, their criminal histories, and even how to simply carry on a basic conversation:

> I always talk about it as soft skills. Things that people take for granted are soft skills, like anyone can have a conversation. People coming out of prison are sometimes not open to having that conversation and you have to draw it out of them. Opening them up about having a conversation, you don't have to talk about your time in prison—no one cares about that. Talk about the weather or the sports game or something. General conversations. If you have questions, ask them and don't just walk away wondering what you have to do.

Indeed, for respondents about to commence a post-release pre-employment program there was much hope that it would provide strategies for discussing their criminal history with prospective employers:

> I'm hoping they [the program leaders] will give me a better way to explain to the employers that they're not much different than myself. They're judgmental because I have the criminal record, [I am the one] with the drugs [in my history]. But [the program may help me get into] a better position to explain to them and you know, to have more of a chance in the job market.

As this participant's words suggest, talking about one's criminal history is a source of stress—probably a factor that makes passing so desirable. This fact leads to another barrier to post-release employment reintegration, widely indicated by participants and evinced in the literature: the criminal record.

## Looking for Work with a Criminal Record

Post-release employment reintegration is complicated by having a criminal record. Many participants indicated that, on multiple occasions, such a record prevented them from being hired:

> Oh yeah, the criminal record. It's killing you everywhere you go. You can't get a decent job.

> The other challenge is the criminal record. There's no way to get around it. I tried to ask for a pardon and they told me there's no way I can ask for a pardon until the next ten years. I'm wondering what have I done to deserve this.

> Yeah, like this last interview [for a job] I did, the two guys [interviewing me] said: "we like your qualifications but if it wasn't for this we would be hiring you in a heartbeat. You're actually a little overqualified for what we need."

As the aforementioned excerpts suggest, the extent to which releasees feel employers avoid hiring individuals with criminal records puts them under a great deal of strain. Many feel they will never find employment, let alone quality employment that will enable them to earn a living wage and is not entry-level, unsafe, or precarious. One participant, asked if he felt discouraged after losing a job placement opportunity after his criminal background was revealed, replied: "At that point no, I was already discouraged, let's be honest. I had already applied for about 200 jobs at the time and at that point it was just the same old thing." In a similar manner, another participant describes the emotional toll of multiple rejected applications:

> My last interview I did on Tuesday, I got a call back that same day to say "Sorry but due to our policies we can't hire you." I got down in the dumps there cause that was the sixth one [rejection] in two weeks. I was at school and I had to leave cause I couldn't deal with the rest of the day. I went home and my mom said to just take it easy and try not to think about it because she knows the first thing that happens, when I keep going over something, [is] I just go into a depression and I don't want to do anything. So [she said]: "Just take it easy, do what you have to do, do some of your home work at least."

As this releasee's words reveal, the constant rejection can be tied to negative feelings and a less than optimal sense of self-worth. Such feelings were not universal, however, as some men and women indicated that their criminal record had not hindered them from securing employment:

> No, I've always worked construction jobs and everyone there has a criminal record, so it's no big deal. I think that it's the financial jobs and things like that where they really care if you have a criminal record or where they ask about their criminal history. Even if they do ask they're not going to pay the $40 for the record check.

As evidenced in the words of this interviewee, the type of work sought affects whether having a criminal record is an issue for individuals or not. Specifically, persons who desired occupations outside of the primary sector tended to feel more hampered by their criminal history, while those who worked in the primary sector, in jobs like construction or in warehouses or basic manufacturing, felt that they were employed in jobs where a criminal history was rather commonplace. It became apparent that unskilled seasonal work, construction, warehouse stocking and in the back-of-house service industry (e.g., dishwashers and line cooks) were common occupations held by parolees. Having a criminal record, however, was believed to pose a problem for other types of work, resulting in the quality of jobs—the safety, stability, skill level, and so on—available to individuals with a criminal record being lower:

> If you have a criminal record, the jobs you can apply for are kind of lowered [sic] down. If you have a good resumé they won't hire you, not because you have a record but because they know you won't stay.

Such realities create new complications for parolees, who, beyond feeling limited in the type of work they are able to acquire, feel restrained in how they should present themselves. Even individuals with "good" resumés (presumably with higher levels of education, qualifications, or employment experience) find themselves struggling to determine to whom they should present their qualifications, as they may be barred from jobs appropriate for their degree of education and experience, but considered overqualified for the jobs they are free to apply for:

> So my issues are [that] I'm not allowed to touch a computer. You can't go to upper management in technologies and where do I go to get work? How do I take the resumé that I have and dumb it down enough that I can do construction with it?

Finally, even if an employer refrains from asking about an applicant's criminal record, simply having the record and the uncertainty that comes with waiting to be exposed—going from discreditable to discredited (Goffman, 1963)—burdens the parolee. For example, one individual explained that, although he lost a job opportunity because he was honest about having a criminal record, if he had not told his possible employers, the stress of not knowing if—or more likely, when—they would find out about his criminal past would have been overwhelming:

> If they didn't ask, I didn't tell. Other places they asked and I said yes. So some places will also ask if you've received a pardon and I was always honest about that. And then other places where they didn't ask and I got to a point where they would offer me a job I would proactively disclose. A lot of them were not-for-profits and I didn't want to have blowback on their operations.... I suffer from anxiety and if I went into a job and didn't tell them then it would be on my mind every day. I would have been fearful every day.

As evinced in the above excerpt, concerns for their employers or personal mental health were both reasons that motivated disclosure. One strategy some parolees used to manage their anxieties and navigate their uncertainties was to initiate the conversation in order to have more control over when and how their criminal history was presented. While it was anxiety-inducing to tell people about their criminal history, many felt it was worth it to have others know and avoid living in fear of being outed. For these reasons, a releasee explained that he stayed at his current job rather than taking a different job offer with better pay because his current employer was already aware and accepting of his criminal record, and he preferred to avoid going through the process of disclosing his criminal history again:

> One of the reasons why I was thinking about the other job was because it was full time, but I thought that it wouldn't be good for me because they didn't know that I had the record and I thought that even though I'm making less money right now I should stay where I am.

As shown here, the parolee's disinclination towards talking about his criminal history with someone new literally translated into monetary losses. The same participant continued to explain, "I had anxiety about starting somewhere else that didn't know that I had a record." He did not want to be discredited, nor did he want to pass; instead he wanted to be working in an environment where he was accepted for who he was, including his criminal history and associated past mistakes.

## Conditions of Parole and Residency

As previously discussed, being on parole comes with obligations and responsibilities, some of which exacerbate the difficulty of entering the workforce post-release. Something as simple as the time commitment, for example, that parole requires in terms of meeting with a parole officer, case workers, or attending programming can leave parolees feeling too restricted to take on full-time work:

> There are so many rules and obligations and meetings and you have to make all these meetings but yet you have to work. Not only do you have to abide by the law but you also have a load of conditions on top of it. It just sucks, and then coming to a halfway house there's even more rules.

Beyond these concerns, as other parolees' words reveal, the conditions and rules imposed vary between different parole officers or residents. As such, confusion is too often experienced by releasees:

> I think the interpretation of conditions from office to office is a bit different, which can be frustrating. If you have financial disclosure [for example], one office doesn't want to see receipts and they say if you spend more than $100.00 on something let me know, and another office wants to see every one. So sometimes they have different rules which can be problematic I think. But the hardest thing for me was all of the switching. But I was ok with it. I think that if anyone doesn't have the right attitude it can be difficult because you make it difficult. If you do that then it's your own fault.

> Living within the expectations of the parole board and the halfway house.... Sometimes they're really clear and that's fine, but sometimes they're not so clear and when they aren't clear that's when it's challenging. I don't want to make a mistake or do something that's a breach. Sometimes it's not clear what constitutes a breach.

As shown here, navigating parole conditions and the rules of a halfway house can complicate parolees' abilities to hold a job as they work to adhere to their other mandated conditions. The amount of time residents are allowed to be away from the house and the travel restrictions imposed by their parole conditions were described as particularly difficult to balance or, as demonstrated below, requiring extra efforts to manage when employed:

> I was able to work around some things because I was working fulltime for a moving company. Pretty much my travel restrictions and my curfew normally would've been an issue but if I contacted the national reporting

centre when my curfew was due and let them know I was still working it wasn't an issue. And my travel, as long as I let my PO know where I was going, it was ok. As long as I let them know ahead of time then it wasn't a problem.

Incarceration, and later, parole, sees releasees displaced from their home communities, whether by their own choice or not, which has adverse effects on their social supports or networks. This fact, in combination with the limitations imposed by parolee conditions and the stigma they bear, not only makes it difficult to expand or develop a new social network, but also can have detrimental effects on their attempts to re-enter the work force. Employment opportunities, for all individuals, are largely affected by whom one knows (see also Graffam et al., 2004; Wilson & Vito, 1988). Without such social networks to draw on for possible employment opportunities, employment reintegration is made more difficult.

## Readjusting/Timing

The feeling that they had to become full and participating members of society faster than they were comfortable with was a recurring theme among participants. Said another way, parolees felt forced to fully reintegrate into social and community living before they were ready. Some participants were required by their release conditions to maintain a job or demonstrate that they were looking for a job. This left many parolees feeling influenced by their parole officers to attain employment before they were ready, and induced feelings of stress. Not surprisingly, many parolees reported becoming overwhelmed. One individual explained that when he first entered an employment reintegration program, he was offered employment almost immediately. He opted to turn it down. Although he first stated he turned the job down because of a physical injury, as the interview continued he revealed that while the injury was an issue, he also found the process to be moving too quickly and felt overwhelmed:

> You know what, the knee is an issue but what we're talking about [the length of time the parolee has been out of prison and what is new in society as a result] is also a concern because I was a little bit overwhelmed. I started this program Monday and I'm thinking that I'd like to see some real job workshop skills, even though it's resumé writing, interview sessions, and seeing what the market is and where I fit in. And then [the employment specialist at the program] had me go and interview the next day and offered me this job.

This quote suggests that the releasee expected the employment reintegration program to proceed slower than it did. Further, he emphasized his knee injury rather than his comfort level or employment readiness to justify why he did not accept the offered employment positions. This suggests the participant felt either shame, inadequacy, or even as though he was failing to show the proper attitude required for reintegration to his case manager because he wanted to take things more slowly. Clearly, the stigma of incarceration and prior criminal engagement was apparent—an underlying challenge with which he had to contend. At multiple points throughout the interview, he reiterated that "the main reason I didn't take that job is because it might be hard on my knee and I want to address that first." Thus, he maintained his story rather consistently, despite revealing the other, perhaps more pressing, reasons he felt unprepared for work.

Addressing the responsibilities and expectations that come with parole, another interviewee explained, "There's sometimes that I feel like I'm being pressured, like I'm trapped in a corner. I don't want to feel like that." This individual continued to note that he expected his search for work to be gradual, with slow steps toward securing employment, yet he found himself comparing the realities of parole to a race:

> I got out, I can take things slowly, that's what I thought could happen. Start off at a YMCA, talk to someone, a job counsellor, a psychologist, something like that just to ease into it right? I don't feel like I've gotten that, they've all been like here, do this, go there and do that and that's what's going to happen. It feels like it's a race, this guy has to go to A, B, and C and come back and show me what you got.... And then I get compared to other people to say they did more time and they were out for as long as me and they're doing good, it feels like a race. I'm not out to impress anybody.

Beyond the pressures parolees experience to start working right away, as evinced in the excerpt above, parolees described participating in employment assistance programs at their parole officers' behest or in response to their parole conditions: "The way I feel is that the parole paper is all the things that I have to do. It feels like if you don't do any of it then you're going back to jail." This parolee's words reveal the pressures adhering to parole conditions can place on a releasee and how their continued freedom appeared to depend on their participation in activities rather than their behaviours on the streets per se.

However, employment too soon after release, before a parolee was ready, was described as a detriment to successful reintegration because of the pressures such experiences can impose and the associated interactions that they would have to learn to navigate before being ready to manage them. To exemplify this experience, a participant who was serving a life sentence described waiting to enter an employment reintegration program for nearly a year after she was paroled, which afforded her some time to readjust to being outside the institution, reconnect with family, and begin the processes of making amends and accepting herself and the consequences of her prior actions. She indicated that this was absolutely necessary: "Well, I had to adjust. It was very overwhelming when I first came out. All I did was cry. And a few times I just wanted to go back because that's familiar, right? I find out here it's very fast for me." She notes that she likely would not have been successful in an employment program if she had enrolled immediately upon her release:

> I think for myself, personally, I think I needed time to adjust. I think if I had been put in right away I don't think I would have done as well. I think, like I said, I was dealing with a lot of overwhelming feelings and I needed to go through an adjustment period. Especially someone like me who's been in a long time.

She reveals here that beginning the program immediately following her release would have been overwhelming. Other participants shared such feelings, again reiterating the theme of needing to take it slowly in order to be successful. This further reinforces that looking for employment, even with the help of employment programming, immediately upon release is overwhelming, given the competing needs and readjustments that come with re-entry into society.

> You're dealing with all kinds of stuff. You're dealing with adjusting to the halfway house, you're dealing with adjusting to the community. Going places by yourself, being more independent, there you're told what to do and you're on a routine. There's a lot of factors there. It's not that simple.... I know it's time for me to grow up and that, but it's going to take time. It's not going to be two weeks or three weeks to get rid of everything I've learned over the past ten years.

Participants further noted, beyond their need to readjust to community living, that they also had to learn how to provide for themselves. They were no longer in an institution where all their basic needs were met and they could make no genuine decisions about their own daily living. Releasees have to find a means to acquire food, clothing, shelter, and to care for themselves—everything from determining which soap to use, coffee to drink or where to do their laundry: "If you don't have a job you can't eat properly, you can't have clothes on your back, you can't have a house. Inside it's all provided for you." Many individuals are penniless upon their release from prison, which as far as their workforce re-entry is concerned, means that they do not have the supplies required to start a job even if they were to find one (or to interview for a position): "I don't have anything at all. And you're throwing me out half naked to go find a job. I don't even have a pair of boots to go to work, and I start next week" or "You gotta get gas money, everything out here is expensive, nothing is cheap." As these respondents' words show, without money, clothing and for some even a contact phone number, they are unlikely to be able to: (1) be called back for a job interview, (2) have something to wear to an interview, or (3) have the clothing or shoes required to work the job if they were to be hired. Such realities can also be felt to further intensify, even make visible, their stigma—the stigma tied to their criminal record and former incarceration. Passing is increasingly difficult without the material required to pass; thus the potential to be discredited may feel insurmountable.

## DISCUSSION

Largely in line with previous research that documents the struggles of securing employment for releasees (see Austin & Hardyman, 2004; Blitz, 2006; Dale, 1976; Graffam et al., 2004; Harrison & Schehr, 2004; Nelson et al., 1999; Richie, 2001), our findings strengthen the body of literature revealing that, after prison, men and women are vulnerable. They are reintegrating into a society that has no intention of being accepting, welcoming, or helpful, and are embarking on a transition that is riddled with uncertainty. Although being offered a job can be a source of esteem for a parolee, it can also be a huge source of stress if they do not yet feel ready for the responsibilities, interactions, and opportunities that come with such a position. Indeed, the financial stability provided by employment for some did not outweigh the anxieties and stress of being discredited if their criminal history were exposed or of trying to manage a job while also navigating free society anew. Thus, although researchers have long shown that employment is likely to reduce the possibility of a person reoffending (Albright & Denq, 1996), not everyone is ready for employment immediately upon release from prison. The transition from prison to community living is embedded in diverse challenges that each person must learn to negotiate and overcome at their own pace.

Parolees also felt hampered in their quest for employment by their lack of prior occupational experiences or valued skills, the fact that they had a criminal record and the associated stigma of that record, the trials of navigating their parole and residency conditions, and—most pronouncedly— their readiness to return to work within the timeframe they believed others had set out for/imposed upon them.

For former prisoners, employment reintegration places them in a precarious position as they await their criminal past to become known. Many feel that once their criminal history becomes known, their social worth or credibility will be tainted in light of the "branding" effect of the stigma they bear (Goffman, 1963). Their *virtual social identity* (Goffman, 1963, p. 4), embedded in the ways citizens perceive former prisoners in light of the stigma they bear, takes precedence and supercedes their *actual social identity*. A stigmatized individual will be negatively affected by the burden of others' judgments, as they must endure the uncertainty and associated vulnerabilities of "not knowing what the others present are 'really' thinking about him" (Goffman, 1963, p. 14). They are left to be constantly "on," actively and thoughtfully managing the impressions they leave on others to an extent beyond the norm. Further, some recognize that their past criminality leaves them in a particularly precarious place. They face the risk of becoming homo sacer if their history becomes known (Agamben, 1995), in that the knowledge of their stigma (i.e., their history of incarceration) might result in the withdrawal of certain opportunities. In having violated a socially maintained ideal by committing some form of crime, former prisoners are at risk of presenting a blemished version of themselves, as a person overshadowed by a past occurrence. The former prisoner then ends up having to fight the constructed depiction of self represented by their particular stigma.

The participation of former prisoners in mainstream society, through the labour market provides those who work alongside them, and who are aware of their status as ex-prisoners, with an opportunity to re-evaluate what it means to be an ex-prisoner. The end result has the potential to create the kind of understanding that would make strides toward stigma reduction and changing the stereotype of who an "offender" is, in actuality. It is in the public's interest to have former prisoners employed in society and working, thus becoming contributing and productive members of society. The former prisoners themselves also have much to gain from employment. Releasees need employment to make ends meet and to successfully integrate into society. Working also serves to teach employees the "ins and outs" of labour force participation—particularly beneficial after, often, years of being removed from the free world—and the nuances of technology (e.g., acquiring and learning to use cellphones and acquiring and learning to use email).

Our findings further suggest that during employment reintegration it is essential to recognize the unique and complex needs of each releasee as they learn to live in society and deal with the anxiety of release prior to seeking and securing employment. As such, employment reintegration must reflect the realities of former prisoners as they seek to negotiate their parole conditions, their reintegration efforts, and their changing life context. The need for individualized approaches to employment processes is clear among our participants, as, clearly, what works for one person may not work for another. With this also comes a need for programming that is wide-ranging and includes strategies for addressing how parolees can discuss their criminal histories with prospective employers. Failing to understand parolee needs may lead to their perceived "failure" on the job or in re-entry employment programming which may, then, negatively impact their sense of self or ability to reintegrate—thus doing more harm than good. Moreover, it is crucial that staff working with parolees, or in pre-employment programming, do their due diligence to ensure all parolees are protected, that their case history remains confidential, and that disclosure is primarily their choice. Overall, these factors, including the ability to purchase goods, to have a job, to contribute to society, and to feel like a citizen (rather than a former prisoner) are fundamental for stigma reduction and successful reintegration, all factors tied to long-term desistance.

## REFERENCES

Agamben, G. (1995). *Homo sacer: Sovereignty and bare life.* (D. Heller-Roazen, Trans.). Stanford, CT: Stanford University Press.

Albright, S., & Denq, F. (1996). Employer attitudes toward hiring ex-offenders. *Prison Journal, 76*(2), 118–137.

Atkinson, D., Fenster, C. A., & Blumberg, A. S. (1976). Employer attitudes toward work-release programs and the hiring of offenders. *Criminal Justice and Behavior, 3*(4), 335–344.

Austin, J., & Hardyman, P. L. (2004). The risks and needs of the returning prisoner population. *Review of Policy Research, 21,* 13–29.

Baldry, E., McDonnell, D., Maplestone, P., & Peeters, M. (2002, May). *Ex-prisoners and accommodation: What bearing do different forms of housing have on social reintegration for ex-prisoners?* Paper presented at the Housing, Crime and Stronger Communities Conference, Australian Housing and Urban Research Institute, Melbourne, Australia.

Berk, R. A., Lenihan, K. J., & Rossi, P. H. (1980). Crime and poverty: Some experimental evidence from ex-offenders. *American Sociological Review,* 766–786.

Blitz, C. L. (2006). Predictors of stable employment among female inmates in New Jersey: Implications for successful reintegration. *Journal of Offender Rehabilitation, 43*(1), 1–22.

Boyatzis, R. (1998). *Transforming qualitative information: Thematic analysis and code development.* Thousand Oaks, CA: Sage Publications.

Buck, M. L. (2000). *Getting back to work: Employment programs for ex-offenders.* New York, NY: Public/Private Ventures.

Corbin, J. M., & Strauss, A. (1990). Grounded theory research: Procedures, canons, and evaluative criteria. *Qualitative Sociology, 13*(1), 3–21.

Curtis, R. L. Jr., & Schulman, S. (1984). Ex-offenders, family relations, and economic supports: The significant women's study of the TARP project. *Crime & Delinquency, 30*(4), 507–528.

Dale, M. W. (1976). Barriers to the rehabilitation of ex-offenders. *Crime & Delinquency, 22*(3), 322–337.

Daly, J., Kellehear, A., & Gliksman, M. (1997). The public health researcher: A methodological approach. Melbourne, Australia: Oxford University Press.

Draine, J., Salzer, M. S., Culhane, D. P., & Hadley, T. R. (2002). Role of social disadvantage in crime, joblessness, and homelessness among persons with serious mental illness. *Psychiatric Services, 53*(5), 565–573.

Fletcher, D. R. (2001). Ex-offenders, the labour market and the new public administration. *Public Administration, 79,* 871–891.

Freeman, Richard. 1992. "Crime and the Employment of Disadvantaged Youths." In George Peterson and William V. Roman (Eds.), *Urban Labor Markets and Job Opportunity.* Washington, DC: Urban Institute Press.

Glaser, B. (1992). *Basics of grounded theory analysis.* Mill Valley, CA: Sociology Press.

Goffman, E. (1963). *Stigma: Notes on the management of spoiled identity.* Englewood Cliffs, NJ: Prentice.

Graffam, J., Shinkfield, A., Lavelle, B., & Mcpherson, W. (2004). Variables affecting successful reintegration as perceived by offenders and professionals. *Journal of Offender Rehabilitation, 40*(1–2), 147–171.

Harlow, C. W. (2003). *Education and correctional populations. Bureau of Justice Statistics, Special Report.* U.S. Department of Justice, Office of Justice Programs. Retrieved from http://www.ojp.usdoj.gov/bjs

Harrison, B., & Schehr, R.C. (2004). Offenders and post-release jobs: Variables influencing success and failure. *Journal of Offender Rehabilitation, 39,* 35–68.

Henry, K. (2000, August 13). A tight labor market is boon to ex-convicts. *Baltimore Sun,* pp. 1D, 4D.

Hollin, C., & Palmer, E. J. (1995). *Assessing prison regimes: A review to inform the development of outcome measures* (Commissioned report for the Planning Group, Her Majesty's Prison Service). London, UK: Home Office.

Kerley, K. R., & Copes, H. (2004). The effects of criminal justice contact on employment stability for white-collar and street-level offenders. *International Journal of Offender Therapy and Comparative Criminology, 48,* 65–84.

Lipsey, M. W., & Derzon, J. H. (1998). Predictors of violent and serious delinquency in adolescence and early adulthood: A synthesis of longitudinal research. In R. Loeber & D. P. Farrington (Eds.), *Serious and violent juvenile offenders: Risk factors and successful interventions* (pp. 86–105). Thousand Oaks, CA: Sage Publications.

Lochner, L. (2004). Education, work, and crime: A human capital approach. *International Economic Review, 45*(3), 811–843.

Lösel, F., & Farrington, D. P. (2012). Direct protective and buffering protective factors in the development of youth violence. *American Journal of Preventive Medicine, 43*(2), S8–S23.

Maruna, S., & Toch, H. (2005). The impact of imprisonment on the desistance process. In J. Travis & C. Visher (Eds.), *Prisoner reentry and crime in America* (pp. 139–178). New York, NY: Cambridge University Press.

Mukamel, D. (2001). *From hard time to full time: Strategies to help move ex-offenders from welfare to work.* Washington, DC: Department of Labor. Retrieved from: http://wtw.doleta.gov/documents/hard.html

Myers, S. L. (1983). Estimating the economic model of crime: Employment versus punishment effects. *Quarterly Journal of Economics, 98*(1), 157–166.

Nagin, D., & Waldfogel, J. (1995). The effects of criminality and conviction on the labor market status of young British offenders. *International Review of Law and Economics, 15*, 109–126.

Nelson, M., Deess, P., & Allen, C. (1999). *The first month out: Post incarceration experiences in New York City.* New York, NY: Vera Institute of Justice.

Pager, D. (2003). The mark of a criminal record. *American Journal of Sociology, 108*(5), 937–975.

Parsons, M. L., & Warner-Robbins, C. (2002). Factors that support women's successful transition to the community following jail/prison. *Healthcare for Women International, 23*, 6–18.

Petersilia, J. (2000). When prisoners return to communities: Political, economic, and social consequences. *Federal Probation, 65*, 3–8.

Rahill-Beuler, C. M., & Kretzer, K. M. T. (1997). Helping offenders find employment. *Federal Probation, 61*(1), 35–37.

Resnick, M. D., Ireland, M., & Borowsky, I. (2004). Youth violence perpetration: What protects? What predicts? Findings from the National Longitudinal Study of Adolescent Health. *Journal of Adolescent Health, 35*(5), 424.e1–10.

Ricciardelli, R. (2014). The inmate code: Looking at men in Canadian penitentiaries. *Journal of Crime and Justice, 37*(2), 234–255. doi:10.1080/07356 48X.2012.746012

Ricciardelli, R., & Moir, M. (2013). Stigmatized among the stigmatized: Sex offenders in Canadian penitentiaries. *Canadian Journal of Criminology and Criminal Justice. 5*, 353–386. doi:10.3138/cjccj.2012.E22

Ricciardelli, R., & Spencer, D. (2014). Exposing 'sex' offenders: Precarity, abjection and violence in the Canadian federal prison system. *British Journal of Criminology, 54*, 428–448. doi:10.1093/bjc/azu012

Ricciardelli, R., & White, P. (2011). Modifying the body: Canadian men's perspectives on appearance and cosmetic surgery. *Qualitative Report, 16*, 949–970.

Rice, P., & Ezzy, D. (1999). *Qualitative research methods: A health focus.* Melbourne, Australia: Oxford University Press.

Richie, B. E. (2001). Challenges incarcerated women face as they return to their communities: Findings from life history interviews. *Crime & Delinquency, 47*, 368–389.

Shapiro, J. P. (2000, November 6). Employers look to the joint to fill jobs. *U.S. News & World Report*, p. 70.

Sharp, J. (1992). *Windham School System and other prison education programs: A performance review, schools behind bars.* Texas Controller Public Account.

Solomon, A. L., Gouvis, C., & Waul, M. (2001). *Summary of focus group with ex-prisoners in the district: Ingredients for successful reintegration.* Urban Institute, Justice Policy Center. Retrieved from http://www. urban.org/uploaded PDF/410492_ExPrisoners.pdf

Spencer, D. (2009). Sex offender as homo sacer. *Punishment & Society, 11*(2), 219–240.

Tripodi, S. J., Kim, J. S., & Bender, K. (2009). Is employment associated with reduced recidivism? The complex relationship between employment and crime. *International Journal of Offender Therapy and Comparative Criminology, 54*, 706–720.

Uggen, C. (2000). Work as a turning point in the life course of criminals: A duration model of age, employment, and recidivism. *American Sociological Review, 65*, 529–546.

Varghese, F. P., Hardin, E. E., & Bauer, R. L. (2009). Factors influencing the employability of Latinos: The roles of ethnicity, criminal history, and qualifications. *Race and Social Problem, 1*, 171–181.

Varghese, F. P., Hardin, E. E., Bauer, R. L., & Morgan, R. D. (2010). Attitudes toward hiring offenders: The roles of criminal history, job qualifications, and race. *International Journal of Offender Therapy and Comparative Criminology, 54*, 769–782.

Visher, C. A., Debus, S., & Yahner, J. (2008). *Employment after prison: A longitudinal study of releases in three states.* Washington, DC: Urban Institute, Justice Policy Center.

Visher, C. A., Kachnowski, V., La Vigne, N. G., & Travis, J. (2004). *Baltimore prisoners' experiences returning home.* Washington, DC: Urban Institute.

Webster, R., Hedderman, C., Turnbull, P. J., & May, T. (2001). *Building bridges to employment for prisoners* (Home Office Research Study 226). London, UK: Communication and Development Unit, Home Office.

Western, B. (2002). The impact of incarceration on wage mobility and inequality. *American Sociological Review, 67*, 526–546.

Wheeler, S., Weisburd, D., Bode, N., & Waring, E. (1988). White-collar crime and criminals. *American Criminal Law Review, 25*, 331–357.

Whiting, B. M., & Winters, E. (1981, November/December). Ex-offenders and job employment in East Central Wisconsin. *Corrections Today, 432*, 82–84.

Wilson, D. G., & Vito, G. F. (1988). Long-term inmates: Special needs and management considerations. *Federal Probation, 52*, 21–26.

# Section III

Employment Reintegration Programming:
Supportive Strategies and Related Outcomes

# CHAPTER 6

# Is Criminal History at the Time of Employment Predictive of Job Performance?
## A Comparison of Disciplinary Actions and Terminations in a Sample of Production Workers

Mark G. Harmon, Laura J. Hickman, Alexandra M. Arneson, and
Ashley M. Hansen

## INTRODUCTION

**T**he number of individuals incarcerated in the United States has risen by more than 500 percent since the 1970s. While the United States accounts for only 5 percent of the world's population, it accounts for 25 percent of its incarcerated population (Alexander, 2010; Bushway, 2004). As a result, every year over 650,000 prisoners are released from prison to communities in the United States (Shivy et al., 2007). These individuals face numerous barriers to success outside of prison, where their access to social welfare programs, housing, education, and employment can be severely restricted (e.g., Solomon, Johnson, Travis, & McBride, 2004).

For individuals with a criminal record, especially a serious felony[1]/indictable conviction, gaining and maintaining employment is one of the most difficult consequences of their record. A well-known longitudinal study by Visher, Debus-Sherrill, and Yahner (2008) sought to document post-prison employment-related experiences using a relatively large sample of 740 previously incarcerated individuals in three states. Within two months of their release from prison, most study participants had been unable to find work, owing to a multitude of challenges, such as limited educational background, limited work experience, and chronic physical and mental-health-related issues. Eight months after release from prison, more than half of the participants were still looking for work, with the majority of them unemployed citing their criminal record as a key impediment (Visher et al., 2008). Of the former prisoners who gained employment, most reported satisfaction with their work, but felt dissatisfied with their wages (Visher et al., 2008). This finding is consistent with other research showing that wages may be negatively affected by a criminal record (Bushway, 1998; Freeman, 1991; Grogger, 1995; Lott, 1992; Waldfogel, 1994).

Findings like these are concerning because employment has been shown to be an important predictor of recidivism, defined both in terms of repeat arrest and return to prison (Bushway, 2004; Travis, 2005; Visher et al., 2008). While the association between employment and recidivism has strong empirical support, theoretical models do not view the relationship as causal. For example, Sampson and Laub (1993, 2005) conceptualize employment as a "life course event" that increases the likelihood that other theoretical mechanisms (social bond and informal social control) will be strengthened and operate to produce desistance. For another example, general strain theory views employment (or the lack thereof) as a factor that can increase or decrease strain (negative emotions) just as criminal behaviour is one of many potential coping mechanisms that function to reduce strain. According to this theory, employment essentially works to supplant crime as the way to decrease strain (Agnew, 1992). Labelling theory addresses the opposite outcome, namely when a criminal label results in the exclusion of a subgroup of individuals from conventional activities, including employment opportunities. Recidivism results when an ostracized individual internalizes the label and behaves consistently with "criminal" expectations (Lemert, 1951; Paternoster & Iovanni, 1989).

While employment plays a role both empirically and theoretically in the prevention of recidivism, obtaining employment requires overcoming substantial barriers. These include the limited qualifications of some former prisoners, and the stigma associated with incarceration and criminal justice involvement generally (Alexander, 2010; Hirschfield & Piquero, 2010; Iguchi et al., 2002; Thompson & Cummings, 2010). Once employment has been obtained, maintaining employment is an additional challenge, an area of research that has received less attention. The absence of empirical data on topics such as ex-prisoner job performance and termination, overall and in specific industries and position types, leaves policymakers and employers with only speculation and anecdotes about how well ex-prisoners might perform relative to similarly qualified employees without a criminal record.

Given the resource-intensive process of bringing in and training new employees and the stigma associated with criminal records (Pager, 2003), it is little wonder that many employers choose to not risk investing in the hiring and training of ex-prisoners.

This study is one of only a few to directly examine employment maintenance among individuals with a criminal record. Specifically, it assesses whether a pre-employment criminal record is related to employee job performance and termination in a sample of 425 production workers. We begin this chapter by first discussing the most pronounced barriers to securing employment for individuals formerly incarcerated. We then turn to an overview of the challenges tied to maintaining employment maintenance for said persons, followed by a discussion of recent developments intended to assist ex-prisoners in gaining and ultimately maintaining employment over time. In the subsequent section, we assess whether the presence of a criminal record has a significant effect on employment performance and outcomes for former prisoners in our sample. Finally, we discuss the implications of these findings for employers interested in "second-chance" employment for individuals formerly incarcerated for serious offences.

## BARRIERS TO SECURING EMPLOYMENT

Despite the potential protective factor against recidivism afforded by employment, a growing number of researchers have found that a criminal conviction serves as an impediment to securing employment (Bushway, 2004; Visher et al., 2008). Barriers to securing employment can be divided into issues/barriers related to (i) the individual seeking the job, and (ii) employer concerns about hiring an individual with a record. Regarding the former (i), on an individual level, major barriers to employment can be classified as belonging to four key domains. These include: (1) a lack of fulfillment of basic needs; (2) health-related problems; (3) familial and personal relational factors; and (4) substance use and/or abuse (Blitz, 2006; Brown, Spencer, & Deakin, 2007; Kethineni & Falcone, 2007; Tonkin, Dickie, Alemagno, & Grove, 2004; Travis, 2005). For example, Tonkin et al. (2004) note that prior to incarceration, individuals involved in the criminal justice system are likely to already be experiencing challenges fulfilling their basic needs like food, shelter, and clothing. Therefore, upon release, securing consistent and sustaining employment is paramount to meet these basic needs. Yet, obtaining a job is made more challenging given the lack of these same basic resources, such as housing and appropriate clothing for job searching. Ex-prisoners also have limited access to many social welfare programs and may lack a driver's licence, thus limiting both their job options and transportation options, particularly in communities lacking mass transit (Thompson & Cummings, 2010; Travis, 2005).

In addition to this lack of basic capital, Kethineni and Falcone (2007) indicate that about 21 percent of prisoners have a medical condition that further limits or diminishes their ability to work. Incarceration can also place strain on and/or result in the dissolution of pre-incarceration familial and personal relationships. Upon release, the absence or weakening of these relationships (and the social and instrumental support that comes with them) can negatively affect employability and employment opportunities post-incarceration.

Finally, substance abuse is common among previously incarcerated individuals (Inciardi, Martin, & Butzin, 2004). For many individuals, integrating back into society without relapsing into drug use can be a significant challenge. For those that do experience relapse, drug use or dependence can have a negative impact on their job performance (Shivy et al., 2007).

If, despite the odds, a job is ultimately secured, maintaining employment can also present a significant struggle for individuals with a criminal history and present additional stressors in their lives. Only a few researchers have undertaken to look at this aspect. Harm and Phillips (2001) conducted interviews with women who had served multiple prison sentences, to identify factors that contributed to their inability to maintain employment and their recidivism. Some of the negative factors identified were low wages, lack of childcare, discrimination in the workplace based on their criminal record, and conflicts with co-workers. While some of these factors mirror those found to affect the chances of gaining employment, the level, size, and relative importance of each are increasingly significant for maintaining employment.

In addition to individual challenges affecting the search for employment, researchers have shown that job candidates with criminal records are less likely to actively be considered for positions by employers, relative to similarly qualified applicants without a record (Bushway, 2004). In some instances, however, it may be unreasonable to expect employers to completely disregard all criminal history information as it pertains to the workplace. For example, it is quite reasonable for employers hiring for financial management positions to consider prior convictions for embezzlement or fraud. Even for employers who welcome applicants with criminal convictions (so called "second-chance" businesses), it is reasonable for them to consider the nature of applicants' prior offences when making hiring decisions. This type of decision-making is in accordance with Glynn's (1998) theory of negligent hiring, which asserts that employers actively take into consideration the potential risk or liability for potential harm caused by their employees (Thompson & Cummings, 2010). In other words, an employer is likely to consider the risk that an employee with a property crime conviction might steal from a customer, or that an employee with a violent criminal conviction might assault a fellow employee at work (Bushway, 2004).

This informal "risk assessment" by potential employers is rarely based on systematic evidence about the relative future risk posed by individual applicants. Instead, it is generally based on assumptions and stereotypes about individuals with a criminal record. Key among these is the assumption that a criminal record signifies an individual who is inherently untrustworthy or threatening (Bushway, 2004; Gaubatz, 1995; Hirschfield & Piquero, 2010). Indeed, researchers have found that honesty was rated as the second most valuable trait among professional workers in general, and that the presence of a criminal record was considered evidence of the absence of this trait (Graffam, Shinkfield, Lavelle, & Hardcastle, 2004). Similarly, Giguere and Dundes (2002) identified considerable hesitation to hire individuals with a criminal record. In a survey of 62 Baltimore-area employers, the top concern was that former prisoners would lack the necessary "people skills" for customer interaction. In addition, the employer respondents described fear of new workplace crimes committed by these potential employees and possible customer discomfort if others learned of an employee's criminal record.

Graffam, Shinkfield, and Hardcastle (2008) found that the belief that a criminal record indicates a "risky person" is a common one. They asked respondents to rate the likelihood that individuals with a criminal record would be able to gain and maintain employment, compared to individuals with other disadvantageous conditions (e.g., physical disability, intellectual disability, chronic illness). They found that employers and other stakeholders rated those with a criminal background the *least* likely to be able to obtain, as well as maintain employment in comparison to the others (Graffam et al., 2008).

In what is now considered a classic experimental demonstration of the impact of criminal record-related stigma on gaining employment, Schwartz and Skolnick (1962) conducted a study to measure the impact that criminal justice system involvement had on ex-prisoners gaining employment. In their experiment, 100 potential employers were divided into four groups. Each group received the resumé of a fictitious applicant, varying *only* by criminal history. Three of the resumés indicated that the applicant had an assault charge that led to: (1) arrest; (2) conviction; or (3) acquittal, while the fourth resumé contained no criminal history. The results revealed a strong association between negative views and criminal justice system involvement. In fact, the findings demonstrated that an applicant acquitted of assault was still viewed less favorably than an applicant with no criminal background.

## "BAN THE BOX" AND OTHER EFFORTS TO INCREASE EMPLOYMENT

Of course, this laundry list of employment-related challenges is not breaking news. Many re-entry researchers have called attention to this broad list of employment-related challenges and the considerable problem of unemployment and underemployment related to the mass incarceration policies in the United States (e.g., Bushway, Stoll, & Weiman, 2007; Clear, 2007; Mears & Cochran, 2015; Petersilia, 2003; Travis, 2005). Consequently, there have been a growing number of efforts undertaken to attempt to reduce the barriers to obtaining and maintaining employment for former prisoners. Some of these efforts target individuals by assisting in overcoming personal barriers (such as the meeting of basic needs, including transportation) and enhancing qualifications. Other efforts are geared towards creating more opportunities by mitigating the impact of stigma in the hiring process by limiting employers' ability to consider records when hiring, and by creating financial incentives for employers hiring individuals with a record (Leukefeld, Webster, Staton-Tindall, & Duvall, 2007).

One example of an effort intended to assist individuals with overcoming barriers to employment after criminal justice involvement is specialized courts. The courts are typically designed to respond to individuals with serious substance abuse and/or mental health needs. These specialized courts often also include programming intended to assist participants in gaining and maintaining employment. Drug courts, for example, may include judge-supervised participation in training for resolving conflicts at work, setting goals, solving problems, and developing life skills related to maintaining employment. Such intervention efforts have shown some positive employment benefits for participants over time, such as reducing drug dependence and parole/probation violation (Leukefeld et al., 2007).

Another example of individually-targeted efforts is the Milwaukee Safe Street Prisoner Release Initiative (PRI). The PRI provided pre-release services such as case management, vocational training, and drug and alcohol treatment for gang members and prisoners who had violent convictions. This was followed by six months of post-release social services and work program subsidies (Cook, Kang, Braga, Ludwig, & O'Brien, 2015). As measured by employment and income, service participants showed statistically better outcomes than control group members. There was no difference, however, in the likelihood of one-year prison-return between the two groups (Cook et al.,

2015). In other words, employment itself did not produce desistance for PRI participants as would be expected by many theoretical models (e.g., Agnew, 1992; Lemert, 1951; Paternoster & Iovanni, 1989; Sampson & Laub, 2005).

As the size of the population that possesses a criminal conviction has grown, so too have movements to increase opportunities for these individuals to secure more long-term employment. Perhaps the best-known employer-directed effort is the "Ban the Box" movement. Citing the unfairly prejudicial nature of criminal conviction information, "Ban the Box" advocates the elimination of the now-standard question about criminal convictions on employment applications (Henry & Jacobs, 2007; Rodriguez & Mehta, 2015). The objective is that all applicants receive the opportunity to be considered based on their qualifications alone, at least in the initial stages of the employment process. Criminal conviction information could still be disclosed at later stages of the process, after the applicant's qualifications have been assessed.

As of 2015, 19 American states and over 100 local jurisdictions had adopted some version of the "Ban the Box" recommendations (Rodriguez & Mehta, 2015). Evidence of the effectiveness of these programs among employers not already open to such hires, however, is lacking. Additionally, some have argued that "Ban the Box" practices could have unintended consequences that potentially harm those without a criminal record. Raphael (2010) argues that when employers are given direct access to criminal records, they are able to examine real information about an individual to determine whether or not they want to hire them. Without access to that information, an employer will often turn to biased heuristics such as a person's race, gender, education, home address, and gaps in their employment history in an attempt to determine any possible link to a criminal background. More specifically, Bushway (2004) expects that if employers are unable to look into criminal histories, discrimination against Black males will increase. Employers may make more wide-reaching generalizations about Black male applicants based on assumptions that this demographic group is the most likely to be criminally involved. Further, Bushway (2004) postulates that employers may assume that job applicants' employment gaps are due to their involvement with the criminal justice system, particularly in the case of Black male applicants. This suggests the possibility of unintended consequences resulting from restricting criminal history information. Therefore, any such efforts should be undertaken in combination with employer education and incentive programs to increase employment opportunities.

In some cases "banning the box" has been shown to have positive impacts. Henry (2008) notes that large cities have been leading the way for the "Ban the Box" movement. In Boston, MA, potential employers are not allowed to ask if a prospective employee has a record. In Boston this has led to measurable increases in employment (Gebo & Norton-Hawk, 2009). While research is lacking on whether these efforts will prove successful, researchers looking at stigmatized populations, such as individuals with mental illness, have promising findings. For example, researchers found that as individuals spend more time with people from these often-stigmatized groups, those within the groups begin to appear less threatening (Corrigan, Green, Lundin, Kubiak, & Penn, 2001; LeBel, 2008). More directly, Giguere and Dundes (2002) found that employers who had spent more time around individuals with a criminal conviction felt less fear of such individuals and were more open to hiring them, relative to employers with less direct contact. Likewise, a large survey conducted by Hirschfield and Piquero (2010) found that time spent with those who have a criminal record was associated with less negative attitudes about criminally involved populations in general. Moreover, they found participants in their sample to be generally open to engaging with formerly incarcerated individuals outside of work. Based on that, they theorize that co-workers may be less concerned about working alongside former prisoners in the workplace than employers assume.

## DAVE'S KILLER BREAD

In addition to the work of movements like "Ban the Box," individual businesses and organizations have also made a commitment to providing employment opportunities for individuals with criminal records. One example is the well-known business "Dave's Killer Bread, Inc.," based in Oregon, USA, a bakery whose namesake is a former prisoner who excelled after being provided the opportunity to work post-incarceration. Dave's Killer Bread has fostered a reputation as a company that is not only willing to hire those with a criminal conviction, but that has actually hired a relatively large number of employees with a criminal conviction. Prior to Oregon's recent adoption of its version of "Ban the Box" application restrictions, Dave's Killer Bread actively encouraged applicants to share their criminal conviction history. In doing so, the company worked to communicate that it does not rule out applicants simply because they have a criminal background. Instead, management considers the full context of an individual's past and encourages applicants to fully divulge and explain their previous convictions.

For Dave's Killer Bread's management, the practice of asking about criminal convictions in the hiring process serves two primary purposes. First, it gives insight into whether an individual has had what the company calls an "ah-ha moment"—the point in time when an individual decided to live his/her life differently and be accountable for his/her actions. This concept is similar to Sampson and Laub's (2005) description of "human agency" as central to the process of desistance from crime. Human agency refers to decision-making by an individual to change their own circumstances (Sampson & Laub, 2005). Second, Dave's Killer Bread uses the candidate's criminal history discussion as an assessment of the applicant's truthfulness. Once an applicant is selected for employment, Dave's Killer Bread runs a full criminal background check as part of the formal hiring process. If any discrepancies are revealed, these concerns are discussed with the potential employee. It is very rare that this process reveals problematic discrepancies and a job offer has almost never been rescinded as a result of information contained in a criminal background check.

Despite its open and non-judgmental approach to individuals with a criminal history, Dave's Killer Bread managers treat this information as private personnel information. The management is supportive of both employees' right to privacy, as well as their right to disclose a criminal history to others at their own discretion. In practice, those with a criminal background and those without work side by side, generally without any knowledge of a co-worker's criminal history, or lack thereof.

As one of their core values, Dave's Killer Bread is committed to providing employment opportunities to individuals with a criminal record. The company views this as a service to the community and also as a positive business decision. The company has seen few negative impacts from hiring those with criminal convictions and Dave's Killer Bread management believes that those employees with a criminal record behave and perform as well as those without such a record. To test this expectation, Dave's Killer Bread sought an independent review of its personnel records that would compare the behavioural and employment-related outcomes of its employees with and without a criminal record. At the request of management, we undertook this analysis independent of the company.[2]

## PRESENT STUDY

To explore the relationship between the presence of a criminal record and employment outcomes, we examined the employment records of individuals working in the production facility of the bakery. The study assessed employment-related performance differences between employees with and without a criminal conviction. The primary analysis consists of a series of $t$-tests and chi-square analyses of the employment records. The results were then contextualized through semi-structured interviews with six key informants who work as bakery floor managers.

## Methods

*Sample Description.* The data for the study consists of de-identified electronic employee records maintained by the Human Resources (HR) department of Dave's Killer Bread. For the purposes of our study, the sample was limited by both employee position type and time period. Dave's Killer Bread is a medium-sized bakery production facility that employs individuals in a variety of capacities, including executives, office workers, line production workers, delivery staff, sales staff, office staff, and production support staff (e.g., janitorial, cleaning, security). According to the HR staff at Dave's Killer Bread, the vast majority of the employees with a criminal record at the time of hire work in production, delivery, and other blue-collar operational positions. To capture adequate variation and avoid position types with too few employees to test for differences, we focused our analysis on these operations position types.

The sample included employment records of all individuals employed at Dave's Killer Bread for some or all of the time between 2012 and 2015. This three-year time period was selected to maximize the sample size due to identified year-to-year variability in business practices. In June 2012, as a result of the change in the ownership of the company, Dave's Killer Bread instituted new record-keeping policies making records prior to that point in time not comparable to the records post–June 2012. Of the 635 individuals employed at Dave's Killer Bread at some point between June 2012 and June 2015, 425 (67 percent) worked in operational positions. This latter group represents the sample for the present study.

*Descriptive Variables.* The available employee data included basic demographic and employment information. Among the demographic information were a series of variables that represented age, gender, race/ethnicity, education, marital status, and military veteran status at the time of hire. There was too little variation in military veteran status (i.e., 13 total individuals) to be included in our analysis.

Because of the highly skewed racial distribution, we collapsed the employee self-identified race/ethnicity categories into White and non-White to avoid the possibility of uniquely identifying individual employees in small categories. For education at the time of employment, we created a dummy variable indicating whether the employee had at least a bachelor's degree (=1) or had less than a bachelor's degree (=0). Gender was coded as a dummy variable (1=male and 0=female), as was marital status (1=married and 0=not married).

Length of employment was constructed as a frequency variable capturing the number of days between the date of hire and the date of termination for those whose employment ended during the three-year study period. In the case of those still employed at the end of the three-year period, length of employment was measured according to number of days between the hire date and the last day of the study period. For ease of interpretation, the number of days employed was converted to years.

The primary independent variable of interest was whether the employee record indicated the presence (=1) or absence (=0) of a felony conviction at the time of hire at Dave's Killer Bread. This served as the sole measure of criminal history since the automated employee records did not contain any additional information on type of conviction, arrest history, incarceration history, or probation or parole status at the time of hire. For simplicity of presentation, "a record" or "criminal history" refers to having a record of at least one felony conviction at the time of hire.

*Disciplinary Dependent Variables.* One of the key components of our analysis was to compare job performance indicators of employees with and without a felony conviction. The personnel records contained documentation of any and all official disciplinary actions taken for each employee since the start of their employment at Dave's Killer Bread. For each disciplinary action, the record contained the date of the incident, the type of incident, and the outcome of the disciplinary action taken by management.

The types of disciplinary incidents fell into three broadly defined HR categories. The first was attendance-related. This included employees failing to show up for a scheduled shift, showing up late, leaving work without permission, and taking leave from work when none was currently available. The second category included violation of company policy; this type of disciplinary action stemmed largely from failing to follow a stated company policy or not performing a required on-the-job procedure. The third category involved individuals disciplined for behavioural issues, typically for behaviour considered disrespectful, indicative of a poor workplace attitude, or for insubordination. Other types of behaviours could also result in behavioural discipline, but were much less common.

We received data from Dave's Killer Bread outlining each documented disciplinary action taken against each employee. We then coded this information into a set of three frequency variables containing the number of disciplinary actions of each type—attendance, policy, and behavioural—for each employee. We created a fourth cumulative variable of all types of disciplinary actions on record. Because the length of employment varied considerably within the sample, comparison of simple frequencies could be misleading. For example, an employee with three attendance-related disciplinary actions over two years of employment would be seen as performing the same as an employee with an equal number of disciplinary actions in two months. We therefore constructed four annual rate variables as a method of standardizing the "time at risk" for disciplinary actions. For each type of incident and for the total incidents variable, we divided the total number of disciplinary actions by the total number of years employed. Using the previous example, the value in the attendance-related variable for the employee with the two-year tenure would be 1.5 per year, compared to a rate of 18.75 per year for the employee with the same number of incidents over two months. In our analysis, we used these four annual rate variables to compare the two groups on total and type of disciplinary actions.

*Termination Variables.* In addition to job performance, the study also sought to examine whether a felony/indictable conviction is related to termination, either voluntary (quitting) or involuntary (being fired). We used two types of variables to capture terminations. One variable captured whether employment was terminated for any reason (=1) or was maintained at the end of the three-year observation period (=0). This variable allowed us to test whether a felony conviction is associated with departure from the company for any reason. Within the employee subgroup that was terminated, we created a variable indicating whether the termination was voluntary (=1; i.e., they quit) or involuntary (=0; i.e., they were fired). This variable allowed us to test whether the two groups differ by reason for termination.

*Key Informant Interviews.* To aid in our understanding of Dave's Killer Bread's hiring and supervision practices, we conducted key informant interviews with six mid-level managers (one from each of the six areas of production) who directly supervised and worked alongside production staff. These managers had both hiring power within their units and could recommend involuntary termination of an employee. They were also responsible for on-the-job performance within their unit and could discipline employees for failing to meet job requirements and expectations.

The purpose of the hour-long semi-structured interviews was to assist the research team in: (1) understanding the hiring and employee management policies and practices of Dave's Killer Bread, (2) interpreting the variables contained in the personal records, and (3) interpreting the results of the quantitative analysis of those records. The key informant interviews were conducted individually with each respondent and questions focused on the clarification of policies and procedures currently and formerly used at Dave's Killer Bread. The interviewees provided context and descriptive information regarding company-wide hiring practices and changes in hiring of employees over time. As the purpose of the interviews was to supply context and deeper understanding of the quantitative analysis and not to collect primary data, no analysis of the six key informant interviews is presented.

## RESULTS

To better explore the relationship between the presence of a criminal record and employment outcomes, we present a comparison of employment records of those with and without a felony offence record in the production facility of the Dave's Killer Bread bakery. The goal of the analysis was to assess whether employment-related performance differences exist between those with a criminal record and those without. The primary analysis consists of a quantitative assessment of employment records using, in the main, a series of $t$-tests and chi-square models.

Table 1 shows the demographic characteristics of the overall group as well as comparisons between the two groups. The majority of production employees were male (81 percent). Among the male employees 47 percent had a felony record at the time of hire, while the proportion of women with a record was lower (38 percent). Regarding race and ethnicity, a larger share of White employees had a felony conviction record relative to non-White employees (47 percent and 38 percent, respectively). Those with a felony conviction were slightly older on average than those without (35.78 years relative to 34.26, respectively). Only 10 percent of production employees

Table 1    Production Employee Demographic Characteristics

|  | No Record<br>n = 234 (55%) | Record<br>n = 191 (45%) | Total<br>N = 425 |
|---|---|---|---|
| **Gender** | | | |
| Female | 51 (62%) | 31 (38%) | 82 (100%) |
| Male | 183 (53%) | 160 (47%) | 343 (100%) |
| **Race/ethnicity** | | | |
| White | 166 (53%) | 149 (47%) | 315 (100%) |
| Non-white | 68 (62%) | 42 (38%) | 110 (100%) |
| **Age at hire** | 34.26<br>(SD = 13.03) | 35.78<br>(SD = 14.05) | 34.93<br>(SD = 14.49) |
| **Married at hire** | 87 (65%)** | 47 (35%)** | 134 (100%) |
| **Bachelor's degree at hire** | 28 (67%) | 14 (33%) | 42 (100%) |
| **Average years employed at DKB** | 3.72**<br>(SD = 0.22) | 2.98**<br>(SD = 0.14) | 3.38<br>(SD = 2.85) |

*p<.05    ** p<.01

had obtained a bachelor's degree by the time of hire, and a larger share of those with a degree had no criminal record (67 percent versus 33 percent). None of these differences in demographic characteristics were significant. We employed *t*-tests to examine the differences between our continuous variables and chi-square tests for the categorical variables. The two groups did differ significantly on marital status. Those without a record were significantly more likely to be married relative to employees with a criminal record (65 percent and 35 percent, respectively).

Lastly, Table 1 presents the average number of years employed with Dave's Killer Bread. This includes both current employees (whose length of employment would be truncated by the date of the 2015 data extraction) and employees who left the company at some point during the study's three-year period. On average, those with a criminal record were employed for 2.98 years relative to a 25 percent longer average tenure of 3.72 years for those with no criminal record. A *t*-test found that the difference is significant ($t=2.66$, $p<.01$). This difference was likely the result of the handful of very long-serving employees (10 years or more) without a criminal record. There was only one employee with a record who had been employed longer than 10 years (10.06 years). Conversely, there were nine employees without a record employed for more than 10 years, with three employed more than 20 years. The longest-serving individual working currently in production had been with Dave's Killer Bread for 26 years at the time of data collection. When these "outliers" were removed, the difference in average years employed between the two groups was no longer significant (2.94 versus 3.12).

## Disciplinary Actions

We compared the rate of disciplinary actions per year taken against employees with a felony conviction with those taken against employees without. Comparing rates (rather than frequencies) helped standardize the length of time at "risk" for disciplinary actions. To compare differences in disciplinary actions, a series of *t*-tests were conducted. Chart 1 shows disciplinary actions overall and in each of the three areas—attendance, policy, and behaviour.

The first assessment conducted was on the overall rate of discipline. Over the course of a year we can expect those without a criminal background to have just under half of a disciplinary action per employee (.44). Those with a criminal background actually had a slightly *lower* rate of disciplinary action taken against them, at .39 disciplinary actions per year. A *t*-test of this difference between the two groups found that the mean difference in rates was not significant and therefore we cannot interpret this as a clear difference ($t=0.68$, $p<.24$). For both attendance and policy-related actions, the annual rate of

Chart 1    Annual Rate of Discipline Actions by Employee Felony Conviction Record Status

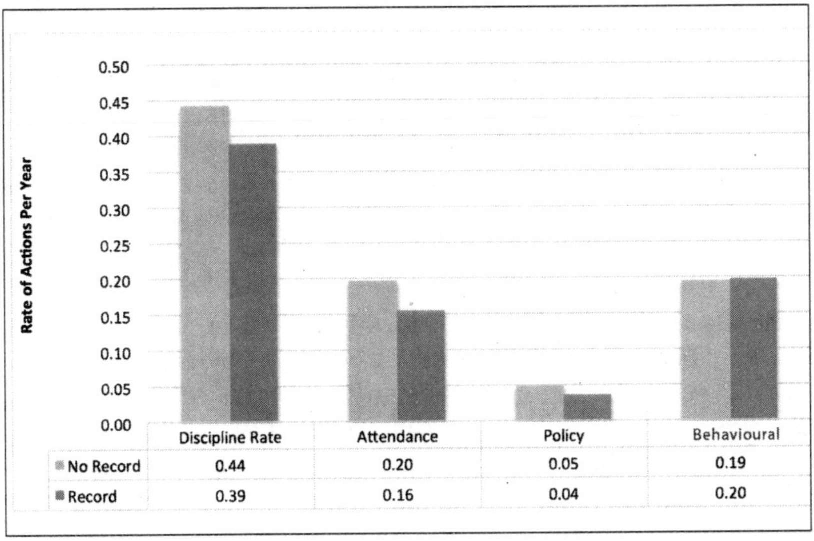

| | Discipline Rate | Attendance | Policy | Behavioural |
|---|---|---|---|---|
| No Record | 0.44 | 0.20 | 0.05 | 0.19 |
| Record | 0.39 | 0.16 | 0.04 | 0.20 |

disciplinary action was slightly higher for those without a felony/indictable offence record relative to those with a record. Behavioural disciplinary rates were, however, very slightly higher for those with a felony conviction than for those without. Like total disciplinary actions, none of the differences between the groups proved significant using $t$-tests.

Overall, the analysis of disciplinary differences indicated that attendance issues were the most common reason for disciplinary action for those without a criminal background, while behavioural actions were the most common among those with a criminal background. Across the four measures, however, differences were rather small, indicating that those with a record and those without are substantively similar with similar disciplinary rates. Overall, this disciplinary analysis suggests that there is no meaningful difference between employees with a criminal background and those without. This was consistent both across overall disciplinary actions and for specific types related to attendance, policy violations, and behavioural problems.

For the sake of comparison, we can think of the disciplinary rates as the rate of expected discipline in a given year. For example, in any given year we can expect one in five employees without a felony offence record to be disciplined for an attendance issue, while we would expect roughly one in six employees with a record to be similarly disciplined. Of course this finding is non-significant and should only be used to illustrate the very modest size of the differences between the two groups over this specific three-year period.

## Terminations

As shown in Table 2, of all 425 individuals employed at Dave's Killer Bread at some point during the three-year study window and included in our analysis, employment ended for 155 (36 percent) during that same window. While those with a felony offence record made up a larger percent of overall employment terminations (39 percent versus 34 percent), the difference between the groups was not significant based on a $t$-test ($t = -0.89$, p < .37) of the percentages.

Table 3 shows the reason for termination for the 155 employees who left Dave's Killer Bread at some point during the study period. Sixty-five percent of terminations overall were involuntary. The table allows a comparison of voluntary and involuntary terminations by group. Of those that voluntarily left the company, 61 percent had no felony offence record, with the remaining 39 percent with a felony conviction. Of those that left the company involuntarily, a greater percentage had a pre-employment felony conviction (72 percent) than did not (59 percent). There was no statistical difference in the distribution of type of termination by record based on a chi-square test ($x^2$=2.60, p<.11).

While comparison across the two groups (as shown in Tables 2 and 3) addresses the key question of this analysis, another method of comparing terminations is to look at the distribution within each group. In other words, among those with a felony offence record, what proportions were terminated voluntarily, involuntarily, or continued to be employed? Chart 2 provides a graphical representation of these proportions within each group. At the

Table 2    Production Employee Terminations by Employee Conviction Record Status

|  | No Record n = 234 | Record n = 191 | Total N = 425 |
|---|---|---|---|
| **Termination for any reason** | 81 (34%) | 74 (39%) | 155 (36%) |

Table 3    Production Employee Involuntary and Voluntary Terminations by Employee Conviction Record Status

|  | No Record n = 81 | Record n = 74 | Total N = 155 |
|---|---|---|---|
| **Voluntary termination** | 33 (41%) | 21 (28%) | 54 (34%) |
| **Involuntary termination** | 48 (59%) | 53 (72%) | 101 (66%) |

end of the study period, 60 percent of those with a felony offence record continued to be employed at Dave's Killer Bread, relative to a slightly higher 64 percent of those without. Employment terminations were voluntary in 12 percent of the felony offence record group, relative to 15 percent of those without a felony offence record. This difference within group proportions is not significant ($t=0.91$, p<.18).

For both employee groups, involuntary terminations were most common. However, a larger percentage of the employees with a felony offence record were involuntarily terminated relative to employees without a pre-employment felony offence conviction (28 percent versus 21 percent). This 7 percent difference between the share of each group experiencing involuntary termination is significant ($t=-1.75$, p<.04). In other words, employees with a felony record were about 7 percent more likely to be fired during the three-year study period than employees without a felony offence record.

One possible reason for this discrepancy was that those with a felony offence record might have experienced more difficulty integrating into the work environment as newer employees, but that over time differences with other employees lessened or disappeared. To test this possibility, we compared the two groups on involuntary terminations by length of time employed. As Chart 3 illustrates, employees in both employee groups were largely not involuntarily terminated for at least six months. Only one person was involuntarily terminated with less than six months on the job. Between

Chart 2    Within-Group Distribution of Termination By Type and Felony Conviction Status

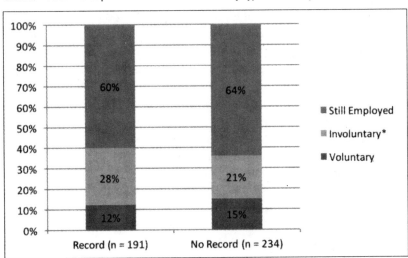

*P<.05

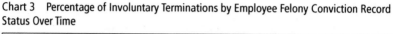

Chart 3   Percentage of Involuntary Terminations by Employee Felony Conviction Record Status Over Time

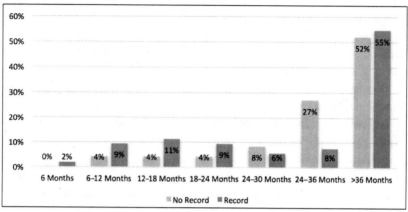

six and 24 months, the number of terminations were substantially higher for employees with a record. A total of 31 percent of the terminations of employees with a record happened within the first two years of employment, while only 12 percent of employees without a record were fired during these first two years. In the two- to three-year period of employment individuals without a record were substantially more likely to be fired. Once either group reaches three years of employment, involuntary termination rates are roughly equal.

## DISCUSSION

In the current study, we set out to analyze employment-related performance differences in a sample of bakery production employees with and without pre-employment felony convictions. Overall, our analysis was consistent with the impressions of Dave's Killer Bread production floor management, and our findings largely oppose much of the prevailing public sentiment that hiring individuals with criminal background is problematic. In our assessment of the 425 employees in operational positions, we could find no significant differences in employee disciplinary actions or voluntary terminations between those with a criminal conviction and those without. In other words, among Dave's Killer Bread's operations employees, those with a criminal record did not stand out as statistically "worse" employees than those without such a record. When compared to employees without a record, employees with a record were not responsible for a statistically greater share of disciplinary actions (overall or specific types) or terminations (either voluntary or involuntary).

Given the limited research in the area of employment maintenance, we further examined employment maintenance within each group of employees. In doing so, we did find a difference in employment between the groups. A larger percentage of employees with a felony offence record experienced an involuntary termination relative to the percentage of those with no prior record. While similar proportions of both groups remained employed at Dave's Killer Bread throughout the study period (60 percent of those with a record and 64 percent of those without), a greater share of terminations were involuntary for those with a prior record (28 percent) compared to those without (21 percent). This difference indicates that for those involuntarily terminated, individuals with a criminal background were about one-third more likely to be fired than those without such a background.

A potential explanation for these findings was suggested during our key informant interviews with production managers. Several managers pointed out that this finding may have been driven by a difference in the potential for securing employment elsewhere. Managers stated that many employees without a felony offence record who were in danger of being fired would have seen "the writing on the wall" and quit voluntarily, expecting to or already having found work elsewhere. More specifically, those employees without a record may have been more willing to quit their job after management had expressed concerns about their work performance, attendance, or other issues, whereas those with a criminal record were less likely to quit as a result. Given the substantial barriers to getting a new job with a felony offence record, those with a criminal record were described as holding onto their job as long as possible, even if they felt an involuntary termination coming. The managers' hypothesis is a very reasonable one and is certainly consistent with the substantial body of evidence documenting the negative impacts of a criminal record on securing employment (e.g., Bushway, 2004; Visher et al., 2008).

While this work represents an informative initial assessment in an area of very limited prior research, the results are restricted in their generalizability outside of the Dave's Killer Bread setting. Dave's Killer Bread actively creates a supportive environment and is open to hiring those with a criminal record. Its unique history may mean that the results of the study may not be representative of other work environments. For example, the *type* of business open to hiring persons with a criminal record can be expected to influence future results. Many of the jobs that Dave's Killer Bread can offer are lower-skilled and require little formal education. It also offers a considerable amount of on-the-job training and support for its employees. These factors make the company particularly adept at working with employees with a criminal record. Dave's Killer Bread also looks to actively promote from within as they create opportunities for lower-level employees to climb up the company ladder. As the interviewed managers noted, this fosters loyalty within the ranks and encourages those with ambition to excel.

It is possible that the supportive work environment created at Dave's Killer Bread substantially limits the generalizability of these results to work places less welcoming and attentive to the special needs of those with a felony record. For example, Dave's Killer Bread supplies its employees with a free shift meal, sick leave, consistent work hours, and a higher wage than competing employers. In addition to the on-the-job training, Dave's Killer Bread has established an employee mentor program. These mentors serve as off-the-clock employee support for everything from finding childcare and transportation to help in the event of substance-abuse relapse. Many of the additional resources at Dave's Killer Bread address a substantial number of the difficulties experienced by those with a criminal background regarding maintaining employment, relative to employers not offering these sorts of employee supports.

Another limitation to the generalizability of the current research is a possible selection bias. Dave's Killer Bread is known as a "second chance" company, accepting of hiring individuals with a criminal record, and because of that, many people with a criminal past apply to work there. Since they have a large applicant pool to choose from, those responsible for hiring employees might be selective in their hiring, and only hire the most qualified from within the ranks of those with a criminal record. Given a less qualified pool of applicants it might be possible that the finding that there is no meaningful difference in discipline rates might look quite different. In this sense the results from Dave's Killer Bread will need to be compared to future research using other samples, regions, industries, and with richer datasets. For example, data on previous employment, types and extent of criminal records, incarceration history, and non-work social data are necessary to help build both theoretical and empirical knowledge in this understudied area.

## CONCLUSION

It is clear from past research that a criminal record may greatly hinder the ability of an individual to reintegrate successfully (Visher et al., 2008). If more employers were willing to offer those with criminal convictions employment opportunities, the negative impact of having a criminal record could potentially be mitigated. Our findings challenge the stigma associated with criminal records found in past research, as well as other stigmas that label those with a criminal record as unfit for the workplace. Disciplinary rates and terminations did not differ by the presence or absence of a felony conviction.

Overall, these results provide no support for the assumption that former prisoners will be trouble at work. The within-group findings also present an opportunity for future research. That is, the study raised the possibility that there may be differential responses to disciplinary actions on the job (quitting versus continuing until being fired) that may stem from unequal opportunities to secure other employment for those with and without a felony record. The data available in the current study do not afford the opportunity to adequately test this possibility, but the issue certainly calls for continued exploration with other data sets and, most likely, original data collection.

While much more research is needed on other former prisoner samples, these results lend support to the concept of "second chance" businesses and programs, and encourages the development of evidence-based approaches to hiring individuals with a criminal background. This is one way to work towards the goal of reducing recidivism by helping employers become more willing to hire those with a criminal past. Dave's Killer Bread and other second-chance employers are offering potential models of hiring and management practices that provide mutually beneficial ways to offer individuals with a criminal record a second chance. This is very important, because as past researchers have shown, employment instability is one of the primary determinants of recidivism. As Solomon and colleagues (2004) argue, recidivism creates a heavy burden on society's resources and reducing its occurrence is invaluable to help society prosper.

## NOTES

1 A felony is an offence defined in the USA as a crime that can result in imprisonment of at least one year. This is legally distinct from Canada's indictable offence. An offence cannot be a felony in Canada.

2 Dave's Killer Bread's management also requested to be identified by name in publications utilizing its data.

## REFERENCES

Agnew, R. (1992). Foundation for a general strain theory of crime and delinquency. *Criminology, 30*, 47–87.

Alexander, M. (2010). *The new Jim Crow: Mass incarceration in the age of color-blindness*. New York, NY: New Press.

Atkinson, D. V., & Lockwood, K. (n.d.). *The benefits of Ban the Box: A case study of Durham, NC*. Durham, NC: Southern Coalition for Social Justice. Retrieved from http://www.southerncoalition.org/wp-content/uploads/2014/10/BantheBox_WhitePaper-2.pdf

Barclay, C. (2004). Future employment outlook: A tool measuring the perceived barriers of incarcerated youth. *Journal of Correctional Education, 55*(2), 133–146.

Beck, A. J., & Shipley, B. E. (1989). *Recidivism of prisoners released in 1983.* Washington, DC: US Department of Justice, Office of Justice Programs, Bureau of Justice Statistics.

Blitz, C. (2006). Predictors of stable employment among female inmates in New Jersey: Implications for successful reintegration. *Journal of Offender Rehabilitation, 43*(1), 1–22.

Brown, K., Spencer, J., & Deakin, J. (2007). The reintegration of sex offenders: Barriers and opportunities for employment. *Howard Journal of Criminal Justice, 46*(1), 32–42.

Bureau of Justice Statistics. (2001). *Correctional populations in the United States, 1998* (Index No. NCJ 192929). Washington, DC: Author.

Bushway, S. D. (1998). The impact of an arrest on the job stability of young White American men. *Journal of Research in Crime and Delinquency, 35*(4), 454–479.

Bushway, S. D. (2004). Labor market effects of permitting employer access to criminal history records. *Journal of Contemporary Criminal Justice, 20*(3), 276–291.

Bushway, S. D., Stoll, M. A., & Weiman, D. F. (2007). *The impact of incarceration on labor market outcomes.* New York, NY: Russell Sage Foundation Press.

Clear, T. R. (2007). Imprisoning communities: How mass incarceration makes disadvantaged neighborhoods worse. Oxford, UK: Oxford University Press.

Cook, P. J., Kang, S., Braga, A. A., Ludwig, J., & O'Brien, M. E. (2015). An experimental evaluation of a comprehensive employment-oriented prisoner re-entry program. *Journal of Quantitative Criminology, 31*(3), 355–382.

Corrigan, P. W., Green, A., Lundin, R., Kubiak, M. A., & Penn, D. L. (2001). Familiarity with and social distance from people who have serious mental illness. *Psychiatric Services, 52*(7), 953–958.

D'Alessio, S., Stolzenberg, L., & Flexon, J. (2015). The effect of Hawaii's Ban the Box law on repeat offending. *American Journal of Criminal Justice, 40*(2), 336–352.

Freeman, R. B. (1991). *Crime and the employment of disadvantaged youths.* Cambridge, MA: National Bureau of Economic Research. doi: 10.3386/w3875

Gaubatz, K. T. (1995). *Crime in the public mind.* Ann Arbor, MI: University of Michigan Press.

Gebo, E., & Norton-Hawk, M. (2009). Criminal record policies and private employers. *Justice Policy Journal, 6*(1), 1–29.

Giguere, R., & Dundes, L. (2002). Help wanted: A survey of employer concerns about hiring ex-convicts. *Criminal Justice Policy Review, 13*(4), 396–408.

Glynn, T. P. (1998). The limited viability of negligent supervision, retention, hiring, and infliction of emotional distress claims in employment discrimination cases in Minnesota. *William Mitchell Law Review, 24*(3), 581–633.

Graffam, J., Shinkfield, A. J., & Hardcastle, L. (2008). The perceived employability of ex-prisoners and offenders. *International Journal of Offender Therapy and Comparative Criminology, 52*(6), 673–685.

Graffam, J., Shinkfield, A., Lavelle, B., & Hardcastle, L. (2004). *Attitudes of employers, corrective services workers, employment support workers, and prisoners and offenders towards employing ex-prisoners and ex-offenders.* Burwood, VIC: Deakin University.

Grogger, J. (1995). The effect of arrests on the employment and earnings of young men. *Quarterly Journal of Economics, 110*(1), 51–71.

Harm, N. J., & Phillips, S. D. (2001). You can't go home again: Women and criminal recidivism. *Journal of Offender Rehabilitation, 32*(3), 3–21.

Henry, J. P., & Odiorne, G. S. (1989). Eleven myths about hiring ex-offenders. *Personnel, 66*(2), 27.

Henry, J. S. (2008). Criminal history on a "need to know" basis: Employment policies that eliminate the criminal history box on employment applications. *Justice Policy Journal, 5*(2), 2–22.

Henry, J. S., & Jacobs, J. B. (2007). Ban the box to promote ex-offender employment. *Criminology & Public Policy, 6*(4), 755–762.

Hirschfield, P. J., & Piquero, A. R. (2010). Normalization and legitimation: Modeling stigmatizing attitudes toward ex-offenders. *Criminology, 48*(1), 27–55.

Homant, R. J., & Kennedy, D. B. (1982). Attitudes toward ex-offenders: A comparison of social stigmas. *Journal of Criminal Justice, 10*(5), 383–391.

Iguchi, M. Y., London, J. A., Forge, N. G., Hickman, L. J., Fain, T., & Riehman, K. (2002). How criminalizing the drug user impacts the health and wellbeing of minority communities. *Public Health Reports, 117*(Supplement 1), 146–150.

Inciardi, J. A., Martin, S. S., & Butzin, C. A. (2004). Five-year outcomes of therapeutic community treatment of drug-involved offenders after release from prison. *Crime & Delinquency, 50*(1), 88–107.

Kethineni, S., & Falcone, D. N. (2007). Employment and ex-offenders in the United States: Effects of legal and extra legal factors. *Probation Journal, 54*(1), 36–51.

Langan, P. A., & Levin, D. J. (2002). *Recidivism of prisoners released in 1994* (NCJ 193427). Washington, DC: US Department of Justice, Bureau of Justice Statistics.

Laub, J. H., & Sampson, R. J. (2003). *Shared beginnings, divergent lives: Delinquent boys to age 70.* Cambridge, MA: Harvard University Press.

LeBel, T. P. (2008). Perceptions of and responses to stigma. *Sociology Compass, 2*(2), 409–432.

Lemert, E. (1951). Social pathology: A systematic approach to the study of sociopathic behavior. New York, NY: McGraw-Hill.

Leukefeld, C., Webster, M., Staton-Tindall, M., & Duvall, J. (2007). Employment and work among drug court clients: 12-month outcomes. *Substance Use & Misuse, 42*(7), 1109–1126.

Lott, J. R. (1992). Do we punish high income criminals too heavily? *Economic Inquiry, 30*(4), 583–608

Maruna, S. (2001). *Making good: How ex-convicts reform and rebuild their lives.* Washington, DC: American Psychological Association.

Mears, D. P., & Cochran, J. C. (2015). *Prisoner reentry in the era of mass incarceration.* Thousand Oaks, CA: Sage Publications.

Orcutt, J. D. (1973). Societal reaction and the response to deviation in small groups. *Social Forces, 52*(2), 259–267.

Pager, D. (2003). The mark of a criminal record. *American Journal of Sociology, 108,* 937–975.

Pager, D., Western, B., & Sugie, N. (2009). Sequencing disadvantage: Barriers to employment facing young black and white men with criminal records. *ANNALS of the American Academy of Political and Social Science, 623*(1), 195–213.

Paternoster, R., & Iovanni, L. (1989). The labeling perspective and delinquency: An elaboration of the theory and an assessment of the evidence. *Justice Quarterly, 6,* 359–394.

Petersilia, J. (2003). *When prisoners come back: Parole and prison reentry.* New York, NY: Oxford University Press.

Raphael, S. (2010). *Improving employment prospects for former prison inmates: Challenges and policy* (Working Paper No. 15874). Cambridge, MA: National Bureau of Economic Research.

Rhodes, J. (2008). Ex-offenders, social ties, and the routes into employment. *Internet Journal of Criminology.* Retrieved from http://www.internetjournalof criminology.com/rhodes%20-%20ex-offenders%20and%20employment.pdf

Rodriguez, M. N., & Mehta, N. (2015). *Ban the Box: U.S. cities, counties, and states adopt fair hiring policies to reduce barriers to employment of people with conviction records.* New York, NY: National Employment Law Project.

Sampson, R. J., & Laub, J. H. (1993). *Crime in the making: Pathways and turning points through life.* Cambridge, MA: Harvard University Press.

Sampson, R. J., & Laub, J. H. (2005). A life-course view of the development of crime. *ANNALS of the American Academy of Political and Social Science, 602*(1), 12–45.

Schwartz, R., & Skolnick, J. (1962). Two Studies of Legal Stigma. *Social Problems, 10*(2), 133–142.

Shivy, V. A., Wu, J. J., Moon, A. E., Mann, S. C., Holland, J. G., & Eacho, C. (2007). Ex-offenders reentering the workforce. *Journal of Counseling Psychology, 54*(4), 466–473.

Solomon, A. L., Johnson, K. D., Travis, J., & McBride, E. C. (2004). *From prison to work: The employment dimensions of prisoner reentry.* Washington, DC: Urban Institute.

Thompson, M. N., & Cummings, D. L. (2010). Enhancing the career development of individuals who have criminal records. *Career Development Quarterly, 58*(3), 209–218.

Tonkin, P., Dickie, J., Alemagno, S., & Grove, W. (2004). Women in jail: "Soft skills" and barriers to employment. *Journal of Offender Rehabilitation, 38*(4), 51–71.

Travis, J. (2005). But they all come back: Facing the challenges of prison reentry. Washington, DC: Urban Institute Press.

Uggen, C., & Thompson, M. (2003). The socioeconomic determinants of ill-gotten gains: Within-person changes in drug use and illegal earnings. *American Journal of Sociology, 109*(1), 146–185.

Visher, C. A., Debus-Sherrill, S., & Yahner, J. (2008). *Employment after prison: A longitudinal study of releasees in three states.* Washington, DC: Urban Institute, Justice Policy Center.

Waldfogel, J. (1994). The effect of criminal conviction on income and the trust "reposed in the workmen." *Journal of Human Resources, 29*(1), 62–81.

Western, B., & Pettit, B. (2000). Incarceration and racial inequality in men's employment. *Industrial and Labor Relations Review, 54*(1), 3–16.

# CHAPTER 7

# Transforming Rehabilitation
## A Critical Evaluation of Barriers Encountered by an Offender Rehabilitation Program for South Asian/Muslim Offenders within the New Probation Service Model

Christine Victoria Hough

I n this chapter, I present observations and outcomes from a proposed evaluation of an offender rehabilitation program, ReachingOut, in the northwest of England, delivered by a third-sector organization, Arooj. As a small, non-profit agency, Arooj works within the wider, established criminal justice system of state, private, and voluntary-sector partnerships that have evolved over time into a universally acknowledged "mixed economy" model of service provision within the criminal justice system (Corcoran & Hucklesby, 2012, p. 1). The term "mixed economy" was first used by Prime Minister Tony Blair, leader of the Labour government from 1997 to 2010, to introduce the government's policy agenda of creating public and private partnerships as a means of funding public sector services. Since then, successive governments have continued to adopt this policy approach of incorporating the role of voluntary, charitable, and non-governmental organizations to an increasing extent, in the delivery of criminal justice services (as well as a range of health and social services). Therefore, the increased involvement of the third sector in providing services to offenders and their families, both in prisons and in communities, is a well-established fact (Meek et al., 2013, p. 340).

Arooj's mentors have worked on a voluntary basis with Her Majesty's Prisons (HMPs) throughout the region and in the local communities, since

2007, to support South Asian/Muslim offenders and ex-offenders through the processes of re-entry and reintegration into their communities after release from prison. Resettlement and reintegration remain contested terms (Meek et al., 2013, p. 359) as, among other arguments, the very words imply that ex-offenders were "well settled or integrated" into their communities before they went into prison, which is often not the case. This experience was illuminated by South Asian/Muslim ex-offenders living in northwest Lancashire who were asked in a 2014 Arooj survey: (1) what they believed led them to offend; (2) their views, after their release from prison, about the support services available; and (3) the consequences of their offending upon their family and community (see Mahmood & Mohammad, 2014, p. 7). In fact, 63 percent of the respondents had been unemployed before they went to prison and over 30 percent had been involved in drug and alcohol misuse (Mahmood & Mohammad, 2014), revealing that there was already a significant amount of "unsettlement" in their lives before they offended.

Arooj's work was initially funded in 2007 by a grant from a private charitable trust, which ended in 2013. In 2014, they were granted further funding from our local Probation Trust in North West England and the National Offender Management Services for the purposes of evaluating Reaching-Out, Arooj's mentoring support program for South Asian/Muslim offenders and ex-offenders. This chapter reflects the obstacles encountered during the first six months of the project's proposed evaluation, which thwarted Arooj's progress and the evaluation process itself. These obstacles are discussed critically with regard to the government's Transforming Rehabilitation agenda and the impact this is now proving to have on the longer-term support available to prisoners and ex-offenders in their re-entry and reintegration after prison. The focus will therefore be on the potentially negative implications of the new Transforming Rehabilitation arrangements for probation supervision nationally and, at a regional level, for the disproportionally high numbers of South Asian/Muslim offenders in the criminal justice system (Mullen & Young, 2014), whose presence in the United Kingdom has almost doubled since 2002.

The successful processes of rehabilitation and desistance are the crucial means by which former prisoners are able to escape the social exclusion too often associated with imprisonment and reclaim the basic elements of social justice, such as regaining access to "accommodation, family relationships and mental health" (Ministry of Justice, 2013b, p. 13) for themselves and their families. As is evidenced from the chapters in this collection, employment is another critical pathway towards reintegration and contributes to desistance from crime. Arooj's mentoring support services are designed to help former prisoners reintegrate into their families and guide them in the processes of preparing for employment, by drawing on the range of their own professional skills and experiences. The mentors provide advice and guidance on: volunteering opportunities offered within Arooj itself; writing business plans to support clients throughout the entire process of starting their own business; accessing benefits and any local council-related allowances (such as council tax and similar); and recommending clients to business contacts within their own community for potential job opportunities. These particular employment-related activities are incredibly important for former prisoners, evidence of which can be found in as the results of Arooj's 2014 survey, which revealed that over 60 percent of the respondents report that being able to work in a self-employed capacity would help them to desist from reoffending (Mahmood & Mohammad, 2014). In response, mentors also provide guidance and help with the process of applying for self-employed status. However, these stages of the re-entry and rehabilitation processes are reached only after Arooj and their clients have negotiated the complex and often protracted processes of the early stages of mentoring, which involve developing trust between client and mentor, assessing clients' needs, and rebuilding bridges between them and their families (Mahmood & Mohammad, 2014).

In this chapter I discuss how the government's Transforming Rehabilitation policies and processes restricted both Arooj's support of South Asian/Muslim former prisoners, and the extent to which these ex-prisoners had their specific rehabilitative and reintegrative needs met. In the absence of any referrals to Arooj's services, which was the direct result of the implementations of the government's policies at regional level—either by local case managers or other local support providers—this particular group of former prisoners will have missed out on the important "building blocks" of support for successful re-entry. These building blocks include religious support, drug and alcohol treatment, as well as employment-related skill building and opportunities. In these times of heightened security awareness globally, these negative outcomes also present a wider cause for consideration. At the time of writing, the reverberations of the November 2015 coordinated terrorist attacks on Café Le Carillon and other public venues in Paris were still being felt across Europe and the rest of the world. As a result of these events, some members of the public have come to indiscriminately associate terrorist groups with individuals of the Muslim faith. Therefore, any central government policies that restrict or prevent community-based support for South Asian/Muslim offenders are in danger of further alienating this group at local, national, and global levels, and of propagating further prejudice against them within the criminal justice system. Problematic outcomes are discussed later in the chapter within the context of the continuing neo-liberal, market-led governmental approach to cost-cutting across public services generally and the criminal justice sector specifically.

## THE OVERREPRESENTATION OF PEOPLE FROM SOUTH ASIAN/MUSLIM COMMUNITIES IN THE CRIMINAL JUSTICE SYSTEM

Researchers have shown that individuals from Black and Asian ethnic minority communities are overrepresented at almost all stages of the criminal justice process (Her Majesty's Chief Inspector of Prisons, 2015; Mullen & Young, 2014; Prison Reform Trust, 2013). The number of Muslim prisoners has doubled in England and Wales since 2002, and the numbers of South Asian female offenders in particular have been increasing in recent years (Prison Reform Trust, 2013). The rising numbers of South Asian/Muslim individuals in the prison population has been further evidenced through research findings: 26 percent of prisoners are South Asian/Muslim, though they make up only 14 percent of the national population; 14 percent of prisoners are Muslim, while only 4 percent of the national population are. South Asian/Muslim prisoners also continue to have a worse experience during incarceration than the rest of the prison population. For example, research shows that former offenders interviewed for a report investigating the Transforming Rehabilitation's impact on minority groups described their experiences in prisons as comprising: discrimination and racism evidenced by differential treatment due to their race, ethnicity, or faith; being stereotyped as drug dealers; and the stereotyping of Muslims as extremists (Mullen & Young, 2014). The interviews for this report were conducted over the span of one year beginning in Autumn 2013, and as such, the data relates to the time immediately prior to the implementation of the Transforming Rehabilitation arrangements (i.e., February 2015). Data was captured through discussion groups with service users, in prison and community settings, and in collaboration with organizations that provide services to them (Mullen & Young, 2014, p. 11).

It is unlikely that the experiences of the former offenders, interviewed for the report, entitled the Young Report, were shaped significantly by the changes afoot under the Transforming Rehabilitation agenda at that time. The recommendations from the report were released in December 2014 and were strongly critical of the "assumptions based on crude stereotyping" (Mullen & Young, 2014, p. 11) encountered by South Asian/Muslim offenders and the negative impact these assumptions have on their ability to resettle and reintegrate successfully. As these reflections are based on data collected before the Transforming Rehabilitation agenda became fully operational, they reflect an already highly negative picture of the prison experiences of South Asian/Muslim offenders. Our experiences with ReachingOut coincided with the introduction of the Transforming Rehabilitation agenda and thus serve to compound this overall negative picture by suggesting a worsening prospect for the re-entry and resettlement outcomes of South Asian/Muslim offenders/ex-offenders.

## The Specific Needs of South Asian/Muslim Offenders and Their Families

The needs of South Asian/Muslim offenders differ from those commonly attributed to the wider population of White, working-class offenders. The factors that contribute to the profile of the wider prison population include: broken homes; drug and alcohol misuse; generational unemployment; abusive relationships; childhoods spent in care; mental illness; and educational failure (Ministry of Justice, 2013b, p. 5). While there will inevitably be some overlap, in addition to the unique needs of South Asian/Muslim offenders mentioned above, Mahmood and Mohammad's (2014) survey revealed that 75 percent of respondents felt they had lost respect with their families as a result of their offending, and 36 percent stated that specialist cultural and religious support would have helped them to stay out of trouble in the future. These are distinctive areas of need for South Asian/Muslim prisoners and ex-offenders. Indeed, while some similarities can be identified between the overall needs of South Asian/Muslim ex-offenders and the seven "reducing reoffending"[1] pathways (Meek et al., 2013), which have underpinned offender management from 2004 in England and Wales, the factors of faith, family respect, and cultural and religious support remain specific to this particular cohort of prisoners and ex-offenders.

Cultural, family, and religious values are particularly significant to many Black and minority ex-offenders in their journey towards desistance from crime (see Calverley, 2013). The significance of these particular factors is evident in what past clients have said about Arooj's work and how valuable it was to them. It is important to say here that the Arooj professionals are South Asian/Muslim themselves, and therefore representative of the community they serve. This fact is prioritized in the Young Review (Mullen et al., 2014), where Baroness Young makes it clear in her introduction that the criminal justice system "does not represent the diverse backgrounds of offenders" (p. 12). As such, the extent to which the involvement of representatives from the offenders' own communities and faiths can play a substantial role in improving confidence in decision-making processes and other procedures is undeniably important. This kind of specialist support can be crucial to a South Asian/Muslim family in overcoming their own cultural and emotional difficulties over a family member's incarceration. As an example, the father of one young South Asian/Muslim prisoner felt he needed Arooj's close support to help him begin to rebuild his relationship with his son. With the assistance of Arooj's mentors, he was able to start the process of supporting his son's reintegration into the family and their community (Vaughan, 2000, as cited in Fitzgibbon & Lea, 2014, p. 34).

## AROOJ'S OFFENDER REHABILITATION MODEL

Arooj is a small charity (or third-sector organization) founded in 2007 to support South Asian/Muslim offenders and ex-offenders in the processes of their re-entry, resettlement, and re-employment during and after their involvement with the criminal justice system (Mahmood & Mohammad, 2014). In the course of their work, Arooj has developed a model of mentoring and support that comprises three stages, each consisting of elements similar to those of an evidence-based model of case management known as assertive outreach (Griffiths & Harris, 2008). Also known as assertive community treatment (ACT), this model of support was originally designed to meet the needs of service users with severe mental illness who did not "readily engage with mainstream mental health services" (Griffiths & Harris, 2008, p. 479). Arooj's clients can be categorized similarly, insofar as without the initial mentoring and befriending support in prison and the referrals to health, drug, and alcohol support groups, clients would be unlikely to seek support for themselves by going through the acknowledged mainstream routes.

During the first stage of what is essentially a three-stage model, the Arooj mentors work toward establishing a relationship of trust with prisoners nearing their release date, in order to establish open lines of communication with prisoners, while they are in prison, and support for them and their families. Arooj's service is independent from the criminal justice system, but mentors have the security clearance needed to go into prison to work directly with South Asian/Muslim prisoners. According to one former Arooj client, Iqram,[2] Arooj is often the only Asian support group working in a prison.

> They provided a non-judgmental ... befriending and mentoring service ... for as long we needed ... without any strings attached.... They were there for our benefit—not their's or the prison's. They would come in every Friday, after Juma prayers ... and arrange to see us separately if there were personal issues. (British Broadcasting Company, 2014, p. 5)

The shape of this service provision is significant to its recipients because their perception is that the Arooj mentors support them individually, rather than as part of the "system" of rehabilitation and resettlement that operates inside prisons.

The second stage of the model is equally significant. Here, Arooj refers their clients to multi-agency groups, such as drug and alcohol support, that offer help toward their rehabilitation and community re-entry. They work closely with clients to help them prepare for employment opportunities and interventions with their families and to encourage their acceptance back into the family network.

The third stage may continue indefinitely, depending on the length of time the offender and their family require, and appear to be benefiting from, Arooj's support. Iqram spoke very positively about this stage of the support:

> One of the Arooj workers came to see me at home upon release … he spoke to my parents and brother and gave reassurances to them that I would not be on my own … he would support me in any way he could … (British Broadcasting Company, 2014. p. 5)

Visiting clients at home and with their families is an integral and important part of Arooj's mentoring services; as demonstrated in Iqram's words: "it is how they continue to build 'bridges' between clients and their families." By extending mentoring support from prison to the home and family, Arooj helps clients make the difficult transition from incarceration back into their family and community network. With this continuum of support, former prisoners are also more likely to act on advice and guidance about future employment opportunities, provided as part of their support services. This holistic support is also a distinctive feature of the original assertive community treatment model developed in the 1970s (Bond, Drake, Mueser, & Latimer, 2001, p. 142), which provides a useful comparison with Arooj's model. With assertive community treatment, the mental health professionals' preferred way to make (and maintain) contact with patients was to visit them "in vivo," or in the "natural settings" where they lived and interacted with family and/or friends. Bond et al. (2001) argue that this is a far more effective approach than trying to maintain contact with patients in hospital or office settings, because the skills "taught in the hospital or clinic do not always transfer well to natural settings" (p. 144). Similar to the range of Arooj's support services, the assertive community treatment model provides patients with help in relation to medication, housing, finances and anything else critical to the practicalities of living and finding employment (Bond et al., 2001).

Although they can be relatively easily defined, Arooj's services are not really offered in discrete stages; it is together that they comprise the holistic model of support that Arooj considers a crucial contributing factor to its success. Through establishing the initial, trusting relationship with their clients in Stage One, the Arooj professionals are then able to contact the individuals' families and support them, both practically and emotionally, through to Stage Two. The families of South Asian/Muslim offenders often have difficulty coming to terms with their own feelings towards their sibling/son/daughter/ partner because of the sense of dishonour that a criminal offence brings upon the family (Calverley, 2013, p. 71). Mohammed's[3] son, for example, was in prison as a result of which Mohammed himself was introduced to Arooj, and he explains how his son's offending had brought shame and dishonor on the family: "I still find it hard to talk to him ... the shame and disgust goes on for years" (British Broadcasting Company, 2014). As a parent, Mohammed gained a great deal of courage from being able to discuss his son's circumstances with Arooj. This helped him to overcome his own (and his family's) feelings of shame towards his son and, with Arooj's support, he felt able to visit his son in prison. "Asian families do not talk freely to outsiders, but Arooj is trustworthy and so the families feel relieved" (British Broadcasting Company, 2014). The fact that Mohammed eventually felt able to visit his son in prison was a significant outcome for him and a reflection of the value of Arooj's support in helping him to address the culturally sensitive issues that underpinned his and his family's feelings of shame.

The links between the assertive outreach model of patient support and Arooj's services show that, overall, both these community-based programs cover clients' holistic needs. I am suggesting that this holistic approach is an important contributory factor to successful, longer-term outcomes regarding the re-entry and employment of ex-offenders. If support and guidance cover clients' emotional, social, health, and practical needs in the non-threatening environment of their homes and communities, they are far more likely to "see through" the processes of full reintegration. The excerpts used here, from Iqram's and Mohammed's stories, are taken from an interview conducted with Arooj, myself and the British Broadcasting Company's Asian radio network, for the purposes of promoting the rehabilitation work Arooj provides to South Asian/Muslim ex-offenders in northwest Lancashire.

Calverley's (2013)[4] research also discusses the significance of the family to minority ethnic offenders in the process of desistance describing it as complex, because it requires the specialist interventions of probation officers who have "insight into the community pressures and dynamics of family obligations facing Indian desisters" (p. 194). The families that the Arooj mentors work with come to regard them as trustworthy confidantes to whom they can talk freely because they share the same culture and faith. Therefore, the involvement of South Asian/Muslim former prisoners' families in the rehabilitation process is an additional, essential factor in Arooj's delivery of their model of support.

Their three-stage model of rehabilitation is predicated on the notions of inclusion and social justice (e.g., social and family networks, employment, and housing) as referred to by Chris Grayling, the former minister for justice, in the original Transforming Rehabilitation document (Ministry of Justice, 2013c, p. 13). The first two stages address the specific needs of offenders and their families in their rehabilitation and resettlement processes. In the transition from stage two to three Arooj continues to empower ex-offenders taking a step from the "transformative issues of welfare provision, such as individual need, diagnosis and rehabilitation" (Clarke, Gerwitz, & McLaughlin, 2000, p. 178) to becoming independent. Arooj mentors have the capacity to help their former prisoner service recipients towards this final stage through sourcing potential employment opportunities. They often do so by drawing on their own contacts within the local business community.

Arooj's holistic model of support resembles the "ethical entitlement"[5] discussed by Frazer et al. (2014), who express concerns that the government's Transforming Rehabilitation agenda proposals may be implemented at the expense of high-quality probation support services for the offender population (p. 94). Burke (2012) explains this further by saying that the support and help for individuals towards achieving a "better life" is not an instrumental, "cause and effect" process; it requires a far more humane approach that acknowledges individuals' rights and needs, rather than focusing on reducing reoffending at the lowest possible cost. The frustrated attempt to conduct the evaluation of Arooj's model of support (discussed in more detail in the next section) indicates that the new payment-by-results structure may well already be bringing about a reduced "ethical entitlement" of support for offenders and former prisoners. The absence of referrals of South Asian/Muslim offenders to Arooj when we attempted to commence the evaluation suggest this particular cohort had no access to support for their own rehabilitative and reintegrative needs, including employment, which in turn suggests they are more likely to reoffend when released from prison. Thus the number of South Asian/Muslim prisoners is likely to remain high.

## TRANSFORMING REHABILITATION AND CHANGES TO THE PROBATION SERVICES

The logistics of conducting the proposed evaluation of Arooj's rehabilitation model required the organization's services to be positioned within the local operational framework of the Community Rehabilitation Company that, at the time (i.e., mid-2014), had been experiencing major structural changes as a result of the government's Transforming Rehabilitation agenda. These changes resulted in a significant curtailment of the modus operandi of Arooj's original model, in order to align with the local Community Rehabilitation Company structure and that of its community-based providers. From January 2013, the coalition government had set in motion fast-paced changes that led to the restructuring of the former Probation Trusts into Community Rehabilitation Companies, followed by the final change: the transfer of the companies "from public to private, voluntary or social sector ownership" (National Offender Management Services, 2014, p. 22). The changes to the way individuals involved in the criminal justice system are to be managed under the new Transforming Rehabilitation arrangements are the outcome of the coalition government's "approach to driving down the rate of reoffending and delivering better value for the taxpayer" (Ministry of Justice, 2013b, p. 3). The role of these newly privatized Community Rehabilitation Companies is to provide community-based case management and rehabilitation services to former prisoners who are assessed as low–medium risk, while those categorized as presenting a high risk of serious harm will remain under the supervision of a publicly managed but newly constituted (and smaller) National Probation Service (Ludlow, 2014, p. 67).

The National Offender Management Services agency was responsible for overseeing the implementation of the Transforming Rehabilitation agenda and the competitive tendering process that led to the application of "contract mechanisms" (Ludlow, 2014, p. 68) to the management of the newly structured probation services. The successful bidders for the 21 Community Rehabilitation Company contracts throughout England and Wales are described as "global security corporations" (Fitzgibbon & Lea, 2014, p. 24) and include Sodexo, A4E, and Ingeus, whose expertise includes the outsourcing of public services—which made them adept at competing for new probation contracts. Fitzgibbon and Lea (2014) perceive this new wave of privatization as reinforcing top-down managerialization processes, introduced into the public sector from the late 1970s, and continuing the deskilling of probation practitioners down to the level of "box-ticking" and "formulaic risk management" (p. 25). A requirement of the competitive bidding process was for these corporations to establish joint ventures with social enterprise groups, charities, and similar voluntary and community organizations. These collaborations were exhorted by Chris Grayling, the former minister of justice, who emphasized that "it will be crucial that providers work closely with all local partners to ensure that the service delivered to achieve the reducing reoffending outcomes are aligned with other local services" (Ministry of Justice, 2013b, p. 14).

Frazer et al. (2014) argue that good rehabilitation can be achieved only if the Community Rehabilitation Companies supply chain "and their own commissioning activity can identify and harness local interventions ... that will respond effectively to offenders' [and former prisoners'] needs and issues ... and help them forge a new, non-criminal identity" (p. 101). This reaffirms the importance of local, third-sector organizations to the successful rehabilitation and resettlement of former prisoners and is reflected in Arooj's mission statement that, at its core, aims to support "the re-entry, resettlement and reintegration of South Asian/Muslim ex-offenders back into society" (Mahmood & Mohammad, 2014, p. 11). These three aims reflect the continuum of support and guidance that Arooj provides to their clients. Their mentoring work is grounded in their local South Asian/Muslim communities wherein they have many networks to draw on in their support of former prisoners (i.e., welfare agencies, the local council, and local businesses) during these processes.

The preferred bidders for the new probation contracts were announced by the minister of justice in October 2014 and the contracts were awarded in December 2014. The outcomes have been that the probation services in England and Wales have now been sold off, in the form of 21 regional Community Rehabilitation Companies, referred to previously, to a small number of corporate "global security companies" who have mostly set up partnerships with the larger national charities (and some with social enterprise groups). Fitzgibbon and Lea (2014) describe this set of changes as a move that will serve to distance the probation and voluntary sector further from their traditional purpose. The rationale here is that the new structure will make "risk management and security strategy" dominate over the more traditional, values-based skill sets that have always characterized the role of the third-sector organizations (p. 29). This eclipsing of the traditional partnership between probation and third-sector organizations by a quantitative, target-driven approach is inevitable under the new payment-by-results system. Fitzgibbon and Lea (2014, p. 32) go so far as to describe this system as portending the death knell of third-sector organizations, and certainly its impact on their demise is a serious consideration in the discussion of the outcomes section later on in this chapter.

Payment-by-results is not a new concept. It was introduced as a policy into the education system in 19th-century Britain with the intention to "bring schools and teachers under the 'laws of supply and demand'" (Jabbar, 2014, p. 220). Jabbar (2014) compares this to the 21st century approach of "incentivizing" teachers through performance-related pay, which she describes as adhering to the "business principles of management" that focus on control

and measureable performance outcomes, such as results in tests and exam-
inations. Opponents of performance-related pay argue that this approach
diminishes, rather than encourages, teachers' intrinsic motivation. In other
words, teachers become focused on "teaching to the test," to produce higher
performance levels, rather than on a more pedagogical, inclusive approach
that addresses the broader aspects of education, such as supporting pupils'
different learning needs (Jabbar, 2014, p. 221). These "business principles
of management" entail centralized control, imposed by the government,
through payment that is dependent on measurable performance outcomes.

This model of management was at the heart of the trend towards the
managerialization of the public sector, which commenced with the Conservative government in the late 1970s and continues across successive governments. Consistent with this, the Transforming Rehabilitation agenda is based
on the managerialistic principle of a centralized control of payment that
depends on the Community Rehabilitation Companies' providers meeting
measurable targets of reduced reoffending through their support of cohorts
of former prisoners. The reduction of costs, resources, and expenditures,
such as those associated with the provision of expensive casework-based
rehabilitative support services, are most likely to be the first priority of the
Community Rehabilitation Companies in order to meet these prescribed
targets of reducing reoffending at the least cost. Thus one of the ultimate outcomes of the Transforming Rehabilitation agenda may well be that voluntary
organizations are absorbed into the system and find themselves curtailing
or "reforming their own advocacy roles and functions in order to facilitate
their involvement" within the Community Rehabilitation Company structure
(Corcoran & Hucklesby, 2012, p. 3). This suggests the potential erosion of
the role of third-sector organizations when incorporated into the corporate
structure of the Community Rehabilitation Companies. Indeed, this reality
comprises a significant outcome of our thwarted small-scale regional project.
The same picture, however, is beginning to emerge nationally, across the third
sector (Clinks, 2015). This cannot help but have a significant negative impact
on the reintegration and employment prospects of South Asian/Muslim former prisoners across the country.

## ORIGINAL AIMS OF THE REACHINGOUT EVALUATION PROJECT

As I have detailed so far, none of the initially proposed analysis work has
taken place, due largely to the major structural changes that have defined
the criminal justice system over the last 12 to 18 months in consequence
of the Transforming Rehabilitation arrangements. The evaluation was to
be a potentially significant piece of research into factors that influence the

reintegration and rehabilitation of South Asian/Muslim prisoners and former prisoners after incarceration. There is a dearth of current research into the cultural and faith-based values that influence the successful/unsuccessful desistance of this cohort, apart from Calverley's (2013) work. With the wider, global implications of the growth of suspicion, stereotyping, and isolation of South Asian/Muslim former prisoners and their families within the criminal justice system (and society at large) this can be seen as, more or less, a sin of omission. The primary research opportunity presented by the funding for ReachingOut would have provided much-needed findings that could have helped to inform the debate about the wider issues faced by South Asian/ Muslim communities locally and nationally. Unfortunately, it is unlikely that an opportunity to conduct an evaluation of ReachingOut will arise in the future as Arooj has ceased to deliver their mentoring model of support to South Asian/Muslim prisoners/former-prisoners. This decision was taken partly in response to the continued absence of funding to support their work but also in light of what they learned from the negative outcomes of our attempt to evaluate ReachingOut. The future for small third-sector organizations that work in the criminal justice system is not promising and it is likely that they will now pursue more consultancy-based work opportunities.

## HOW THE TRANSFORMING REHABILITATION ARRANGEMENTS MAY ALREADY BE REDUCING THE QUALITY OF SUPPORT FOR EX-PRISONERS

A combination of factors, including the uncertainty of the future roles of the former probation officers now incorporated into the new Community Rehabilitation Companies and the sheer speed with which the Transforming Rehabilitation changes were imposed, precluded the evaluation of Arooj's support program. Before the attempt at the evaluation had even begun, the new Transforming Rehabilitation arrangements meant that the local Community Rehabilitation Companies needed to incorporate Arooj's services into a pilot, regional program for reducing reoffending. This resulted in the subjugation of Arooj's role from that of an established community-based service provider to that of an organization "in waiting." During the first six months of the project, we felt we were waiting for Arooj's services to be launched within the operation of the local Community Rehabilitation Companies, but this never happened. First, at the outset of ReachingOut, the Community Rehabilitation Companies reduced Arooj's three-stage model of rehabilitation of support to one, which meant that offenders would be referred to them only after their release from prison. As a consequence, Arooj was unable to select respondents for the ReachingOut evaluation, due to the lack of opportunity to establish relationships with offenders prior to their release from prison.

Second, the pilot program of local third-sector organizations and rehabilitation providers—convened to provide a dry run for the new Transforming Rehabilitation arrangements—provided no official guidance to the other partners as to how they might refer any South Asian/Muslim ex-offenders for Arooj's specialist rehabilitation services. Arooj's history of working to support South Asian/Muslim prisoners and former prisoners in their social rehabilitation has had positive outcomes for many because, as a small third-sector organization they have been able to work independently of centrally imposed systems and processes. As such, they are able to focus on the more values-based issues, such as strengthening, or mending, the relationships between service recipients and their families. The payment-by-results system that underpins the Transforming Rehabilitation arrangements has already been pressuring Community Rehabilitation Companies to focus on cost cutting in order to produce the most financial benefit. This "leveraging" of resources, or securing of a "bigger bang for the buck" (Hamel & Prahalad, 1993, p. 75), will inevitably begin to squeeze out many of the smaller third-sector organizations from the new corporate model of offender rehabilitation, because they will find themselves competing with the larger charitable organizations for contracts with the Community Rehabilitation Companies.

This discouraging picture is also reflected in the findings from a recent survey conducted by Clinks (2015) in which third-sector organizations were asked to provide responses to questions about how the Transforming Rehabilitation agenda was affecting their own future prospects. The responses reflected the third-sector organizations' concerns that the new Community Rehabilitation Company contracts were very restrictive and that they would be forced to change their service to "fit the contract." Others said that while their contracts had been extended by the Community Rehabilitation Companies, there was no guarantee of work in the future (Clinks, 2015, pp. 6–7). Although these are early days, these recent survey findings and the unsuccessful attempt at evaluating ReachingOut, fail to paint a promising picture for third-sector organizations in the new world of Transforming Rehabilitation. Community Rehabilitation Companies are still in the process of restructuring their services, which has already involved terminating existing contracts, usually for smaller third-sector organizations, and creating "redundancies" among the probation officers they employed from the former Probation Trusts.

This latter issue has been taken up vigorously by the general secretary of the National Association of Probation Officers. At a recent national conference, Lawrence (2015) announced that some Community Rehabilitation

Companies are still struggling to recruit staff, despite the number of current vacancies for former prisoner managers. A number of Community Rehabilitation Companies have already made significant numbers of case manager positions redundant (Lawrence, 2015, p. 2), which doubtlessly reduces the effectiveness with which referrals are made to community-based rehabilitation support groups. These developments have contributed to growing feelings of uncertainty about the future among former probation officers and will, in turn, have a negative impact on the longer-term outcomes of the reintegration and employment of all former offenders under the new payment-by-results regime.

## DISCUSSION OF THE OUTCOMES OF REACHINGOUT
### Impact of the Payment-by-Results System
Since June 2015, the new contract holders/owners of the Community Rehabilitation Companies throughout England and Wales have become subject to the payment-by-results system. The income for these new contractors will now be dependent, to a large part, on their meeting the quantitative targets and outcomes, set by the Ministry of Justice (2013c), to show that they are reducing "re-offending rates significantly beyond historic levels" (p. 7). To be eligible for the payment-by-results bonus payments, service providers are expected to demonstrate: "both an agreed reduction in the number of offenders who go on to commit further offences and a reduction in the number of further offences committed by the cohort of offenders for which they are responsible" (Ministry of Justice, 2013c, p. 15). The former is described as the frequency metric that "measures the rate of offences committed by offenders within a cohort within a 12- month period" and the latter as the "binary metric" that measures the "percentage of offenders that are convicted of an offence within a 12 month period.... Payment-by-results payments will be allocated on the basis of performance against the binary measure and the frequency measure, with a percentage of the total funding available linked to each" (Ministry of Justice, 2013c, p. 8). Therefore service providers will "only be paid for frequency reductions as long as the binary reoffending rate at least stays constant and does not increase" over 12 months (Frazer et al., 2014, p. 97). According to Frazer et al. (2014), the required binary measure is in danger of encouraging the new providers to concentrate only on ensuring a reduction in reoffending across this "relatively short period of time," instead of "supporting the more complex and uneven [and longer-term] processes of secondary desistance" (p. 98).

For the purposes of this chapter, the question arises whether this payment-by-results system of "pass/fail" performance metric is the most effective means of evaluating the process of desistance and, ultimately, the rehabilitation, reintegration and employment prospects of former prisoners. An ex-prisoner's journey towards desistance can be subject to many complex and intangible factors, such as the psychosocial aspects of their behaviour and their (often chaotic) personal circumstances. Researchers emphasize "the role of the individual agent in the desistance process" (King, 2013, p. 142) which elucidates that an individual's willpower to desist/not desist is a significant consideration. These types of influences are very difficult to quantify because they are linked intrinsically to an individual's own agency or motivation and are, perforce, closely aligned to their personal values and beliefs. In this context, Frazer and colleagues (2014) describe the process of rehabilitation as an increasingly "complex process that can support or hamper, but cannot command or compel" (p. 96), which also applies to the value of the advocacy support that Arooj provided to their clients.

As mentors, Arooj support ex-prisoners through a medium of trust, rather than through threat or coercion. Therefore their clients work with them on a voluntary basis. This is one of the reasons why Arooj's past clients feel they are effectively supported, as demonstrated earlier in the comments from Iqram and Mohammed. Their clients are encouraged to want to desist from reoffending and are supported individually at all stages of the rehabilitation journey. Such an approach is expensive, in terms of time and resources, so is likely to prove incompatible with the payment-by-results regime of cost-cutting, value-for-money and meeting targets within a specific timeframe. Under the payment-by-results system, success will be determined based on whether the Community Rehabilitation Companies achieve a quantifiable measure of reductions in reoffending within a specified timeframe, rather than addressing the reasons why clients reoffend. This was apparent in the regional pilot partnership that Arooj was attached to, evidenced through the reduction from their three-stage model of support to a one-stage model.

### Primary and Secondary Desistance
King (2013) describes primary desistance as "a crime-free gap or lull in offending" (immediately after release from prison) and secondary desistance as involving "the assumption of a non-offender identity" (p. 137). Secondary desistance is the longer-term process and is more "complex and uneven," as described by Frazer et al. (2014). Using this understanding of desistance, it is possible to see how, through their three-stage model of rehabilitation, Arooj works to address aspects of both primary and secondary processes of desistance. They help clients through the early stages of re-entry preparation while they are still in prison, "through the gate," and then, in the longer term,

through their intervention with families and multi-agency support groups and, ultimately, through their contacts within the wider community, to explore potential opportunities for employment. Fitzgibbon and Lea (2014) caution that the payment-by-results system is in danger of providing "an incentive, on the part of all concerned, to fail to report breaches and reoffending" (p. 33) because the corporate providers are likely to view the process of making significant reductions in recidivism as "a high-stakes gamble" on which they will be loath to risk large amounts of money in those areas of provision that will not guarantee the bonus payment that is their main incentive. The expense of providing support for longer-term, secondary desistance may prove too much of a financial risk and, thus, the Community Rehabilitation Company providers may focus all their attention on the shorter-term, primary desistance programs that are unlikely to be sustainable in the longer term. This may reduce the ability of ex-prisoners to successfully reintegrate into their communities and access opportunities for potential employment.

## Erosion of the Role of Third-Sector Organizations under the Transforming Rehabilitation Arrangements

Fitzgibbon and Lea (2014) foresee the opening up of the probation services to a mix of providers as potentially damaging to the future of the voluntary sector. These new alliances, forged between the Community Rehabilitation Companies and smaller voluntary and social enterprise groups, will result in open competition for funding where the larger, corporate providers (who have won the Community Rehabilitation Company contracts) are all experienced contractors (A4E, Capita, and Sodexo, among others). They have a wealth of experience in bidding for contracts, subcontracting out a range of services, and are better placed to withstand the financial risk tied to providing initial capital outlay in comparison to smaller third-sector organizations, that mostly depend on short-term streams of funding to support their work (Clinks, 2015).

The consequences of the competitive bidding process for the Community Rehabilitation Company contracts will very likely mean the inevitable erosion of the traditional role of third-sector organizations, which is one of non-judgmental advocacy. In the new world of Transforming Rehabilitation and the marketization of the probation services, the traditional role of the third-sector organizations is in danger of being subsumed into a range of operational processes, such as classification, risk assessment, and resource management (Clarke et al., 2000)—traits that now characterize the business-based working model of the new contract holders that presently own the Community Rehabilitation Companies.

In contrast, the work of voluntary groups such as Arooj have historically focused on more "'transformative issues' like individual need, diagnosis and rehabilitation" (Clarke et al., 2000, p. 178). However, there is the danger that, far from harnessing "local interventions ... that will respond effectively to [offenders'] needs and issues" (Frazer et al., 2014, p. 101), the Transforming Rehabilitation agenda may reduce even further the likelihood of any commonality between the vision and aims of third-sector organizations and those of the Community Rehabilitation Companies. "Since the 1980s, successive governments have seen contractual mechanisms ... as a route to more efficient and effective public services" (Gash & Panchamia, 2013, p. 3). The term "marketization" refers to the opening up of "service provision to competition" across both "corporate (for profit) and voluntary (not for profit) providers" (Clarke et al., 2000, p. 3) and this was the basis of the competitive bid process for the new Community Rehabilitation Company contract holders. Different governments, since the mid-1980s, have insisted that restructuring public services to conform to a more business-based model will provide greater value, effectiveness, and efficiency for money spent (Fitzgibbon & Lea, 2014; Gash & Panchamia 2013; Ministry of Justice, 2013a). Efficiency and effectiveness, however, imply a focus on the relationships between inputs, outputs, and outcomes (Mandl, Dierx, & Iltzkovitz, 2008), which is an approach better suited to quantifiable, manufactured items and products rather than the complexities of human agency and well-being. Therefore, this kind of business model is not an appropriate means for evaluating the quality of services specifically provided to meet the needs of vulnerable groups and individuals (such as prisoners or former prisoners and their families). The terms "outputs" and "performance" imply that the processes of rehabilitation and desistance from crime can be measured or quantified, but this reductionist approach belies the complexity and multi-faceted nature of the welfare needs of this vulnerable cohort of service users. Gash and Panchamia (2013) discuss the complications that arise when trying to measure the value multiagency providers, like health services, add. It becomes difficult to assess whether an outcome was generated by the provider, would have happened anyway, or was the outcome of the collaborative actions of other service providers.

Under the new Transforming Rehabilitation structure, then, the need for Community Rehabilitation Companies to be accountable for their rehabilitation services may become problematic, as evidenced in our attempt to evaluate Arooj's ReachingOut model of support. The Community Rehabilitation Companies now operate by commissioning the services of different community-based support services for their cohort of offender clients, many of whom will have physical and mental health difficulties, such as drug and alcohol dependence. These needs create challenges for many releasees as they try to conform to the day-to-day requirements of resettlement. Many former prisoners follow mental health, drugs, and/or alcohol treatments and other support programs while incarcerated, which they continue with after their release. Therefore, there will often be a range of different agencies (such as Arooj) involved in the overall rehabilitative support of releasees in the community. The work of these agencies comes at an additional cost to the Community Rehabilitation Companies, and their contribution to any resettlement and reintegration may be piecemeal and fragmented. This would make it difficult for the Community Rehabilitation Companies to account for how they attribute service outcomes to which provider and thus measure success/failure in terms of the input of these different agencies. In light of this, the Community Rehabilitation Companies may well decide to forego these additional agencies' services, which might prove an attractive option as a means of cutting costs. In turn, this would mean the smaller, local-community, third-sector organizations will cease to exist if they cannot access new streams of funding to continue their rehabilitative support work. The Clinks (2015) report on the role of the voluntary sector in the new Transforming Rehabilitation arrangements already reveals this emerging trend in the voluntary sector, to which the ReachingOut experiences now add further evidence.

## REFLECTIONS

The outcomes of the proposed ReachingOut project are based on a small-scale, regionally-based set of experiences and therefore cannot provide the basis for any general assertions or deductions about the impact of the Transforming Rehabilitation agenda nationally. These experiences, however, have already had a profound impact on Arooj's proposed future work and determining if their work as service providers for South Asian/Muslim releasees working toward desistance, reintegration, and employment—the aims at the core of Arooj's work—is sustainable. How and where their expertise in this area develops will depend on the direction they choose to take in the future, although it is highly likely that they will cease to work as front-line providers of rehabilitation services because of the lack of funding made available to them under the new Transforming Rehabilitation arrangements.

In this chapter, I have outlined some of the troubling outcomes from yet another government policy initiative to outsource and marketize a significant area of provision in public services, the criminal justice system. With its drive toward cutting costs and adopting a more business-based model of payment to providers, I highlighted some of the more drastic implications these changes will bring to bear on the holistic support offered to releasees in the processes of resettlement, reintegration, and employment. It is therefore perhaps fitting to leave the last word with a Member of Her Majesty's government, the British Labour Party Member of Parliament for Aberavon, Stephen Kinnock. Recently in session at the Westminster Hall Commons Chamber (Kinnock, 2015), he spoke disparagingly about the lack of consultation that preceded the unseemly haste with which the Transforming Rehabilitation changes were introduced. He berates the government's decision to dismantle the former probation services in England and Wales, which were of outstanding quality, and replace them with a new, business-based model of provision that lacks coherence and disenfranchizes third-sector organizations.

## NOTES

1  These seven pathways were formulated from a list of factors that had been identified as influencing reoffending (Social Exclusion Unit, 2002) and formed the basis of the service provision for offenders' re-entry as provided by National Offender Management Services (NOMS) from 2004. The pathways include: accommodation; education, employment and training; health; drugs and alcohol; finance, debt and benefit; children and families; attitudes, thinking and behaviour (Meek et al., 2013, p. 339).
2  Name is fictitious.
3  Name is fictitious.
4  Calverley's research was published just before the CRCs took over the Probation Trusts.
5  "Policy debates around probation practice cannot and should not be merely limited to instrumental means. Supporting and helping individuals towards achieving a better life and treating them with humanity is an ethical entitlement and not one contingent upon reducing reoffending at the lowest possible cost" (Burke, 2012: 319).

## REFERENCES

Annison, J., Burke, L., & Senior, P. (2014). Transforming Rehabilitation: Another example of English "exceptionalism" or a blueprint for the rest of Europe? *European Journal of Probation, 6*(1), 6–23.

BBC (British Broadcasting Company). (2014, August). *BBC Asian Network interview, ReachingOut.* Transcript available on request from author.

Bond, R., Drake, R. E., Mueser, K. T., & Latimer, E. (2001). Assertive community treatment for people with severe mental illness. *Dis Manage Health Outcomes, 9*(3), 141–159.

Burke, L. (2012). Pause for thought? *Probation Journal, 59*(4), 317–322.

Calverley, A. (2013). *Cultures of desistance: Rehabilitation, reintegration and ethnic minorities.* Oxon, UK: Routledge.

Clarke J., Gerwitz, S., & McLaughlin, E. (Eds.). (2000). *New managerialism new welfare?* London, UK: Sage Publications.

Clinks. (2015). *Early doors: The voluntary sector's role in Transforming Rehabilitation.* London, UK: Author. Retrieved from http://www.clinks.org/resources-reports/ early-doors-voluntary-sector%E2%80%99s-role-transforming-rehabilitation

Corcoran, M., & Hucklesby, A. (2012). *The third sector in criminal justice.* University of Leeds. Retrieved from http://www.law.leeds.ac.uk/assets/files/research/ ccjs/130703-thirdsec-crimjust-briefing-2013.pdf

Department of Deputy Prime Minister. (2002). *The Social Exclusion Unit*. Retrieved from: http://webarchive.nationalarchives.gov.uk/+/http:/www.cabinetoffice .gov.uk/media/cabinetoffice/social_exclusion_task_force/assets/publications _1997_to_2006/seu_leaflet.pdf

Fitzgibbon, W., & Lea, J. (2014). Defending probation: Beyond privatisation and security. *European Journal of Probation, 6*(1), 24–41.

Frazer, L., Drinkwater, N., Mullen, J., Hayes, C., O'Donoghue, K., & Cumbo, E. (2014). Rehabilitation: What does good look like anyway? *European Journal of Probation, 6*(2), 92–111.

Gash, T., & Panchamia, N. (2013). *When to contract: Which service features affect the ease of government contracting?* London, UK: Institute for Government. Retrieved from http://www.instituteforgovernment.org.uk/publications/ when-contract

Griffiths, R., & Harris, N. (2008). The compatibility of psychosocial interventions (PSI) and assertive outreach: A survey of managers and PSI-trained staff working in UK assertive outreach teams. *Journal of Psychiatric and Mental Health Nursing, 15*, 479–483.

Hamel, G., & Prahalad, C. K. (1993). Strategy as stretch and leverage. *Harvard Business Review 71*(2), 75–84.

Her Majesty's Chief Inspector of Prisons. (2015). *Annual Report 2014–15*. London, UK: Stationery Office. Retrieved from https://www.gov.uk/government/ uploads/system/uploads/attachment_data/file/444785/hmip-2014-15.pdf

Hough, C. V. (2010). *Every child matters: A small scale enquiry into policy and practice*. (Unpublished dissertation). Universities of Lancaster and Cumbria.

Jabbar, H. (2014). The case of "payment-by-results": Re-examining the effects of an incentive program in nineteenth-century English schools. *Journal of Educational Administration and History 45*, 220–243.

Kiegelmann, M. (2009). Making oneself vulnerable to discovery. *Forum: Qualitative Social Research, 10*(2), 3.

King, S. (2013). Assisted desistance and experiences of probation supervision. *Probation Journal, 6*(2), 136–151.

Kinnock, S. (2015). *House of Commons Session Westminster Hall*. Retrieved from http://www.parliamentlive.tv/Event/Index/f6b09b24-5e5b-404b -b7f5-88d5e5fdff60

Lavalette, M., & Pratt, A. (Eds.). (2006). *Social policy, theories, concepts and issues*. London, UK: Sage Publications.

Lawrence, I. (2015). *Transforming rehabilitation: Making it work*. [Speech made by NAPO General Secretary, at "Transforming Rehabilitation: Making it Work" conference hosted by No Offence.] Retrieved from https://www.napo.org.uk/ news/napo-general-secretary-sets-out-probation-members-post-tr-position -stark-terms

Ludlow, A. (2014). Transforming Rehabilitation: What lessons might be learned from prison privatisation? *European Journal of Probation, 6*(1) 76–81.

Mahmood, T., & Mohammad, H., (2014) *Arooj: Reducing offending within South Asian/Muslim communities. A research report*. UK: Arooj (available on request).

Mandl, U., Dierx, A., & Iltzkovitz, F. (2008). The effectiveness and efficiency of public spending. *Economic Papers, 301*. Brussels, Belgium: European Commission.

Meek R., Gojkovic D., & Mills A. (2013). The involvement of nonprofit organizations in prisoner reentry in the UK: Prisoner awareness and engagement, *Journal of Offender Rehabilitation, 52*(5), 338–357.

Ministry of Justice. (2013a). *Rehabilitation program market engagement, May 2013, Payment mechanism—Straw man.* Retrieved from http://webarchive .nationalarchives.gov.uk/20130128112038/http://www.justice.gov.uk/ transforming-rehabilitation/prior-information-notice

Ministry of Justice. (2013b). *Transforming Rehabilitation: A revolution in the way we manage offenders.* Norwich, UK: TSO.

Ministry of Justice. (2013c). *Transforming Rehabilitation: A strategy for reform response to consultation.* Norwich, UK: TSO.

Mullen J., Clinks, BTEG and Barrow Cadbury. (2014). *The Young Review: Improving outcomes for young Black and/or Muslim men in the criminal justice system.* Retrieved from: http://www.youngreview.org.uk/

National Offender Management Service. (2014). *Business plan 2014–2015.* London, UK: Author.

Prison Reform Trust. (2013). *Bromley Briefings: Prison factfile autumn 2013.* London, UK: Author.

Social Exclusion Unit. (2002). Reducing re-offending by ex-prisoners. London, UK: Office of the Deputy Prime Minister. Retrieved from http://www.bristol.ac.uk/ poverty/downloads/keyofficialdocuments/Reducing%20Reoffending.pdf

# Promoting Employment Opportunities through Mentorship for Gang-Involved Youth Reintegrating into the Community

Adrienne M. F. Peters

In the present economic environment, many young people are un- or underemployed, as obtaining work that suits their interests and is permanent and full-time is increasingly challenging. By the end of 2015, the unemployment rate among 15–24 year olds in Canada was approximately 13 percent, where for the overall population the unemployment rate was lower, at only 7 percent (Statistics Canada, 2015). Young people who are employed hold jobs that fail to align with their training or education, thus youth employment appears to be neither gainful nor consistent with youth aptitudes. For young people who have had involvement with the police and youth justice system, securing and maintaining a job can be even more difficult. Like many adult former prisoners, youth who have been involved in the justice system experience several barriers when seeking employment— beyond the presence of a provisional youth record.

First, youth involvement in the justice system can interrupt attendance at school and participation in related activities (e.g., Altschuler & Brash, 2004; Hagan, 1997). The consequences of this absenteeism appear to continue into adulthood, as researchers in the United States demonstrate that adult offenders' rates of high school completion were lower than those of the general population (Uggen, Wakefield, & Western, 2005). Furthermore, these youth may not have the requisite skills or training to qualify for many jobs; in consequence, the challenges they encounter in school (and/or that result from their exclusion from traditional classroom learning) may explain why they later, as adult offenders, are also less likely to have been employed full-time when in the community (Uggen et al., 2005).

A second barrier to employment is the court-imposed conditions that comprise the community portion of a youth's custodial sentence under the *Youth Criminal Justice Act (YCJA)*. Upon completion of the custodial portion of their youth sentence—which comprises the first two-thirds of a youth custodial sentence, with the remaining one-third served on a community supervision order—youth in Canada have numerous restrictions they are required to abide by when released. These conditions include no-go orders and curfews that limit their mobility and freedom and, effectively, influence work possibilities. Third, resulting from present Canadian legislation that mandates only the most serious forms of offending to be addressed through the formal court system, many young people involved in the youth justice system are identified as living with numerous risk factors (e.g., unstable living situations, mental health issues, and/or substance abuse; Corrado & Peters, 2013; McClelland, Elkington, Teplin, & Abram, 2004) that may interfere with their ability to gain employment. Lastly, the desire to earn money may, for select youth, be so overwhelming that they participate in criminal activities or join a criminal organization for this reason (Lachman, Roman, & Cahill, 2013). In this context, youth associated with gang members may also perceive their access to legitimate opportunities as blocked and feel their only venue to earn money is through illegitimate activities (Short, Rivera, & Tennyson, 1965). For these diverse reasons, it is important that youth justice systems acknowledge the presence of these barriers and work with youth to reduce the resulting harm such experiences and constraints impose.

## THEORETICAL EXPLANATIONS ON THE LINK BETWEEN YOUTH OFFENDING AND EMPLOYMENT

The developmental/life-course framework builds on existing social control theories and outlines how employment acts as a central turning point by nurturing existing relationships and leading to the acquisition of positive social capital (Laub & Sampson, 2003). Moffitt's (1993) developmental taxonomy, for example, proposed two dominant pathways individuals who engage in criminal behaviours follow: (1) the adolescent-limited pathway, and (2) the life-course persistent pathway. While a very select proportion of youth meet the latter group criteria—engaging in persistent offending throughout their adolescent and adult life—the majority of criminally involved individuals fall into the category of adolescent-limited. These individuals' delinquency is initiated during the teenage years, typically as a result of the age group's propensity towards risk-taking behaviour and access to deviant peers. As youth begin to exit this life stage and mature, they will seek other sources of attachment (e.g., pro-social romantic partners and colleagues) and means to become involved with conventional society. Thus, these later genuine commitments foster the desistance process. Like Moffitt, Sampson, and Laub (2005) further put forth that employment expands youth's relationships, increases their investment in social capital or in valued social institutions, thereby preventing their involvement in delinquent behaviours.

To examine unemployment experiences among vulnerable young people, Baron (2008) used data from a sample of street-involved youth living in Western Canada and found that older sample participants expressed higher levels of anger due to their unemployment and were more likely to commit drug trafficking offences. Beyond the obvious strain that this presents for young people, older youth are also more inclined to desire the attainment of more meaningful connections, such as those offered through work. Assistance in accessing employment could therefore increase the likelihood that older youth will engage with the programming, ultimately leading to a smoother transition back into free society. Related to developmental theories as well, Caspi, Wright, Moffitt, and Silva (1998) looked at whether higher levels of social capital earlier in life—defined as "social relationships that provide access and control over various types of resources" (Caspi et al., 1998, p. 428)—had a significant relationship to youth (ages 15 to 21) unemployment. Using family-structure measures and age-appropriate indicators of social capital, their results supported that youth who were unemployed tended to be raised in single-parent families, experienced conflict within the family environment, and had weak parental attachment and school involvement (Caspi et al., 1998).

Researchers have revealed that the importance of the parent–child relationship persists into adulthood and encourages the desistance process, particularly for children who do not develop romantic relationships (Schroeder, Giordano, & Cernkovich, 2010). Still other researchers, however, have suggested that when individuals mature and assume their own parental responsibilities, greater challenges may arise in the absence of employment. Fader (2008), for example, found that when fathers could not obtain a job, the resulting frustration pushed them to commit new crimes for which they were ultimately reincarcerated. Hence, while romantic relationships and family can provide important attachments and social capital, employment-related barriers encountered by former prisoners can present additional stressors when individuals cannot provide for their family.

## CANADIAN YOUTH JUSTICE LEGISLATION ON REHABILITATION AND REINTEGRATION

The government of Canada has been a leader in the movement away from a youth justice philosophy founded on punitive responses. Since the enactment of the *Youth Criminal Justice Act* (2002) in 2003, the numbers of young people who are formally charged, tried in youth court, and sentenced to youth custody has decreased (Bala, Carrington, & Roberts, 2009). In 2013/14, for example, 15 percent of youth court cases where the young person was found guilty resulted in a custodial sentence, representing a 7 percent decline since 2003/04 (Alam, 2015). These sentences are also characteristically short; in 2013/14, youth sentences of one year or more were imposed in only 2 percent of cases (Alam, 2015). Instead, the majority of young people (58 percent) sentenced in youth court in Canada receive a probation sentence and the median length of these sentences in 2013/14 was one year. Even among young people who received a custodial sentence and entered the youth correctional system in 2013/14, more than 70 percent had first spent time supervised in the community (Correctional Services Program, 2015). There is evidently a discernable path between each of these criminal justice settings for youth in conflict with the law for serious offences in Canada.

As part of its rehabilitative goal, the *Youth Criminal Justice Act* delineates the practice of assembling relevant community members and criminal justice staff to participate in the planning and delivery of rehabilitation programs for youth who have come into contact with the justice system. For those youth who are sentenced to incarceration, this extends to successful community reintegration, by providing some youth with the option to go on reintegrative leave in the community, and all formerly incarcerated youth with automatic community supervision orders. Given that 62 percent of the young people who were formally charged with a crime in Canada in 2013/14 were nearing the end of adolescence (i.e., were 16 or 17 years of age) when they appeared in youth court (Alam, 2015), these youth likely need both school/educational programming and vocational training and employment assistance (Altschuler & Brash, 2004). Such assistance will better prepare them for community reintegration post-incarceration. Researchers show that incarcerated youth in Canada encounter challenges in school, ranging from low achievement, behavioural problems, and difficulties with peers (Peters & Corrado, 2013), thus a slightly greater proportion of these youth have directed their future goals towards attaining employment compared to further schooling (Peters & Corrado, 2014).

Youth who spend longer periods in a youth detention centre are often assessed as high risk and high needs, presenting with a range of mental health and substance-abuse-related needs, either in isolation or co-morbidly (Odgers, Burnette, Chauhan, Moretti, & Reppucci, 2005; Teplin et al., 2006). They are often from socially disorganized neighbourhoods and communities, and many are of Indigenous heritage (Corrado & Cohen, 2002). Essential programming is therefore needed to address the risk profiles of youth who have been convicted of more serious offences. Even in the rare cases when a young person receives a lengthy custodial sentence, they will eventually be released and expected to reintegrate into their communities.

While the emphasis on education is important, additional schooling may not be a realistic option for all youth. For older adolescents in particular, life and job skills training, as well as supported employment may be more meaningful (Altschuler & Brash, 2004; Uggen, 2000). Indeed, researchers have demonstrated that youth who attend school and work several hours per week have higher rates of delinquency, substance use, and behavioural problems compared to youth who work at a lower intensity, which is attributed to greater exposure to opportunities to engage in crime. Continued research, however, revealed that by adding pre-employment measures, this link disappeared (see Paternoster, Bushway, Brame, & Apel, 2003). Due to these inconsistencies, alternatively, concentrating the majority of youth's energy on *one* of these may be the most beneficial to their future success.

## THE EMPIRICAL RELATIONSHIP BETWEEN RE-ENTRY, EMPLOYMENT, AND RECIDIVISM

Compared to the attention paid to the linkage between adult employment and recidivism, less attention has been paid to youth unemployment due to employment's construction as an adult pursuit. Past researchers, however, indicate that joblessness at a young age among the general youth population is worrying since unemployment in youth lowers an individuals' probability of being employed later in life (Lynch, 1989). This link also applies to employees' wages: wages are likely to be lower for individuals who have periods of unemployment in their work histories than individuals without such gaps in employment (Baker & Elias, 1991).

As abovementioned, social capital and relationships are central to successful reintegration. Although many researchers' focus rather exclusively on familial relationships (e.g., Berg & Huebner, 2011), social capital can be derived from various individuals interacting with young people. The importance of these relationships, along with networks of family and friends, also translates to non-familial important others who may assume a supportive and/or mentoring role for the young person (Caspi et al., 1998; Laub & Sampson, 2003; Uggen, Wakefield, & Western, 2005). In this sense, youth workers, program staff, and/or employers working with youth in employment programs become social capital. The association between a youth's relationships and their accomplishments also extends to the neighbourhood level; young people who live in affluent neighbourhoods are more likely to earn higher grades in school, as they are exposed to employed others who act as role models (Chung, Mulvey, & Steinberg, 2011). Youth in conflict with the law who spend notable amounts of time with positive role models through specialized programming and at work can thus have a comparable effect.

Wright and Cullen (2004) relied on data from waves 5 and 6[1] of the National Youth Survey to assess pro-social co-workers' influence on youth's relationships with delinquent peers, as well as on their delinquent and criminal behaviour (e.g., drug use), and found that with time the relationships developed with pro-social co-workers became more important than those with delinquent peer networks, which in turn led to lower rates of adult offending. In addition, there was a significant relationship found between hours worked per week and total weeks working, with the latter being negatively predictive of offending. This study therefore provides empirical support for the learning and adoption of noncriminal values and behaviours over time.[2] Older youth, in addition to being more mature, may be in jobs where they are exposed to older peers and co-workers who exhibit pro-social attitudes and serve as role models for conventional lifestyles and values.

Young serious offenders associated with gangs can present an even more complex re-entry situation where the youth must decide to either rejoin the gang or seek legitimate employment. Even for youth peripherally involved in the gang, the commitment they feel to the group may surpass their commitment to society and conventional activities. Some gang members, after prolonged contact with gang associates and their law-violating attitudes, adopt similar thinking patterns and are likely to highly value their connection to the gang. In consequence they bear a greater likelihood of reconnecting with their gang upon release (Boduszek, Dhingra, & Hirschfield, 2015). Young people who work for mid-level, and more organized criminal groups are also compensated well for their services to the gang, like drug-distribution (see Thompson & Uggen, 2012), and as a result, it can be difficult to induce the search for legitimate employment opportunities, which are likely to result in reduced earnings. Offering support in programming that combines life skills training, employment mentoring, and subsidized employment could help in "knifing off" existent antisocial influences and (re-)establishing pro-social attachments (see Maruna & Roy, 2007).

A recent evaluation of an employment-focused re-entry program found that, when young, high-risk former prisoners (i.e., with a history of violence or gang involvement), were provided with jobs and wraparound services, they ended up with higher rates of employment, higher incomes, and lower odds of being re-arrested compared to the control group (Cook, Kang, Braga, Ludwig, & O'Brien, 2015). The researchers concluded that intervention services started while youth were still incarcerated, and continued when they were released from custody, together increased their human capital and successes related to employment and recidivism. Unlike other studies that examined the impact of subsidized employment by itself and found no significant results, Cook et al.'s (2015) work highlights the encouraging results attainable by "reaching-in," or initiating employment planning prior to release from custody.

To expound on the findings introduced above, Boduszek et al. (2015) used a series of important risk and gang-related variables collected as part of the Pathways to Desistance Study to assess their ability to predict youths' intention to rejoin their gang upon release. Results indicated that the importance of the gang to youth was the strongest predictor of young people's intention to return to the group after detention. By designing and providing access to vocational training and employment interventions that provide youth with credible alternatives, program coordinators can reframe how youth visualize the gang *and* how they envision a life without the gang. Such programming provides an opportunity to counsel gang members about the unfortunate, but all too common, consequences of continuing their relationship with the gang—for themselves and their family—and can present them with alternative options that can lead to success through conventional means. Such assistance, in addition to housing assistance and substance abuse treatment, can reduce reoffending among gang members (Braga & Weisburd, 2012). It is evident that concepts derived from developmental theories play a critical role in supporting youth transition out of the gang and into adulthood, as contributing members of society.

Despite the abundance of research available on the effectiveness of targeting youth educational issues and delinquency through mentorship (see Tolan et al., 2013), empirical research that evaluates the influence of social capital, mentorship, and youth employment programming is less common (see McDonald, Erickson, Johnson, & Elder, 2007), especially in the contexts of employer mentorship and re-entry. Although likely explained by researchers' focusing on educational attainment for this age group and the challenges inherent to conducting experimental research in the area, a lacuna in the literature remains.

The relationship between mentoring and employment is multifarious. Family, friends, teachers, and other relationships that youth have external to work can serve as informal mentors for youth in achieving full-time employ-ment, especially for young men (McDonald et al., 2007). While non-work mentors can encourage the attainment and maintenance of employment, alternatively, employment can present opportunities to develop new men-toring relationships with colleagues and employers. Researchers have found, however, that work-related mentor–mentee relationships are less common than those with non-work mentors and as a result, youth often have closer attachments with non-work role models (McDonald et al., 2007).

Nonetheless, some of the cessation of offending, from adolescence to adulthood, is attributable to the natural maturation process rather than time- and resource-intense programming. Furthermore, researchers continue to highlight the persistence of an offending trajectory for serious/violent youth who begin offending early and develop chronic offending patterns over time (Baglivio, Jackowski, Greenwald, & Howell, 2014; Yessine & Bonta, 2012). Youth who have had contact with the justice system in Canada are a highly vulnerable group. They require supplementary support in school, in voca-tional training or with job preparation if they are to avoid the continuation of these stressors into adulthood. To this end, I now present a description of a youth employment program that operated in Vancouver, British Columbia, from 2009 to 2014. I accompany this description with the case study of one young person who, as a result of engaging with this program, established strong social capital and productively reintegrated into the law-abiding community.

## PLEA COMMUNITY SERVICES EMPLOYMENT PROGRAM

In 2010, I began a research project entitled the *Study on Specialized Commu-nity Case Management of Young Offenders* in Vancouver, British Columbia (BC) where I examined the impact of intensive probation caseloads for seri-ous/violent, gang-involved, and mentally disordered youth in Lower Main-land, British Columbia. As part of this larger study, I formed a relationship with PLEA Community Services, which is based in Vancouver and delivers a range of programming to at-risk and justice-involved young people and their families. One such program was Career Path, which originated in 2009 with the goal of connecting youth associated with criminal organizations to mentorship, vocational training, and employment opportunities. A youth probation officer working closely with gang-involved youth recognized a gap in services for these young men who had steady sources of illegitimate income and were offered endless law-abiding incentives through their gang connections—but never through legitimate means. As suggested by develop-mental theories of offending, a lack of attachment to and/or supervision from adults left these youth seeking attention and guidance from other sources. Sadly, specifically for slightly older, criminally entrenched young men, their societal isolation in conjunction with their developing gang relationship underpinned a process of subtle grooming for gang-related delinquent and criminal activities.

While PLEA had a long-standing employment program that had been serving youth with criminal involvement—officially known as Creative Urban Employment or the Q Program—there was no program that catered to the unique needs of gang-associated youth. Career Path was distinctive from the Q Program in that referrals were accepted for youth who had ties to criminal organizations in the Lower Mainland, and whose offending appeared influenced by these relationships. Like Q, it also focused on providing youth with vocational training and linking them to work. Career Path, however, introduced an even more individualized career-oriented component; rather than simply finding a job for the youth, Career Path staff developed a program where they worked closely with youth to first determine their interests and aspirations, and then helped them search for longer-term employment opportunities that aligned with said interests and aspirations. Career Path coordinators therefore devoted considerable time to building relationships with potential employers in the community, so they could engage in repeated employment collaborations that benefited youth referred to the program.

Employers were sought after based on their profession/field of work, personal commitment to the program's objectives, and openness to assuming a strong mentoring role for the youth. Career Path then paid the young people's wages for ten weeks, at which point the company could hire the youth. Based on this model, and the unwavering commitment of staff and employers, Career Path has been responsible for several youth being successful on their path to desistance (see Peters & Corrado, 2015). To share one of the program's success stories, I contacted one of the Career Path coordinators and conducted a one-hour informal interview about the program and one particular youth's experience.

## SAM'S STORY

My informal interview with PLEA's Q Program and Career Path program coordinator focused primarily on the case of a 17-year-old Indigenous male, Sam,[3] who was nearing completion of PLEA's Career Path program. At the time, Sam had been successfully employed for approximately four months. Sam was a young man with severe anger and hostility issues, who often acted defiantly and felt frustrated. Despite his young age, Sam is the father of two children and was involved in an Indigenous gang on the Downtown Eastside of Vancouver, Canada. After becoming entrenched in this gang—in which his other family members were also active—and selling narcotics, Sam was arrested, charged, and convicted of a series of related offences. He served a portion of his sentence in custody, as legislated by the *YCJA*, and was then released to be supervised in the community by a youth probation officer. It was this officer who referred him to PLEA's Career Path program.

Many youths' community order conditions require them to attend school or work. Since Sam had not been attending school, employment became the more appropriate option. His social worker secured him a stable address through a program in Vancouver called Directions Youth Services; living stability is of utmost importance for young people generally, and particularly so if they are to have any success in PLEA's employment programs. Sometimes the youth referred to PLEA are in temporary (i.e., unstable) housing situations. If their housing breaks down, it is likely they will also lose their job and then have difficulty finding future work.

Once stable housing was in place, Sam began Career Path's employment program curriculum. When he was initially accepted into the program, the staff conducted an assessment (including an examination of his goals) and reviewed the program objectives with Sam. Although Sam agreed to engage in the Career Path curriculum, he was initially defiant and expressed an immediate interest in securing a job rather than following the curriculum. At each meeting he continued to exhibit defiant attitudes and resistance to the job-training curriculum. While the Career Path program aimed to equip youth with valuable skills related to developing resumés, interviewing, and other employability-related factors, Sam experienced repeated difficulties remaining focused in the classroom. Career Path staff worked with Sam, but eventually recognized that the curriculum portion of the program was ineffective for this particular youth. Staff acknowledge that they receive this aversion to the classroom from time to time as it reminds some youth of traditional schooling—a place where they had perhaps been unsuccessful and/or had had negative experiences. The coordinators also recognize that, for some youth, skills learned in the classroom can also be learned on the job. Furthermore, there are many skills that are not learned in a classroom and can be practised only once employed, such as waking up early, preparing a lunch, arriving to work on time, and following the directions of others. Ultimately, "doing" is how young people, and many former prisoners, gain critical work experience. In acknowledgement of this, Career Path staff does not compel every youth to complete the entire program curriculum. Instead they deliver the program using an individualized approach that ensures they reach and assist a broad range of youth who, although all capable of retaining

employment, have diverse needs and risks. This flexibility is an essential program element, yet not something that Career Path openly publicizes. Instead
they present the curriculum as important to encourage the majority of youth
to complete it—they opt to not give youth an "out" prematurely, but try to
push them to follow the curriculum. Still, the primary focus of Career Path
is to help young people find work and support them on the job, by pairing
them with an employer-mentor who provides regular support.

After a few failed attempts to incite participation in the curriculum, the
Career Path program coordinator and staff agreed to initiate the process of
getting Sam a job. They presented Sam with potential employers and very
briefly rehearsed standard interview protocols. Sam had expressed interest in
working at a warehouse, and so a coordinator secured him a warehouse position. Although they knew that the selected companies would agree to employ
Sam in light of their standing relationship from previous program participants, Sam was not privy to this information. He met with the employer, had
an interview, and was offered a job. Shortly after attaining his first position,
however, it became apparent that the arrangement was not a suitable match
and Sam ultimately quit. Soon thereafter, a Career Path Program coordinator
secured Sam a second job, building long boards in a warehouse. Sam quickly
developed a strong rapport with his colleagues and enjoyed the work. Every
morning, he would wake extremely early to catch the bus from downtown
Vancouver to North Vancouver, which was a notable transition for a youth
who formerly had more flexible hours selling drugs and no commitments
until the afternoon. Although difficult, as it would be for the majority of
people, Sam committed himself to this job and finished his contract with
the company. Unfortunately, due to financial constraints, the company could
not continue to employ Sam after the Career Path program's ten weeks. Staff
share that this event, although disappointing, was a good learning experience
for Sam, as the position provided an opportunity to practise fundamental
skills associated with working, such as waking up early in the morning, saving
money for bus fair and purchasing bus tickets, and many other day-to-day
practices that the average person takes for granted, but that many ex-prisoners have to learn and experience.

Following this second setback, Sam maintained his desire to work and
expressed that he would like to try working in construction. When advised
that construction workers began their workday even earlier than warehouse
employees, Sam surprised everyone by agreeing to this anticipated requirement. Staff from Career Path, therefore, continued to support Sam in his
employment pursuits and contacted their main construction employer. Construction is described as especially appealing for young people who have been

involved in criminal organizations and drug trafficking since the wages are among the highest for individuals with their skill level (see also Schaeffer et al., 2014), employment experience, and criminal history—and the industry is thriving in the Lower Mainland, British Columbia. A Career Path coordinator successfully arranged an ironworker placement with one of the larger Lower Mainland construction companies they had previously worked with and with which they had experienced positive outcomes. When Sam commenced this position, he again had to adjust to early-morning commutes. The main incentive for Sam was the $15 hourly wage with the potential for a raise. Career Path staff work closely with all youth employers; they regularly receive time sheets and track the hours youth attend work. Aside from minor setbacks in the beginning when Sam missed a few days and left early, he quickly ensured he made it to work every day. During the transition period, when he was still adjusting to the new job and hours, the employer was understanding of his circumstances and continued to work with him to support his employment, and, in effect, his commitment to distancing himself from the criminal lifestyle.

It was admittedly difficult for Sam to leave the lucrative drug market where he made $500 per day. Nevertheless, a Career Path coordinator suggests that one of the central motivating factors for reaching this turning point in Sam's life was his children. Although Sam did not have custody of his children, he would regularly spend time with his daughters and spoke highly of them. A second incentive to leave the gang and seek legitimate employment was safety. Many gang members live with a constant fear, which leads to "always looking over their shoulder," or an anxiousness about others trying to "rip them off." A Career Path coordinator explained that for many youth "the switch just goes, 'I can't do this anymore'" (Career Path coordinator, personal communication, September 15, 2015). Based on my prior research, this view is shared among many youth justice personnel and programming staff. Young people who have had prolonged, serious contact with the youth justice system necessitate the most intensive supervision and intervention, yet many attempts to reduce their reoffending may be futile. Youth who have experienced more success in transitioning out of this lifestyle have often been described as "being ready" to commit to a change, often instigated by what some youth probation officers refer to as "hitting rock bottom." Rock bottom can derive from various experiences, including going to youth detention, overdosing on a substance, placing less importance on their gang associations, or feeling overwhelmingly helpless. Regardless of the source, this provides an opportunity for youth support and program workers to engage the young person in meaningful, individualized programming like that offered by Career Path.

Sam's case, and others like his, reveals that Career Path offers its participants continual support delivered in several ways, from driving youth to their work during early days, to paying the first ten weeks of wages, to assisting youth who require multiple placements. They also "put out fires" through ongoing meetings between the youth and their employer-mentor, caregivers, and other youth support workers to organize the young person's schedule, brainstorm how to best assist the youth, and outline each person's/ agency's role. Program staff further listened and responded to the concerns of the youth and/or any individuals collaborating in the support of the young person. In Sam's case, program staff also provided him with the necessary work clothing.

Owing to all of this support, Sam successfully completed the ten-week employment period funded by Career Path, after which the construction company continued to employ him, adding him to their payroll. Four months later, it was reported that Sam was doing really well. "Just the gratification, the smile on their faces; we bring him a cheque for $1200, he was getting those cheques consistently as well, and really couldn't believe it. He knew how much he was making, but once you actually see the cheque, it's like 'wow.' It's a huge motivator" (Career Path coordinator, personal communication, September 15, 2015). During a recent check in, Sam shared that his employer had presented him with the opportunity to be trained as a project lead if he continued his commitment and hard work over the subsequent six months. At the time of my interview, Sam was working towards attaining this goal. He had already learned a number of new skills related to the construction industry and, despite the high turnover in the construction industry, he had made significant progress and established important relationships with his employer-mentor and colleagues: "Like all of us, you have to connect with people; it makes it a lot easier. And that was key for him in the job as well" (Career Path coordinator, personal communication, September 15, 2015). This is further evidence that a positive relationship with co-workers and employers strengthens individuals' social capital, which in effect fosters commitment to pro-social activities like employment.

Despite the challenges that many of the youth in the program presented, employers assumed strong mentorship roles, sometimes as a result of their own involvement with the law when they were young or simply their desire to give back to their communities. The employment program coordinators were attentive to protecting youth's offending profiles and information on their youth justice involvement; nevertheless, because their wage was paid by an external source, other site workers quickly learned of this and made inferences about the youth's circumstances. Thus, while the mentors were required to maintain confidentiality regarding the young person's circumstances, the youth themselves were often more forthcoming about their own histories, as well as their appointments with their youth probation officers, and often self-identified as being involved in the youth justice system. Consequently, employers and supervisors heard their stories and often connected with the youth on a deeper level, mentoring them on how to do the job well (e.g., what to do on a job site, how to stay safe at work), and more generally how to work with other people. Beyond the employers, other workers on the sites also assumed mentorship roles, due to similar backgrounds or their ability to identify with the young people. Essential here was the care taken by workplace mentors not to label the youth, and to give them the freedom to work independently and prove themselves. For example, one of the more successful employer-mentors with Career Path was an individual who assigned the youth responsibility and treated him like everyone else on the site.

Among the other services that PLEA delivers to justice-involved youth is their Intensive Support and Supervision Program (ISSP). Career Path staff therefore worked closely with ISSP workers and youth probation officers to collect collateral information on the young people in their programs. ISSP workers can also assist in transporting youth to and from work; and similarly to the employer-mentor, they have the opportunity to develop a closer relationship with the young people because they spend time participating in pro-social activities with the youth. Career Path coordinators give much time-intensive support to youth when they start the program; however, their role is reduced once the young person secures employment. ISSP workers, however, remain continuously involved with the young person in the community (and in custody if the youth is incarcerated), extending to a period of six months or more. ISSP workers reinforce pro-social attitudes and behaviours, support youth in abiding by their court conditions, and ensure that they remain committed to their work and any other obligations.

Sam was fortunate to have been in an area in British Columbia where he could be referred to Career Path, as its staff stood by him during two failed job attempts and then during his success securing a longer-term position. Sam is also positively involved in his children's lives and working to develop and sustain this relationship while providing some financial support:

> We're just so excited for this guy, for being 17 and doing what he's doing; it blew us away ... a lot of times that type of story happens to our kids who

are 19, that are a little bit older and might not have as many barriers, and for him to be doing that is huge ... you're always competing with family values and community values, where they're from and what happens. We're trying to instil some different values. If you're going home everyday to an environment that's got different values and they're reinforced, those values tend to trump what you're trying to do. So for him to move away from that as well, you can see all the barriers in front of him ... we're really happy for him. (Career Path coordinator, personal communication, September 15, 2015)

The coordinator expounded on the positive outcomes of Sam's employment, stating that PLEA's programs assisted Sam in nurturing relationships with his children, and that PLEA's employment and mentoring services can help "break the cycle" for a few young people. Sam is also giving back to society and his community as an employed taxpayer.

Since being referred to Career Path, Sam has discontinued his associations with the gang he was formerly involved with, and to the best of the staff's knowledge, he no longer sells drugs. He has been receiving a good wage for his work and officially finished the Career Path portion of his job towards the end of January 2016. At this point, the youth no longer has any formal obligations to the program. When young people successfully complete the program, Career Path staff may take the youth out for lunch or dinner to celebrate their successful program completion and employment. There is also a six-month discharge follow-up conducted, whenever possible, to assess how the young person is doing in a number of areas of their life through a casual conversation with PLEA staff. A very small proportion of youth visit the program following their successful completion to update staff on their progress, while another small percentage have lost their jobs following their discharge from the employment program and request a second referral to PLEA's job-related services.

Although not all youth who are referred to Career Path achieve the same positive outcomes as Sam, his case is emblematic of the successes of youth who have reached a point at which they are willing to commit to a lifestyle change. As stated earlier, for some young people, once they reach a certain age, or experience a certain life event, such as being sentenced to a lengthy custodial sentence, having children, or surviving an attack on their life, their mindset undergoes a transformation, through which they can visualize another type of life, in which they can live freely in the community, support their family, and experience happiness as a result of their own legitimate hard work and commitment.

## DISCUSSION

By relying on existing youth justice legislation, such as Canada's *Youth Criminal Justice Act*, probation officers and rehabilitative programming staff can play a pivotal role in youth reintegration. This should commence with release planning and coordination as soon as a young person enters a youth facility. Canada's youth justice legislation outlines very different youth detention practices and alternatives from those in the United States and other Western countries, including England and Australia. It explicitly provides professional discretion to grant the young offender the opportunity for reintegrative leave, and even early release, to initiate youth's transition into free society and their new roles. This should be used more frequently in cases where youth have expressed interest in seeking employment upon release and have exhibited good behaviour and commitment to programming in custody. Further, all youth sentenced to custody in Canada are supervised by a youth probation officer throughout their entire sentence and more closely in the community for the final portion of their sentence. During this time, the officer works collaboratively with the young person and other service providers on the formulated case management plan to assist the youth in working towards their established goals. Such planning should incorporate input from individuals working with the young person in the custodial centre and in the community.

Youth case managers and probation officers in British Columbia have been resourceful in making use of these legislative provisions by referring some youth to the Career Path program while they are still in youth detention and starting the intake process during this time. Youth who demonstrate good behaviour and commitment to programming in custody can be granted reintegrative leaves, and in a small number of cases, youth may receive approval for early release to begin their employment. In other cases, youth probation officers can discuss programming options, such as PLEA's employment programs, with young people while they are serving the custodial portion of their sentence and then make the referral once the youth has been released from detention. Each of these scenarios highlights the importance of collaborative, individualized case planning. Youth probation officers, as well as any previously engaged program staff, should dedicate time to visiting young people in custody even in cases where they have received lengthy custodial sentences. Some youth workers may mistakenly overlook the importance of this practice assuming instead that the youth detention staff responsible for case managing incarcerated youth are sufficient. As youth typically receive relatively short custodial sentences (Alam, 2015), probation officers would benefit from supervising all young people with a certain degree of forethought. This is particularly important during a young person's initial involvement with the justice system and/or for a youth who has been newly assigned to the officer's caseload. Upon developing early rapport with youth and individuals attached to them (both personally and professionally), youth probation officers can determine which approach (e.g., reintegrative leaves, early release, or program referral pre- or post-release) would be in the best interests of the young person.

Furthermore, early release planning in combination with specific programming can assist individuals in building their knowledge-base and skills, and therefore increase their employability (e.g., Cook et al., 2015) in preparation for their release. This can help youth in the formulation of future goals and realization strategies. Case planning should also equip youth with strategies to deal with any setbacks they may encounter throughout the re-entry process, as incarcerated youth have been found to lack concrete executions for the plans conceived of pre release (see Clinkinbeard & Zohra, 2012). I argue then that youth probation officers and correctional staff should further work to maintain youth's existing networks in the community and any employment for when they are released.

Although Sam had strained family relationships and was unmarried, he had experienced a type of identity transformation consistent with the developmental framework; when he became a father he committed to his children and the associated social capital. His bonds to his daughters and his desire to support them instilled a sense of responsibility distinct perhaps from that experienced by youth who have not undertaken such a duty. This fostered a second turning point whereby Sam wished to exit his gang and seek legitimate employment. Sam was not dissuaded by the scope of such an endeavour, despite the fact that successful re-entry can be especially challenging for individuals who are fathers and view themselves as providers (Fader, 2008).

Vocational and employment interventions should therefore take each of these issues under consideration when registering young people for their programs, and work with the young people, as well as their families, to offer the most beneficial types of support for their particular needs. In this regard, the individualized strategy used by Career Path is essential. Young people are balancing a number of identities as they transition from adolescence to adulthood and any reintegration interventions should also attempt to balance the positive and/or negative impact of family and peers on a youth's re-entry. Employment-based interventions should further initiate a process of networking for young people, connecting them to employers working in fields of interest and promote connections that can be translated to future employment opportunities.

PLEA's Career Path provides a strong model for employment programs that can service older, high-risk youth during community reintegration. The key program elements underlying program success include: ensuring the youth have stable housing, and providing individualized case plans, inter-est-based employment opportunities, mentoring, supported subsidized employment, multi-program/agency collaborations, and tenacity from both program staff and the youth. Sam's story highlighted each of these as he nav-igated his way out of the gang lifestyle into a conventional life despite several barriers presented to him during the reintegration process. Based on my observations and this case study, youth appear to benefit the greatest from dependable support and pro-social role models who reinforce conventional attitudes and behaviours. Wright and Cullen's (2004) earlier work comparing the influence of youth's relationships with co-workers to their relationships with delinquent peers importantly corroborates my assertion that Career Path's use of pro-social employer/colleague mentors is an important factor to the program's success; the new pro-social bonds and role modelling pre-sented by colleagues can in fact supersede the influence delinquent peers have on a young person's behaviour. Just as individuals engaging in law-break-ing activities often have mentors who encourage such behaviours and provide profitable opportunities, pro-social mentors at work can promote conven-tional behaviours. Colleagues and employers who share their own personal stories with youth can begin to foster a relationship and demonstrate their confidence in the young person. When youth are exposed to such reliable individuals, who are also on time for work shifts, follow supervisors' direc-tions, and value their job, youth are likely to adopt similar attitudes and practices. These influences can then be applied by youth in both work and non-work settings.

With regard to gang-involved youth specifically, since criminal organi-zations offer youth desired relational supports, pro-social co-workers and an encouraging employer-mentor can nurture new relationships with youth and, over time, reduce the importance placed on retaining membership in the gang (Boduszek et al., 2015). When combined with stable housing and substance-use interventions (see Braga & Weisburd, 2012), as required, youth with ties to criminal organizations can be offered a promising opportunity to reintegrate post-incarceration. Stable housing, again, was a central compo-nent of Sam's success in Career Path, and although substance use was not, it is often a factor in determining whether or not a young person can enter one of PLEA's employment programs. I therefore encourage youth reintegrative programming coordinators to be cognizant of youth's multiple vulnerability factors and be discriminatory in their program referrals. More specifically, interventions should be offered selectively, targeting the dominant need of youth rather than attempting to address several needs, thus increasing the potential to overwhelm the young person. As each risk factor is successfully managed, program coordinators can refer youth to subsequent programming.

Beyond relational considerations, another central programming component highlighted through Sam's story was the provision of economic support, such as subsidized employment. By providing young people who have access to gang resources and illegal drug earnings with reasonable wages, the field of construction was a promising option for Sam, and may be for other youth like him, who do not have post-secondary education; it compensates workers well compared to other jobs requiring the same skill and experience level, and it offers opportunities for advancement to those who exhibit strong commitment.

A related recommendation is that agencies delivering youth programming should strive to offer a range of reintegrative services, or at the very least, work closely with other community-based organizations to offer the range of programming options required by many justice involved young people. The standing relationships with employers in the community, as well as their internal Intensive Support and Supervision Program workers, were essential to youth's success in Career Path. The communication that was consequently made possible within PLEA between its various youth justice, employment, and residential programs was also valuable to the successful case management of formerly incarcerated youth and to their successful community reintegration. Collaborations with youth probation officers and social workers provided additional assistance to developing a case plan for Sam and other youth who have participated in the employment program.

## CONCLUSION

Sam's case story and the related youth programming literature highlight a number of issues concerning young people, offending, employment, and recidivism that should not be overlooked. Supporting youth as they build conventional ties to pro-social role models and their communities, while potentially tenuous at the beginning, presents important opportunities to realign their pathways and encourage commitment to legitimate work and lifestyles. Employment programs should target older adolescents who have begun the process of maturation, visualizing their futures, and internalizing adult roles. PLEA has successfully delivered tailored employment services as part of Career Path and now the Q Program, through flexible planning and supported, subsidized employment offered through the collaborations between other internal program staff, youth probation officers, and professionals who work with the youth in the community. Sam's story encourages criminal justice personnel, community-based service providers, as well as young people, to adopt positive attitudes to reintegration and employment, and have faith in their abilities to pursue opportunities, achieve personal satisfaction, and lead a successful life.

## NOTES

1 The researchers selected these waves due to respondents' ages (15–21 years of age and 18–24 years of age, respectively), thereby representing important transitional periods in young people's lives.
2 This is in contrast to the research evidence linking youth's employment to increased offending risk due to exposure to delinquent peers who are also working in low-paying jobs (e.g., Ploeger, 1997).
3 Name changed to protect youth's identity.

## REFERENCES

Alam, S. (2015). *Youth court statistics in Canada, 2013/2014.* Statistics Canada. Retrieved from http://www.statcan.gc.ca/pub/85-002-x/2015001/article/14224-eng.htm

Altschuler, D. M., & Brash, R. (2004). Adolescent and teenage offenders confronting the challenges and opportunities of reentry. *Youth Violence and Juvenile Justice, 2,* 72–87. doi: 10.1177/1541204003260048

Baglivio, M. T., Jackowski, K., Greenwald, M. A., & Howell, J. C. (2014). Serious, violent, and chronic juvenile offenders: A statewide analysis of prevalence and prediction of subsequent recidivism using risk and protective factors. *Criminology & Public Policy, 13,* 83–116.

Baker, M., & Elias, P. (1991). Youth unemployment and work histories. In S. Dex (Ed.), *Life and work history analyses: Qualitative and quantitative developments* (pp. 214–244). London, UK: Routledge.

Bala, N., Carrington, P. J., & Roberts, J. V. (2009). Evaluating the Youth Criminal Justice Act after five years: A qualified success. *Canadian Journal of Criminology and Criminal Justice, 51,* 131–167. doi:10.3138/cjccj.51.2.131

Baron, S. W. (2008). Street youth, unemployment, and crime: Is it that simple? Using general strain theory to untangle the relationship. *Canadian Journal of Criminology and Criminal Justice, 50,* 399–434.

Basso, R. V. J., Graham, J., Pelech, W., DeYoung, R., & Cardey, R. (2004). Children's street connections in a Canadian community. *International Journal of Offender Therapy and Comparative Criminology, 48,* 189–202.

Berg, M. T., & Huebner, B. M. (2011). Reentry and the ties that bind: An examination of social ties, employment, and recidivism. *Justice Quarterly, 28,* 382–410. doi:10.1080/07418825.2010.498383

Boduszek, D., Dhingra, K., & Hirschfield, A. (2015). Gang reengagement intentions among incarcerated serious juvenile offenders. *Journal of Criminology, 2015,* 1–10. doi:http://dx.doi.org/10.1155/2015/494562

Braga, A. A., & Weisburd, D. L. (2012). The effects of "pulling levers" focused deterrence strategies on crime. *Campbell Systematic Reviews, 8*(6), 1–90.

Caspi, A., Wright, B. R. E., Moffitt, T. E., & Silva, P. A. (1998). Early failure in the labor market: Childhood and adolescent predictors of unemployment in the transition to adulthood. *American Sociological Review, 63*, 424–451.

Chung, H. L., Mulvey, E. P., & Steinberg, L. (2011). Understanding the school outcomes of juvenile offenders: An exploration of neighborhood influences and motivational resources. *Journal of Youth and Adolescence, 40*, 1025–1038. doi:10.1007/s10964-010-9626-2

Clinkinbeard, S. S., & Zohra, T. (2012). Expectations, fears, and strategies: Juvenile offender thoughts on a future outside of incarceration. *Youth & Society, 44*, 236–257. doi:10.1177/0044118X11398365

Cook, P. J., Kang, S., Braga, A. A., Ludwig, J., & O'Brien, M. E. (2015). An experimental evaluation of a comprehensive employment-oriented prisoner reentry program. *Journal of Quantitative Criminology, 31*, 355–382. doi:10.1007/s10940-014-9242-5

Corrado, R. R., & Cohen, I. M. (2002). A needs profile of serious and/or violent Aboriginal youth in prison. *FORUM on Corrections Research, 14*(3), 20–24.

Corrado, R. R., & Peters, A. M. F. (2013). The relationship between a Schneider-based measure of remorse and chronic offending in a sample of incarcerated young offenders. *Canadian Journal of Criminology and Criminal Justice, 55*, 101–136. doi:10.3138/cjccj.2011.E.50

Correctional Services Program. (2015). *Youth correctional statistics in Canada, 2013/2014.* Retrieved from http://www.statcan.gc.ca/pub/85-002-x/2015001/article/14164-eng.htm#n08

Fader, J. J. (2008). *Inside and out: Community reentry, continuity and change among formerly incarcerated urban youth* (Published doctoral dissertation). Retrieved from http://search.proquest.com/docview/304505759/132A84DA6A616C95A79/1?accountid=4485)

Forste, R., Clarke, L., & Bahr, S. (2011). Staying out of trouble: Intentions of young male offenders. *International Journal of Offender Therapy and Comparative Criminology, 55*, 430–444.

Hagan, J. (1997). Defiance and despair: Subcultural and structural linkages between delinquency and despair in the life course. *Social Forces, 76*, 119–134.

Lachman, P., Roman, C. G., & Cahill, M. (2013). Assessing youth motivations for joining a peer group as risk factors for delinquent and gang behaviour. *Youth Violence and Juvenile Justice, 11*, 212–229.

Laub, J. H., & Sampson, R. J. (2003). *Shared beginnings, divergent lives: Delinquent boys to age 70.* Cambridge, MA: Harvard University Press.

Lipsey, M. W., & Wilson, D. B. (1998). Effective intervention for serious juvenile offenders: A synthesis of research. In R. Loeber & D. P. Farrington (Eds.), *Serious & violent juvenile offenders: Risk factors and successful interventions* (pp. 313–345). Thousand Oaks, CA: Sage Publications.

Lynch, L. M. (1989). The youth labor market in the eighties: Determinants of re-employment probabilities for young men and women. *Review of Economics and Statistics, 71*, 37–45.

Maruna, S., & Roy, K. (2007). Amputation or reconstruction? Notes on the concept of "knifing off" and desistance from crime. *Journal of Contemporary Criminal Justice, 23*, 104–124. doi:10.1177/1043986206298951

McClelland, G. M., Elkington, K. S., Teplin, L. A., & Abram, K. M. (2004). Multiple substance use disorders in juvenile detainees. *Journal of the American Academy of Child Adolescent Psychiatry, 43,* 1215–1224.

McDonald, S., Erickson, L. D., Johnson, M. K., & Elder, G. H. (2007). Informal mentoring and young adult employment. *Social Science Research, 36,* 1328–1347. doi:10.1016/j.ssresearch.2007.01.008

Moffitt, T. E. (1993). Adolescence-limited and life-course-persistent antisocial behavior: A developmental taxonomy. *Psychological Review, 100,* 674–701.

Odgers, C. L., Burnette, M. L., Chauhan, P., Moretti, M. M., & Reppucci, N. D. (2005). Misdiagnosing the problem: Mental health profiles of incarcerated juveniles. *Journal of the Canadian Academy of Child and Adolescent Psychiatry, 14,* 26–29.

Paternoster, R., Bushway, S., Brame, R., & Apel, R. (2003). The effect of teenage employment on delinquency and problem behaviors. *Social Forces, 82,* 297–335.

Peters, A. M. F., & Corrado, R. R. (2013). An examination of the early "strains" of imprisonment among young offenders incarcerated for serious crimes. *Journal of Juvenile Justice, 2,* 76–94.

Peters, A. M. F., & Corrado, R. R. (2014, November 20). *Exploring the utilization of custodial programming among a Canadian sample of incarcerated serious/violent young offenders.* Paper presented at the 70th American Society of Criminology Annual Conference, San Francisco, CA.

Peters, A. M. F., & Corrado, R. R. (2015). *Participation in PLEA's youth justice, addictions, education, and employment programming among serious-violent and mentally disordered young offenders: Profiles and recidivism.* Report submitted to PLEA Community Services, Vancouver, BC.

Ploeger, M. (1997). Youth employment and delinquency: Reconsidering a problematic relationship. *Criminology, 35,* 659–675.

Sampson, R. J., & Laub, J. H. (2005). A life-course view of the development of crime. *Annals of the American Academy of Political and Social Science, 602,* 12–45.

Schaeffer, C. M., Henggeler, S. W., Ford, J. D., Mann, M., Chang, R., & Chapman, J. E. (2014). RCT of a promising vocational/employment program for high-risk juvenile offenders. *Journal of Substance Abuse Treatment, 46*(2), 134–143.

Schroeder, R. D., Giordano, P. C., & Cernkovich, S. A. (2010). Adult child–parent bonds and life course criminality. *Journal of Criminal Justice, 38,* 562–571.

Short, J. F. Jr., Rivera, R., & Tennyson, R. A. (1965). Perceived opportunities, gang membership, and delinquency. *American Sociological Review, 30,* 56–67.

Statistics Canada. (2015, August 7). Labour Force Survey, July 2015. *The Daily.* Retrieved from http://www.statcan.gc.ca/daily-quotidien/150807/dq150807a-eng.htm

Teplin, L. A., Abram, K. M., McClelland, G. M., Mericle, A. A., Dulcan, M. K., & Washburn, J. J. (2006). *Psychiatric disorders of youth in detention.* (NCJ No. 210331). Washington, DC: Office of Juvenile Justice and Delinquency Prevention, US Department of Justice.

Thompson, M., & Uggen, C. (2012). Dealers, thieves, and common determinants of illegal earnings. *Criminology, 50,* 1057–1087.

Tolan, P., Henry, D., Schoeny, M., Bass, A., Lovegrove, P., & Nichols, E. (2013). Mentoring interventions to affect juvenile delinquency and associated problems: A systematic review. *Campbell Systematic Reviews, 10.* doi:10.4073/csr.2013.10

Uggen, C. (2000). Work as a turning point in the life course of criminals: A duration model of age, employment, and recidivism. *American Sociological Review, 67,* 529–546.

Uggen, C., Wakefield, S., & Western, B. (2005). Work and family perspectives on reentry. In J. Travis & C. Visher (Eds.), *Prisoner reentry and crime in America* (pp. 209–243). New York, NY: Cambridge University Press.

Wright, J. P., & Cullen, F. T. (2004). Employment, peers, and lifecourse transitions. *Justice Quarterly, 21,* 183–205. doi:10.1080/07418820400095781

Yessine, A. K., & Bonta, J. (2012). *The offending trajectories of youth probationers from early adolescence to middle adulthood.* Ottawa, ON: National Crime Prevention Centre, Public Safety Canada. Retrieved from https://www.public safety.gc.ca/cnt/rsrcs/pblctns/2012-04-typ/2012-04-typ-eng.pdf

## Statutes Cited

*Youth Criminal Justice Act*, SC 2002, c 1, preamble.

# CHAPTER 9

## Barriers to Community Reintegration
## The Benefits of Client-Centred Case Management and Pre-Employment Skills Training

Ashley Brown

**A**n important component for service providers supporting former prisoners in their successful transition from prison back into the community is the use of evidence-based interventions rooted in the principles of the Risk–Need–Responsivity (RNR) model. This approach has proven valuable in guiding criminal justice employees' safe and effective risk assessments, decision-making and risk-management practices. While the RNR principles have shown reductions in recidivism when applied correctly (Andrews & Bonta, 2006), Crossroads Day Reporting Centre (CDRC) staff in Toronto, Ontario, argue that effective risk management should also pay detailed attention to specific responsivity factors that may act as barriers to service and parolee participation. Further, effective risk management incorporates the use of core correctional practices that highlight the need for positive relationships, pro-social modelling, and an appropriate use of authority. As a re-entry program, it is important to integrate person-centred, strength-based practices that emphasize collaborative and flexible case management processes, and to offer pre-employment training within this framework. These processes help to support the development of positive relationships between staff and former prisoners and encourage the latters' engagement, which is needed to effectively target criminogenic needs and individual risk for reoffending.

## PROMINENT MODELS OF EFFECTIVE CORRECTIONAL INTERVENTION

The RNR model of offender assessment and rehabilitation is an evidence-based model used to guide practitioners in their assessment and treatment of offenders. It is recognized among correctional professionals as an effective model of reintegration (Andrews & Bonta, 1998; Andrews et al., 1990). The RNR model is comprised of three main principles that, if applied as intended, demonstrate reductions in recidivism in the range of 26–30 percent (Andrews et al., 1990; Andrews & Bonta, 2006; Smith, Gendreau, & Swartz, 2009). First, the *risk principle* contends that an individual's recidivism risk can be accurately assessed and used to guide the frequency and intensity of treatment, operating with the assumption that treatment that is proportionate to the individual's level of risk for recidivism will be the most effective (i.e., lower-risk offenders receive less frequent and intensive services, while offenders assessed as higher risk receive the most intensive interventions). The second principle, the *need principle*, states that for programming to have a positive impact on risk, the practitioner should target criminogenic needs (e.g., anti-social attitudes, anti-social peers, and impulsivity) that contribute to the individual's offence cycle and overall likelihood to engage in crime. Lastly, the *responsivity principle* argues that for an offender to truly integrate treatment interventions, these interventions must match his/her identified learning style.

The *responsivity principle* can further be broken down into general and specific responsivity. General responsivity asserts that cognitive behavioural and social learning approaches, such as those found in core correctional practices (e.g., problem solving, pro-social modelling), produce the greatest changes in criminogenic behaviours (Dowden & Andrews, 2004). Specific responsivity, on the other hand, relates to individual factors, such as motivation level, learning disabilities, ethnicity, culture, and gender, that can impact treatment interventions by impeding an individual's ability to meaningfully engage in programming (Bonta & Andrews, 2007). Both general and specific responsivity are central to delivering effective programming and services for former prisoners. While commitment to the RNR principles has demonstrated a reliable reduction in recidivism, it is also important to consider what, if any, additional factors are also present in an individual's decision to desist from crime and meaningfully engage in programming and rehabilitation (Laws & Ward, 2010; Maruna, 2001; Sapouna, Bisset, & Conlong, 2011).

For releasees, helpful working relationships with programming staff and views of staff as encouraging are established important features in psychotherapy and for reducing reoffending (Bachelor & Horvath, 1999; Horvath & Symonds, 1991; Martin, Garske, & Davis, 2000; Shirk & Karver, 2003;

Wampold, 2001). Positive relationships between staff and prison releasees can be particularly advantageous when working with former prisoners who have been mandated to participate in re-entry programming and who therefore already experience limited autonomy in their daily lives (McNeill, Batchelor, Burnett, & Knox, 2005). Research conducted by Trotter (2007) suggests that positive staff characteristics influence individuals involved in the correctional system and may contribute to decreased rates of recidivism. Andrews and Bonta (2006) also emphasized that the relationship principle (e.g., relationships built on warmth, respect, and collaboration), as well as the structuring principle (e.g., appropriate modelling, reinforcement) were essential subcomponents of the RNR model and offender rehabilitation. Further, Andrews and Kiessling (1980) identified five dimensions for effective correctional treatment, later called core correctional practices (see Dowden & Andrews, 2004), which include the effective use of authority, appropriate modelling and reinforcement, problem solving, community resources, and quality of interpersonal relationships. They assert that a positive working relationship is the most influential of all five of these dimensions and must be present for the core correctional practices to be effective.

In a meta-analysis, Dowden and Andrews (2004) examined the impact of core correctional practices and found that not only did the staff's program delivery method affect treatment outcome, but that the therapist's interpersonal style of delivery was also influential. Additionally, the findings suggested that reductions in recidivism were strongest when RNR principles were combined with core correctional practices. Although a positive relationship occurring in isolation is not enough to produce reductions in recidivism (Dowden & Andrews, 2004), a professional relationship founded on sincerity, respect, and fairness is beneficial to both staff and the releasee (Wampold, 2001; Willis, Yates, Gannon, & Ward, 2013). Practising these skills can assist staff to effectively challenge thinking and behaviour, enhance former prisoners' receptiveness to role modelling, increase program retention and, perhaps most importantly, affect the overall outcome of treatment (Bachelor & Horvath, 1999; Bonta & Andrews, 2007; Horvath & Symonds, 1991).

The Good Lives Model (GLM) is another leading theory of offender rehabilitation which offers a strength-based model of prisoner re-entry. GLM is founded on the assertion that all individuals "fashion their lives around their core values and follow some sort of (often implicit) Good Life Plan" (Willis et al., 2013, p. 125). It contends that criminal behaviour occurs as a result of individuals attempting to fulfil specific needs in an inappropriate, harmful, and socially unacceptable way. As a result, GLM is viewed as seeking to assist individuals in achieving these goals pro-socially and, as a result, enhancing both the individual's well-being and their community safety. This model also stresses the respect and dignity of persons receiving support by emphasizing autonomy, each releasee's values, and collaborative goal-setting while minimizing labelling and punitive strategies for treatment (Willis et al., 2013).

Proponents of the Good Lives Model argue that the RNR model, while effective, does not adequately motivate individuals to sincerely participate in treatment or programming (Ward, 2002; Ward & Maruna, 2007). In this context, the RNR model has been criticized for its narrow focus on criminogenic risk and need factors, in the light of which the former prisoner's re-entry and rehabilitation is primarily viewed from a perspective of liability and supervision rather than the former prisoners being seen as individuals who can be positive, contributing members of their communities (Bazemore, 1996; Burnett & Maruna, 2006). Re-entry programs and services can therefore benefit from incorporating elements of both the Risk–Need–Responsivity and Good Lives Model of offender rehabilitation.

## CASE MANAGEMENT AT THE ST. LEONARD'S SOCIETY OF TORONTO'S CROSSROADS DAY REPORTING CENTRE

The Crossroads Day Reporting Centre in Toronto provides former prisoners with case management practices that focus on RNR application, strong therapeutic relationships, and personal strengths. This is fundamental to achieving the agency's overarching goals—to provide support for former prisoners during reintegration, including employment reintegration. The Crossroads Day Reporting Centre serves to assist federally sentenced men and women as they re-enter and subsequently live in the community while on conditional release. Former prisoners access the services of the centre through referrals from their parole officers who feel these individuals would benefit from increased supervision and/or additional support as they work to achieve greater stability and access to resources in the community. For those attending the Crossroads Day Reporting Centre, increased stability can include finding secure employment, safe and affordable housing, and/or access to financial assistance, such as Ontario Works or Ontario Disability Support System. Additionally, some individuals may need support or advocacy in accessing resources, like mental health services, which may prove challenging or even impossible to navigate independently. The goal of Crossroads Day Reporting Centre staff is to maintain the safety of the community by supporting ex-prisoners in their adherence to their parole conditions and to create an individualized case management plan that meets each releasee's unique needs.

That said, a significant portion of individuals receiving services from the Crossroads Day Reporting Centre are part of the population believed to be at a greater risk for recidivism and, thus, are directed to attend the program for additional supervision and support. For example, in the 2013/2014 fiscal year approximately 80 percent of individuals referred to the Crossroads Day Reporting Centre were released into the community on statutory release (SR).[1] This number is significant as prisoners who remain in custody until their statutory release date often are more challenging and higher risk. Indeed, they have not achieved discretionary release types such as day parole and full parole. According to the Review Panel (2007), individuals released on statutory release are more likely

> to have a history of substance abuse, a previous criminal history, a previous negative correctional history (escape, segregation, revocation of parole), low program completion rates and higher levels of imposed residency conditions at release. (p. 109)

Further, former prisoners with an imposed residency condition (i.e., statutory release with residency [SRR]) are considered to be at higher risk of committing serious injury, and actions resulting in the readmission into a federal institution (Grant, Johnson, & Muirhead, 2000). Beyond the high incidence of former prisoners on statutory release, 41 percent of the total Crossroads Day Reporting Centre releasees served during this same time were assessed as moderate/high and high-risk releases (St. Leonard's Society of Toronto, 2014).

It is evident that the majority of former prisoners at the Crossroads Day Reporting Centre present with unique challenges that increase the risk for recidivism. To meet these needs, staff practice an eclectic approach to care and case management that is consistent and includes the RNR model of rehabilitation in combination with a person-centred practice and strength-based approaches. Staff work to create lasting relationships built on trust to gain releasees' attention and respect, as well as to limit barriers to engagement such as frustration and anxiety. These methods not only emphasize individual and community safety, but also highlight the need for strong, positive working relationships and a collaborative process in short- and long-term goal development, all consistent with core correctional practices.

## Case Management
In addition to the RNR model of offender rehabilitation, the Crossroads Day Reporting Centre also follows a strength-based practice that emphasizes principles of individual autonomy, dignity, collaboration, and respect. The

positive impacts of these principles on offender rehabilitation are emphasized within the Good Lives Model discussed above. The Crossroads Day Reporting Centre uses a combination of both the RNR model of offender rehabilitation and strength-based case management similar to the Good Lives Model. Staff believe that safe and effective reintegration requires both the effective monitoring of risk, need, and responsivity, as well as a supportive environment that emphasizes respect and dignity as a means to motivate individuals to participate in programming. Other strength-based approaches to offender rehabilitation, such as those offered by Burnett and Maruna (2006) assert that former prisoners need to be given opportunities to "develop pro-social self-concepts and identity, generally in the form of rewarding work that is helpful to others" (p. 20). The emphasis on positive therapeutic relationships, collaborative goal setting, and the development of positive self-concepts echoed above are important values integrated within Crossroads Day Reporting Centre case management practices.

From the initial stages of involvement and throughout the course of participation, case management strategies focus on the strengths and resources of those referred rather than deficit-based approaches that are problem-focused. Case workers assist their service recipients as they evaluate their internal and external resources, along with other strengths they view as important for their well-being. The challenge they experience in daily life, often tied to criminogenic needs, are not viewed as independent of one another, but are instead seen as interconnected, with each need influencing every other. For example, an individual who committed an offence for financial gain may encounter challenges in securing employment due to a history of job instability and limited education and experience. The releasee may also experience low self-esteem, periods of extreme anxiety, poor problem-solving skills, literacy challenges, and chronic substance use that further affect their ability to find a stable job and to maintain any pro-social change. Here, Crossroads Day Reporting Centre case management practices would address client needs from a holistic perspective that can be divided into several stages, including *Intake/Assessment, Collaboration/Goal Development, Action Plan, Maintenance*, and *Discharge*.

During the initial *Intake/Assessment* phase of case management, time is dedicated to becoming acquainted and building rapport with the referred individual, thereby setting the foundation for a trusting and open relationship. This is accomplished through extensive information gathering, including semi-structured interviews that support the exploration of the former prisoner's expectations, needs, and goals over the course of their participation. The process also assists the individual in becoming familiar with staff and provides an opportunity to ask any questions related to program guide-lines and expectations (Shively & Ulrich, 2014). Core correctional practices should guide each part of this process. Any resistance to programming and support, observed by staff during the *Intake/Assessment* stage of Crossroads Day Reporting Centre involvement, can represent a lack of engagement, inconsistent or nonexistent attendance, and general indifference toward short and long-term goal development. Former prisoners who have been referred to the centre may also be angry that they are expected to attend the program at a pre-established rate of frequency, while others may arrive with ambiva-lence and possess little motivation to engage with staff (Ulrich, Ricciardelli, & Brown, 2012). Such circumstances present additional challenges that staff then have to seek strategies to address.

In the experience of Crossroads Day Reporting Centre staff, this type of resistance is not uncommon among former prisoners involved in mandated programming and who may experience a lack of self-efficacy and autonomy in their lives—a result of years of incarceration. For example, from 2008 to the present day, approximately one-third of all releasees who have received assis-tance from the Crossroads Day Reporting Centre resided at local shelters, with limited financial resources and pro-social family and social supports when released from prison (St. Leonard's Society of Toronto, 2014). Former prisoners face barriers related to their most basic needs when re-entering the community, such as access to food, stable housing, safety, and freedom from fear (Griffiths, Dandurand, & Murdoch, 2007; Taxman, 2004; Young, 2000). These barriers, until successfully addressed, make it more challenging for releasees to adequately focus and engage in other areas of their correctional programming. As such, it is vital that Crossroads Day Reporting Centre staff understand the obstacles former prisoners face, particularly during the ini-tial stages of contact when trust is being developed. In other words, respect for the individual and their opinions is a fundamental value of Crossroads Day Reporting Centre programming. Being respectful includes respecting former prisoners' autonomy and identifying what they feel is most helpful in the reintegration process (see Taxman, 2014; Young, 2000). Empowering the individual to exercise autonomy also means accepting that the client's ideas and values toward programming will not always align with those of the staff. Crossroads Day Reporting Centre staff recognize that, where pos-sible, flexibility can be an important factor in supporting releasees as they re-establish their independence and maintain their progress toward goals (Brown & Ward, 2004).

To exemplify, in 2012 a released prisoner who was participating in the Crossroads Day Reporting Centre program was experiencing challenges balancing both the expectations of his employer to be on-site and perform his required work hours, and those of his correctional plan where he was to provide a sample for urinalysis with little prior notice. For this individual, attempting to meet the expectations of his employer and his parole officer caused a conflict of responsibilities. In this case the individual had been successful in the community for several years and had established a degree of trust and accountability with Crossroads Day Reporting Centre staff and the local parole office. As such, staff felt confident in their ability to advocate on behalf of the individual to the parole office by encouraging the exploration of alternative measures that could meet the individual's needs, as well as the needs of the parole office and the employer. This included reevaluating the frequency of urinalysis testing and proposing increased visual check-ins by Crossroads Day Reporting Centre staff outside of regular office hours to accommodate the individual's work schedule. In this way, the Crossroads Day Reporting Centre's flexibility can reduce some of the frustration and angst a releasee may otherwise feel when confined by rigid program guidelines. It is therefore important for staff to work in partnership with parole officers to ensure clear communication and understanding of the releasee's goals and priorities, as well as to review any staff concerns or safety issues with the individual such as a drug/alcohol-related relapse. Working together as a team, the parole officer, the former prisoner, and the Crossroads Day Reporting Centre staff employ flexibility to meet each party's needs and the obligations of parole.

During the *Collaboration/Goal Development* and *Action* stages of case management, Crossroads Day Reporting Centre staff do not adhere to a one-size-fits-all, prescribed model of care that can limit program flexibility and individualized case plans. The former prisoner's goals are prioritized collaboratively with the premise that engagement must come from a sincere desire to make changes. In addition to RNR principles, motivational interviewing techniques that recognize and resolve resistance to change (Thigpen, Beauclair, Brown, & Guevara, 2012) and trauma-informed practice that acknowledges the importance of safety, choice, and empowerment in care (Benedict, 2014; Bloom, Owen, & Covington, 2005) are also used. This is done to elicit trust, self-determination, and the need to make lasting changes from the releasee's own perspective and drive, especially when working with clients who arrive at the Crossroads Day Reporting Centre ambivalent about their goals or in a pre-contemplative stage of change.

Similarly, the development of an action plan is also a collaborative process in which the releasee can continually renegotiate how and when their goals are achieved (Willis et al., 2013). In an effort to ensure consistency between staff, the needs, goals, and challenges of the former prisoner are discussed between all members of the case management team to solicit feedback and suggestions; this also, of course, assists in avoiding the potential duplication of services. Ongoing communication between all staff involved in the case is viewed as an essential piece of effective case management and community safety promotion. Furthermore, in addition to advocating on the releasee's behalf, Crossroads Day Reporting Centre staff have opportunities to provide updates to other correctional staff regarding any potential changes in the individual's behaviour that may signal an elevation in risk (e.g., recent drug or alcohol use). When an elevation in risk is perceived, the staff make a concerted effort to directly address any identified concerns with the individual, rather than immediately employing a more punitive response (e.g., suspension of parole, revocation of community privileges, or increased restrictions). Staff believe it necessary to first have a sincere, transparent conversation with the releasee about recently made decisions and their potential consequences, as well as how these choices can impact the former prisoner's ability to attain his/her goals. By relying on this type of approach, these situations serve as learning opportunities where the individual is encouraged to generate and explore multiple options for facing future obstacles and gain insight into their own behaviour, rather than immediately facing extreme disciplinary measures.

By the *Maintenance* case management stage, participants have typically demonstrated a certain degree of commitment to working toward their goals. They present as more stable within the community; however, stability is unique to each person and can manifest through a variety of outcomes. This can range from a pattern of parole condition compliance to the development of pro-social supports, to continued involvement in education or volunteer work, a lengthy period of employment, and/or continued abstinence from drugs or alcohol. As a releasee demonstrates increased stability in the community over time, the required frequency of contact with Crossroads Day Reporting Centre staff should gradually decrease. The rate of this decrease is largely determined by the case management team and can be discussed at the request of the parole officer, a Crossroads Day Reporting Centre staff member, or the individual receiving support. For individuals who are deemed to be moderate- to high-risk, periods of stability must be observed over longer periods of time before a decision for reduced contact or a complete discharge can be made. The timeframe for each person is different, based on several factors such as their pattern of criminal history, motivation level, accountability, and other aforementioned stability factors.

A releasee's *Discharge* from the Crossroads Day Reporting program can occur for positive or negative reasons, including if a client has reached his/her warrant expiry date, is considered stable enough to withdraw from support, has been returned to custody for a breach of parole conditions, or is transferred after moving to another jurisdiction. In 2013–2014, approximately 43 percent of individuals receiving support through the Crossroads Day Reporting Centre reached their warrant expiry date, 41 percent returned to custody, 8 percent were transferred to another jurisdiction, and 8 percent were discharged. This division between discharge types has been relatively consistent from year to year and the similarity in numbers between those who return to custody and those who reach their Warrant Expiry Date may be attributed to the higher level of risk and the complex needs of former prisoners referred to the Crossroads Day Reporting Centre. Indeed, a portion of the Crossroads Day Reporting Centre population is referred only after an escalation of risk has already occurred, usually as a means to add increased support or supervision to their case. This occurrence, however, often leads to individuals viewing the Crossroads Day Reporting Centre as a punishment, which can limit their willingness to engage and, unfortunately, create challenges in forming a positive working relationship with staff. Instead, staff are afforded only a short opportunity to meaningfully engage with each former prisoner before any escalation in risk continues and they are returned to custody.

### Pre-Employment Programming

Former prisoners at the Crossroads Day Reporting Centre self-disclose a range of outstanding needs, related to negative associates, unstable housing, continued substance use, or educational issues, to name a few, that impact their ability to successfully reintegrate into the community. Not surprisingly, employment remains the most commonly cited need of CDRC releasees (St. Leonard's Society of Toronto, 2014).[2] The related literature further indicates that the positive association between ex-prisoner reintegration and employment is undeniable—employment is a need after incarceration (Erez, 1987; Gillis, Robinson, & Porporino, 1996; Lipsey, 1995; Visher, Debus & Yahner, 2008). As such, a pre-employment program was initiated at the Crossroads Day Reporting Centre in 2013 to directly address this need area and to examine how staff could best prepare individuals to secure and maintain long-term employment. The pre-employment programming was designed to better educate releasees on employability techniques such as interviewing, networking, resumé development, and problem solving, as well as to provide them with the same level of person-centred support that is offered throughout all stages of Crossroads Day Reporting Centre case management.

From the perspective of staff, it is important to acknowledge that participants' consistent and long-term employment can represent added structure, the potential for safe housing, improved finances, the ease of parole restrictions, reunification with family/children, among many other positive achievements. Unfortunately, a multitude of challenges can preclude former prisoners from securing meaningful employment, such as the use of criminal record screenings, their limited employment history, and/or their impulsivity and poor emotional management skills (Correctional Service Canada, 2007; Griffiths et al., 2007; Young, 2000). For some participants, the direct experience they gain through the program may be their first exposure to employment, or their first exposure to it in many years. As a result, staff at the Crossroads Day Reporting Centre are expected to have an appropriate understanding of the specific responsivity factors that can have an impact on participation and ask questions such as: *Does the participant have an understanding of public transit? How has technology changed over the course of their sentence? How is the participant coping with anxiety after serving a very lengthy sentence?* While these factors may seem inconsequential, they have the potential to profoundly influence an individual's self-esteem and resilience.

Accurately assessing a former prisoner's *readiness* to participate, in addition to their *motivation* to participate, can provide a clearer picture of what type of staff interventions are required (Woodier, 2013; Young, 2000). This includes assessing and targeting his/her needs for more general skills, like communicating, problem solving, and working with numbers (see Latendresse & Cortoni, 2005, p. 2), versus more job-specific training, in, for example, computer literacy or trade-specific skills. For example, when first returning to the community, many former prisoners identify feeling anxious around large crowds or express embarrassment with their lack of familiarity with the progression of technology and limited understanding of smart phones, social media websites, and email. Some releasees fail to understand why most companies now require an online submission for a job application rather than the formerly common method of submitting resumés in person. Thus, assessing for both employment readiness and motivation provides a clearer picture of the person's current state (i.e., are they overwhelmed or comfortable in the community?), as well as their strengths, resources, and areas in need of improvement. Without such assessment and support the ex-prisoner may be set up for disappointment and frustration, particularly given the immediate expectations they are under to find and maintain employment—even if they are not yet ready or able to sustain said employment. As such, and in line with the aforementioned core correctional practice, it is important to assist former prisoners in identifying available tools and resources in support of their goals and in strengthening skills that better prepare them to anticipate and deal with unexpected obstacles.

Program flexibility and ongoing staff support are also essential for the participants' success and the pre-employment/employment support program in general. Program flexibility was established by having employers and policies that could easily adapt to parole expectations, such as providing time off for urinalysis provisions, as previously discussed, or for attendance at mandatory programming (e.g., anger management). Crossroads Day Reporting Centre staff felt that incorporating flexible policies and practices would provide the client with more latitude in meeting other aspects of his/her correctional plan. In the past, staff have witnessed clients unable to attain jobs or quickly lose newly acquired employment due to being unprepared for employment either in light of needs tied to re-entry generally, or to employment specifically. Adaptability in this area was considered crucial for reducing client frustration and preventing unnecessary obstacles for maintaining employment. In addition, it has been found that difficulties with impulsivity or poor problem-solving skills can impede client success (Andrews & Bonta, 2006). The hope is that with ongoing support and direct employer contact, staff can assist clients by providing feedback on behaviour (as evaluated by employer), helping them learn new coping strategies, and encouraging them to generate solutions to emergent workplace challenges.

Stable, long-term employment provides many benefits, such as financial security, responsibility, a sense of agency and belonging, and increased social capital (Bierens & Carvalho, 2011; Gillis et al., 1996; Eley, 2007; Graffam, Shinkfield, Lavelle, & Hardcastle, 2004; Sapouna et al., 2011). Former prisoners enrolled in the pre-employment program are placed in a work environment where the employer understands that the client may have periods when she or he struggles to apply their newly acquired skills. Through this programming, clients can benefit from trial and error as they cultivate skills without the fear of reprimand found in traditional work environments. With more opportunities to experiment safely, clients can become more comfortable and independent in fulfilling their responsibilities and taking chances. In addition, there is the prospect that the client can begin to combat unemployment and underemployment by obtaining recent job references and continually building on their experiences. The pre-employment program seeks to not only engage employers to remove the stigma of a criminal past, but to also provide Crossroads Day Reporting Centre service users with the best possible opportunity for future success.

## CONCLUSION

Providing effective services and support to individuals accessing services through the Crossroads Day Reporting Centre, particularly those with complex and extensive needs, can pose many challenges for service professionals. These challenges include a lack of client engagement, rigid program guidelines, poor client attendance, and limited access to community resources. A lack of self-determination and agency, which is too often experienced by former prisoners, may further complicate individuals' re-entry and relationships with their service provider (Willis et al., 2013; Taxman, 2004). Establishing positive working relationships alongside individualized and collaborative programs designed to respond to the unique needs of clients should go far toward securing client involvement in their programming (Bonta & Andrews, 2007; Willis et al., 2013) and strengthening their overall resiliency to daily challenges.

Crossroads Day Reporting Centre staff believe client-centred case management that aims to reduce program barriers and focus on individuals' strengths and resources is an important complement to correctional supervision, particularly within the RNR model of offender rehabilitation. By adhering to such practices, former prisoners can have improved opportunities for successful community re-entry. Access to employment remains a primary need for those using Crossroads Day Reporting Centre support and a significant factor in achieving community stability for those reintegrating into the community. It is therefore argued that positioning the outlined program values and practices within pre-employment programming can be helpful in supporting former prisoners as they strive to strengthen their employability skills.

## NOTES

1  Statutory release is a mandatory release by law, after the individual serves two-thirds of their sentence. This does not apply to those serving a life or indeterminate sentence. Statutory release can be revoked and the individual returned to jail if they do not abide by their conditions of release (Department of Justice, 2012).

2  A CDRC referral may be considered "unseen" or "pending" if the former prisoner experiences a parole revocation prior to attending the program, is transferred to a jurisdiction outside Toronto, ON, or has not yet been released to the community from the institution. Eleven percent of the 2014 caseload fell into this classification.

## REFERENCES

Andrews, D. A., & Bonta, J. (1998). *The psychology of criminal conduct* (2nd ed.). Cincinnati, OH: Anderson.

Andrews, D. A., & Bonta, J. (2006). *The psychology of criminal conduct* (4th ed.). Newark, NJ: LexisNexis.

Andrews, D. A., & Carvell, C. (1998). *Core correctional treatment—Core correctional supervision and counseling: Theory, research, assessment and practice.* Ottawa, ON: Carleton University.

Andrews, D. A., & Kiessling, J. (1980). Program structure and effective correctional-practices: A summary of the CaVIC research. In R. Ross & P. Gendreau (Eds.), *Effective correctional treatment* (pp. 439–463). Toronto, ON: Butterworth.

Andrews, D. A., Zinger, I., Hoge, R. D., Bonta, J., Gendreau, P., & Cullen, F. T. (1990). Does correctional treatment work? A clinically relevant and psychologically informed meta-analysis. *Criminology, 28*(3), 369–404.

Bachelor, A., & Horvath, A. (1999). The therapeutic relationship. In M. A. Hubble, B. L. Duncan, & S. D. Miller (Eds.), *The heart and soul of change: What works in therapy.* Washington, DC: American Psychological Association.

Bazemore, G. (1996). Three paradigms for juvenile justice. In J. Hudson and B. Galaway (Ed.), *Restorative Justice: International Perspectives.* Monsey, NY: Criminal Justice Press.

Benedict, A. (2014). Using trauma-informed practices to enhance safety and security in women's correctional facilities. *National Resource Center on Justice Involved Women.* Retrieved from http://cjinvolvedwomen.org/wp-content/uploads/2015/09/Using-Trauma-Informed-Practices-Apr-14.pdf

Bierens, H. J., & Carvalho, J. R. (2011) Job search, conditional treatment and recidivism: The employment services for ex-offenders program reconsidered. *Journal of Economic Analysis & Policy, 11*(1), 1–38.

Bloom, B. E., Owen, B. A., & Covington, S. (2005). *Gender-responsive strategies for women offenders: A summary of research, practice, and guiding principles for women offenders.* Washington, DC: US Department of Justice, National Institute of Corrections. Retrieved from: http://nicic.gov/library/020418

Bonta, J., & Andrews, D. A. (2007). Risk–need–responsivity model for offender assessment and rehabilitation. *Rehabilitation, 6,* 1–22.

Brown, M., & Ward, T. (2004). The good lives model and conceptual issues in offender rehabilitation. *Psychology, Crime & Law, 10*(3), 243–257.

Burnett, R., & Maruna, S. (2006) The kindness of prisoners: Strength-based resettlement in theory and in action, *Criminology and Criminal Justice, 6*(1), 83–106.

Correctional Service Canada. (2007). *Glube and panel recommendation review.* Ottawa, ON. Retrieved from http://www.csc-scc.gc.ca/publications/005007-9008-eng.shtml.

CSC Review Panel. (2007). *A roadmap to strengthening public safety.* Ottawa, ON: Minister of Public Works and Government Services Canada, Government of Canada.

Department of Justice. (2012). *Statutory release.* Ottawa, ON: Ministry of Public Safety and Solicitor General, Government of Canada. Retrieved from http://www.victimsinfo.ca/en/after-sentencing/offender-release/statutory-release

Dowden, C., & Andrews, A. D. (2004). The importance of staff practice in delivering effective correctional treatment: A meta-analytic review of core correctional practice. *International Journal of Offender Therapy and Comparative Criminology, 48*(203), 203–214.

Eley, S. (2007). Job searching with a history of drugs and crime. *Howard Journal, 46*(2), 162–175.

Erez, E. (1987). Rehabilitation in justice: The prisoner's perspective. *Journal of Offender Counselling, Services and Rehabilitation, 11*(2), 5–19.

Gillis, C., Robinson, D., & Porporino, F. (1996). Inmate employment: The increasingly influential role of generic work skills. *Forum on Corrections Research, 8*(1), 18–20.

Graffam, J., Shinkfield, A., Lavelle, B., & Hardcastle, L. (2004). *Attitudes of employers, corrective services workers, employment support workers, and prisoners and offenders towards employing ex-prisoners and ex-offenders.* Victoria, Australia: Deakin University.

Grant, A. B., Johnson, L. S., & Muirhead, M. (2000). *Use of the residency condition with statutory release: A descriptive analysis.* Ottawa, ON: Research Branch, Correctional Service of Canada.

Griffiths, C., T., Dandurand, Y., & Murdoch, D. (2007). *The social reintegration of offenders and crime prevention.* Ottawa, ON: Public Safety Canada.

Horvath, A. O., & Symonds, B. D. (1991). Relation between working alliance and outcome in psychotherapy: A meta-analysis. *Journal of Counselling Psychology, 38*(2), 139–149.

Latendresse, M., & Cortoni, F. (2005). *Increasing employability related skills among federal male offenders: A preliminary analysis of the National Employability Skills Program.* Ottawa, ON: Research Branch, Correctional Service Canada.

Laws, D. R., & Ward, T. (2010). *Desistance and sexual offending: Alternatives to throwing away the keys.* New York, NY: Guilford Press.

Lipsey, M. (1995). What do we learn from 400 research studies on the effectiveness of treatment with juvenile delinquents? In J. McGuire (Ed.), *What works: Reducing Reoffending—Guidelines from Research and Practice* (pp. 63–78). Chichester, UK: John Wiley and Sons.

Martin, D. J., Garske, J. P., & Davis M. K. (2000). Relation of the therapeutic alliance with outcome and other variables: A meta-analytic review. *Journal of Consulting Clinical Psychology, 68*(3), 438–450.

Maruna, S. (2001) *Making good: How ex-convicts reform and rebuild their lives.* Washington, DC: American Psychological Association.

McNeill, F., Batchelor, S., Burnett, R., & Knox, J. (2005). *21st century social work: Reducing reoffending—key practice skills* (pp. 1–16). Edinburgh, UK: Scottish Executive.

Sapouna, M., Bisset, C., & Conlong, A-M. (2011). What works to reduce reoffending: A summary of the evidence. Edinburgh, UK: Justice Analytical Services, Scottish Government. Retrieved from http://www.gov.scot/Resource/0038/00385880.pdf

Shirk, S. R., & Karver, M. (2003). Predictions of treatment outcomes from relationship variables in child and adolescent psychotherapy: A meta-analytic review. *Journal of Consulting and Clinical Psychology, 71,* 452–464.

Shively, R., & Ulrich, M. (2014). The importance of relationship in working with clients. *Journal of Community Corrections, 23*(2), 9–14.

Smith, P., Gendreau, P., & Swartz, K. (2009). Validating the principles of effective intervention: A systematic review of the contributions of meta-analysis in the field of corrections. *Victims & Offenders, 4*(2), 148–169.

St. Leonard's Society of Toronto. (2014). *Crossroads Day Reporting Centre Annual Report. 2013–2014 Annual Report.* Toronto, ON: Author.

Taxman, F. S. (2004). The offender and reentry: Supporting active participation in reintegration. *Federal Probation, 68*(2), 31–35.

Thigpen, M. L., Beauclair, M., J., Brown. R., & Guevara, M. (2012). *Motivational interviewing in corrections: A comprehensive guide to implementing MI in corrections.* Washington, DC: National Institute of Corrections.

Trotter, C. (2007). Parole and probation, *What Works with Women Offenders* (pp.124–141). Cullompton, UK: Willan Publishing.

Ulrich, M. S., Ricciardelli, R., & Brown, A. (2012). Offender rehabilitation: Toward an understanding of the therapeutic alliance in successful transition and reintegration efforts—The Crossroads Day Reporting Centre Experience. *Journal of Community Corrections, 21*(4), 4–11.

Visher, C., Debus, S., & Yahner, J. (2008). Employment after prison: A longitudinal study of releasees in three states. *Urban Institute: Justice Police Center.* Retrieved from http://www.urban.org/sites/default/files/alfresco/publication -pdfs/411778-Employment-after-Prison-A-Longitudinal-Study-of-Releasees -in-Three-States.PDF

Wampold, B. E. (2001). *The great psychotherapy debate: Models, methods, and findings.* Mahwah, NJ: Erlbaum.

Ward, T. (2002). Good lives and the rehabilitation of offenders: Promises and problems.*Aggression and Violent Behavior, 7*(5), 513–528.

Ward, T., & Maruna, S. (2007) *Rehabilitation: Beyond the risk paradigm.* London, UK: Routledge.

Willis, G. M., Yates, P. M., Gannon, T. A., & Ward, T. (2013). How to integrate the Good Lives Model into treatment programs for sexual offending: An introduction and overview. *Sexual Abuse, 25*(2), 123–142.

Woodier, N. (2013). *Employment, reintegration and reducing re-offending resettlement within Europe. EuroVista, 2*(3), 132–141.

Young, N. K. (2000). *Integrating substance abuse treatment and vocational services: Treatment improvement protocol (TIP) series.* Rockville, MD: Substance Abuse and Mental Health Services Administration, Center for Substance Abuse Treatment. Retrieved from http://adaiclearinghouse.org/downloads/ TIP-38-Integrating-Substance-Abuse-Treatment-and-Vocational-Services-56 .pdf

# Section IV

The Employment Reintegration of Unique Populations

# CHAPTER 10

# "Between a Rock and Hard Place"
## How Being a "Convict" Hinders Finding Work in the Neo-Liberal, Late-Capitalist Economy

Dale C. Spencer

## INTRODUCTION

T he brunt of the precarity induced by late capitalism and the brutal effects of neo-liberal reason on the workplace, politics, and culture are most felt by the homeless in contemporary post-industrial cities. Criminalized and undereducated, the homeless struggle to find work and flourish. Drawing on 70 in-depth life-story interviews with homeless males in Winnipeg, Manitoba, and Chicago, Illinois, I examine the struggles of formerly incarcerated men to find work in the post-industrial economy. Within the context of neo-liberal revision of society and late capitalism, I consider the impact of incarceration on these men. I probe how homeless males perceive the mark of a criminal record and the challenges of living on the streets after release while trying to find meaningful, long-term work. I explore their levels of education, vocational training, and past employment and how each of these influences their ability to transition from the streets to work. Specifically, I analyze how these men interpret both the institutional and community-based responses to their plight and how they see the effectiveness of the programs. Finally, based on the insights gained through these men's narratives, I offer suggestions for future reintegration efforts for men that have seemingly been unable to successfully reintegrate into society.

This chapter is structured in four main sections. In the first, I probe the nexus between post-industrial capitalism, neo-liberalism, and incarceration.

The second section briefly reviews the literature on employment and reintegration, while in the third I offer an overview of the methods of this study.
The final section elucidates how the participants' criminal record affects their
ability to find meaningful, long-term work, their transition out of homelessness, and their evaluation of programs aimed at finding them education,
housing, and work.

## THE RUB: LATE CAPITALISM, NEO-LIBERALISM AND PRECARIOUS LABOUR

In the period following WW II, numerous debates have taken place over the
evolution of capitalism, its unparalleled global reach, and the move from
production to consumption as the primary mode of social organization (e.g.,
Bell, 1976; Deleuze & Guattari, 1987; Jameson, 1992; Lash & Urry, 1993).
Lash and Urry (1993) note a change in capitalism from an organized Fordist
division of labour to a post-Fordist knowledge economy. They characterize
this development as an "informationalization," both in terms of the labour
process and in terms of what is produced.

   This shift to late capitalism did not come without significant social and
economic ramifications. As eloquently put by Bauman (2003), "For something to be created, something else must be consigned to waste" (p. 21).
The solidities of the production economies and the routinization of labour
associated with factory life (Bauman, 2000; Sennett, 2011) have in some cases
corroded, while in other cases, the types of jobs associated with this work
have been relocated to the Global South. The reasonably well-paying, low-
skilled jobs associated with the Fordist mass production model[1] have been
greatly diminished.

   Since the 1970s, the political economic philosophy of neo-liberalism
has swept across the globe. Neo-liberalism is generally regarded as enacting
an aggregate of economic policies that align with its sacrosanct axiom of
affirming and defending free markets. This includes, but is not limited to,
changes oriented to the following: the deregulation of industries and capital
flows; drastic reduction in welfare state provisions and protections for the
poor; privatization and outsourcing of public goods, including education,
parks, postal services, roads, social welfare, prisons, and militaries (Berlant,
2011; Connolly, 2013). Neo-liberalism is not just signified by a change in
government policies and social programs, but is marked by a widespread shift
in understandings of government and self-governance (see Rose, 1999). For
Brown (2015), as a "normative order of reason developed over three decades
into a widely and deeply disseminated governing rationality, neo-liberalism
transmogrifies every human domain and endeavour along with humans

themselves, according to a specific image of the economic" (pp. 9–10). The citizen is transformed into *homo economicus*, where their labour is no longer merely a figure of exchange, but takes shape as human capital seeking to strengthen its competitive positioning and appreciate its value. That is, in order to stay competitive and survive in the late-capitalist economy, citizens must continuously train and (re)educate to be of worth in current and potential labour markets. To challenge the discourse related to neo-liberalism is to challenge the contemporary doxa of the inviolability of the market (see Bourdieu, 2010).

Such market-driven conditions are none too kind to abject populations. The situation is particularly acute for homeless, formerly incarcerated populations. Rather than just facing the stigma and challenges of reintegration (see below), homeless, formerly incarcerated persons face the double pincer of conditions associated with late capitalism and neo-liberalism that, as a political economic governance regime, is brutally opposed to providing "handouts" to the poor. To quote Bauman (2003) once more, the "society of consumers has no room for flawed, incomplete, unfulfilled consumers" (p. 14); said another way, the homeless body is not valued because its bearer does not participate in the economy. The disenfranchised possess insufficient levels of cultural, social, and intellectual capital to participate in well-paid occupations and, in many cases, have forms of negative social capital through their adversarial relationships to criminal justice institutions and embeddedness in ethnically marginalized communities (Portes, 2014; Wacquant, 1998). In addition, as abject bodies, the homeless face manifold forms of regulation and violence in their everyday lives and lack the protections accorded to housed citizens by virtue of being homeless (Huey, 2012). On the other hand, the criminalization of the homeless population is predicated on homelessness as a "moral pestilence" that upsets the smooth operation of consumption and social order (Bauman, 2000, 2003). Homeless populations are pushed to the margins of neo-liberal cities in the name of, *inter alia*, public health and safety, gentrification, order, and civility.

In relation to those most vulnerable to the double pincer of late capitalism and neo-liberalism, the problem lies in the decrease in job security. This induces precarity, a condition of existence that is marked by a lack of material security due to underemployment (Wacquant, 2001a, 2014). Precarity, to echo Bourdieu (2010), is "now everywhere" (p. 149). Precarity is found in both the private and public sectors, and has increased the volume of temporary, part-time, and casual positions in Canada (Vosko, 2006) and other Western nations (Bauman, 2000). Freed from the labour restrictions of the welfare era, employers are also able to reach out to an ever-increasing number of temporary labour organizations and avoid having to go through the "messy" work of hiring workers. Homeless males, like those in this study, fill the rank and file of this precarious labour force, if they are able to find work at all. As will be shown, this is particularly problematic as precarious forms of labour are low paying and offer little way for already vulnerable homeless males to escape the streets.

## REINTEGRATION, EMPLOYMENT, AND HOMELESSNESS

It is uncontroversial to suggest that the punishment of offenders has cascading effects. Individuals convicted and sentenced for crimes face the hardships related to separation from their families and communities and the harsh perils of surviving incarceration (Ricciardelli, 2014). The spouses or partners and families of prisoners suffer from lost intimacy and emotional support and reduced income (Clear, 2009; Mauer & Chesney-Lind, 2003; Murray, 2007). These cascading effects of incarceration do not begin and end with incarceration. Rather, the mark of incarceration and related forms of marginalization continue for the considerable majority of former prisoners, well after they are released from custody.

The dire view is that for a former prisoner on parole or on probation, a return to society is almost impossible and a return to prison almost certain (Bauman, 2003). For Garland (2001), the "interests of convicted offenders, insofar as they are considered at all, are viewed as fundamentally opposed to those of the public" (p. 180). While this view may be hyperbolic (and unsubstantiated; see Hutchinson, 2006), scholars have suggested a multitude of challenges in reintegrating parolees with their families and communities. Several "collateral" consequences tied to the cycling of parolees in and out of the community, including community cohesion and social disorganization, work and economic well-being, family matters, mental and physical health, political alienation, and housing and homelessness have been identified (Brisman, 2003; Clear, 2009; Hagan & Dinovitzer, 1999; Mauer & Chesney-Lind, 2003; Murray, 2007). These challenges are further complicated by the racialization of incarceration in the United States and Canada (Bracken, Deane, & Morrissette, 2009; Tonry, 2012), where disadvantaged childhoods, unstable home lives, bad educations, and lack of employable skills contribute to conflict with the law in the first place.

In some American states, former prisoners can apply to have their records expunged; in Canada, former offenders can apply for a record suspension (formerly known as a pardon).[2] Despite this fact, few individuals with criminal records make an application for these formal forms of forgiveness

(Ruddell & Winfree, 2006). The paperwork-intensive process of receiving a record suspension is often described as overwhelming and difficult (see State Appellate Defender, 2015). As such, the mark of a criminal record (and loss of civil rights; Miller & Spillane, 2012) sticks to offenders in Canada much as they do in the United States. The experience of imprisonment is inscribed on the body well after leaving prisons (Moran, 2012) and despite aims to overwrite these inscriptions, the mark of "convict" follows formerly incarcerated men (Miller, 2014; Tica & Roth, 2012). Status degradation continues well after their release and the necessary rituals for reintegration are wholly lacking (Maruna, 2011). As Tonry (1995, 2012) has shown time and again, such, primarily racialized,[3] males become subject to disproportionate criminal justice interventions and poor management regimes in urban centres (see also Miller 2014; Wacquant 1998, 2001a, 2001b, 2009).

While legislation and types of policies regarding rehabilitation and reintegration vary between the United States and Canada (based on federal, state, and provincial dispositions; see Maruna, Immarigeon, & Lebel, 2013; Petersilia, 2001; Ruddell & Winfree, 2006; Wormith et al., 2007), it is particularly salient to recognize that policy does not always translate into ground-level practice (see Meyer & O'Malley, 2005). That is, the messy actualities of former prisoners' attempts to reintegrate and find employment in neo-liberal late capitalism merit an exploration of their own. In this chapter, I respond to this need by examining these actualities as an ongoing process rather than a final end. My contribution offers an account of the lives of homeless, formerly incarcerated men and their attempts to get back on their proverbial feet. Findings suggest that some former prisoners see their incarceration as insignificant or "normal," while others see it as utterly crippling.

In addition, and perhaps most notably, it is imperative that attention be paid to the broader social, cultural and economic context in which men are attempting to reintegrate and find work. Lastly, attention to the broader context allows for an acknowledgement of the gender differences in terms of access to resources in the community (Hannah-Moffat, 2004) and the reality that adult men are, primarily, the face of homelessness in Canada and the United States (Gaetz, Donaldson, & Gullver, 2013; Henry, Cortes, & Morris, 2013). Adult males arguably face a harsher reality than their female counterparts as a result of the lack of resources specifically for formerly incarcerated men in the community and society's mental disposition of conjoining dangerousness with this group (see Miller, 1996; Spohn & Holleran, 2000; Tator & Henry, 2006).

## METHOD

Between April 2013 and April 2014, 70 semi-structured interviews were conducted in Winnipeg, Manitoba, and Chicago, Illinois, with adult males who were patrons of local drop-in centres and homeless shelters or clients of housing organizations dedicated to aiding marginalized and homeless people. Inclusion criteria for this study consisted of being a homeless or underhoused adult male at the time of the interview and a patron of the drop-in centres and/or homeless shelters in Winnipeg or Chicago. Winnipeg and Chicago were chosen as cases qua sites for data collection for three main reasons. First, at the time of the interviews both Winnipeg and Chicago had the highest number of murders in major cities in their respective countries, suggesting they constituted "violent" cities. Second, they both had high levels of homelessness at the time of the interviews and still do today, particularly among their respective marginalized populations (Gaetz et al., 2013; Henry et al., 2013; Goudie & Markoff, 2015). Third, both cities have passed ordinances that ban panhandling and other laws discriminating against homeless people; laws evincing the view of homeless persons as a blight on the city (Bowen, 2012; Graser, 2000).

Participants' ages ranged between 16 and 65 (with a mean age of 41). Interviewees in Winnipeg identified as Canadian (12), Indigenous (18—including self-identification as Aboriginal, Native, Metis, Ojibwe, and Cree), Scottish (1), British (1), Zimbabwean Canadian (1), and Nigerian (1). Interviewees in Chicago identified as African American (26), Black (3), American (3), Hungarian Gypsy (1), American Indian (1), White (1), and one respondent did not want to state his ethnic background. At the time of the interview, 48 self-reported being single and 22 were in a relationship with a woman. Two self-identified as gay, one as bisexual, and two did not want to state their sexuality. Further, 38 men were fathers. A majority of the males in this study had criminal records (n=62),[4] with convictions ranging from drug trafficking to assault and aggravated assault.

The interviews' foci were intentionally wide-ranging and covered topics including experiences of homelessness, (un)employment, violence, and exclusion. Interviewees were asked about social assistance, their social networks, people important to them, and substance use patterns, including both drugs and alcohol. Several questions focused on their engagements with and experiences of violence and victimization. In addition, interviewees were asked about their perceptions of their health and whether they had been diagnosed with some physical or mental health problems. The interviews were digitally voice recorded and ranged from 25 to 90 minutes in length, averaging 45 minutes. Pseudonyms were assigned to all participants, who also received an honorarium as a thank-you for their time and willingness to participate.

In approaching interview data my concerns rested with *what* respondents said as much as *how* they said it. I listened to the interviews and read the transcribed interviews multiple times. At points, I returned to the audio version of the interview to note how respondents voiced their words and concerns. This mattered insofar as homeless males' responses to particular questions, at times, involve inflections that highlighted moments where they emphasized certain aspects of their experiences of the streets (raising their voices) or hesitancies in their response. Interviews were transcribed verbatim and transcripts were thematically coded (Charmaz, 2014; Flick, 2014; Marshall & Rossman, 2011). I engaged in further analysis through a critical hermeneutic approach (Gadamer, 2004) to the coded themes that often involved moving between interviewees' narratives and the quoted theme to understand how the "parts" fit within the "whole" (see Freeman, 2011; Schwandt, 1999). Particular attention is paid to how homeless men with criminal records narrate their struggles to find work and attempts to form alternative identities to their criminalized self.

## TRYING TO FIND AND KEEP WORK AS A "CRIMINAL"

Both time in prison and modest to poor educational backgrounds among the racialized men in this study made it extremely difficult for them to find work. This was combined with limited availability of full-time low-skilled jobs[5] and inadequate training and education programs available to these men. This finding echoes the work done by Trimbur (2013) in New York who avers that "anti-black racism in employment procedures and the lack of existing wage labour combine to limit the availability of adequate work for young men of colour" (p. 20). For most of these men, pursuing alternative means of income, through criminalized activities like drug trafficking, was seen as a last resort, as most were trying to get their lives "back on track." This is not to say that the men in the present study did not engage in such criminalized activities, especially when they needed to eat, but getting "on track" meant actively seeking paid "legitimate" work—exposing oneself to all the pain, anguish, and rejection related to job searches and modes of subjectification (Butler, 1990; Foucault, 1990) associated with participation in the neo-liberal late-capitalist economy. As a mode of subjection, the applicant, the homeless male in this case, is subjected to the norms of the market and must refashion himself as a suitable worker. Here I analyze how (primarily) racialized men with criminal records try to transfigure themselves into suitable workers and the broader forces that stand against such attempts. As much as homeless males are (re)socialized into street life (Arrigo, 1999), said processes are countered by the continual "pull" to life off of the streets, into "normalcy." This pull is evidenced in their attempts to get their lives in "order." Specifically, as I will demonstrate, modes of survival on the streets and modes of "normal" work life in the neo-liberal, post-industrial economy become intertwined in the men's narratives and provide a glimpse into the difficulties in finding work with a criminal record.

## Running into Barriers

The homeless men in this study encountered numerous barriers to obtaining and sustaining legitimate, long-term work, which are personal and broader, more structural in nature. At the extreme end, this is limited to obtaining work through temporary labour agencies:

> Finn: Shittiest fuckin' thing I've ever done was work for a temp agency. Shitty ... shitty man, they take like ... you make, let's see they'll put you at like 12 an hour ... sometimes you work a whole week, sometimes not, and be expecting, at most, after deductions, $376.
>
> Dale: Yeah, so they're skimming off the top of your, your paycheque, is what you're telling me?
>
> Finn: Well, especially if you use their things, if you use their equipment and you don't have equipment, they garnish it hard, especially if you don't have a way to get there that comes off your cheque, so yeah it's your, it's your issue if you don't have the tools and you have the fare or the way to get there, they get more of your money ... they take like 50 bucks for them finding you a job, oh because they found it for you they're taking this much, oh and then you got to pay into fuckin' what CPP, EI, shit like that.

Finn explains how temporary labour corporations, working as an intermediary between workers and employers, both underpay him and gratuitously deduct fees from his paycheque. The move towards temporary labour is part and parcel of the neo-liberal "flexibilization" of labour markets and employment strategies across the globe (Coyle, 2005; Fraser, 2003; Barbieri & Scherer 2009; Purcell 1998). With very few options at their disposal, men with criminal records too often must subject themselves to the exploitation associated with selling their labour to temporary labour corporations. This type of work is irregular and, as homeless males explain, they could show up, wait three hours, only to not be given any work. The net result of working for temporary labour corporations for men with criminal records is a high level of precarity and an income that is insufficient to exit life on the streets.

There is also the contextual basis for men not being able to put their proverbial best foot forward. This basis is beyond the practical limitations of having neither a permanent address to place on job applications nor adequate dress, and it is based on the nature of homelessness and street life more broadly. With few exceptions, the shelters require men to take their belongings with them when they leave the shelters in the morning, sometimes as early as 5 a.m. Paul and Calvin suggest this presents a number of problems:

> Paul:    See, you know most jobs, they won't, I don't think they would want to hire you. No, most of them wouldn't want to hire you because if a person sees that you are lugging stuff around, they are going to be thinking to themselves: "Is this guy homeless? This guy is like a hoarder."
>
> Calvin:  For people staying in shelters, I say one big thing is where do they put their stuff? You show up to work with a duffle bag and backpack, you can't be carrying that stuff around on the job site. There is no washer or dryer here. This is very problematic, especially no washer and dryer, if you are working it could be three weeks before you get paid and you will be wearing the same clothes every day. Where are you going to wash your clothes if you ain't got no money?

Paul's view reflects the generalized disposition towards the homeless that are carrying everything they own with them. Like the hobo of the turn of the 20th century (Anderson, 1923), they are met with suspicion, having some compulsive disorder that separates them from the norm. The carrying of belongings to and from work without anywhere to put them, as shown in Calvin's words, also presents particular problems for men trying to sustain employment. The presentation of self required in late-capitalist workplaces is of a worker who is fast, lean, and nimble (Moody, 1997), unhampered by carrying around all their worldly possessions. It also requires a self that is kempt and reflective of the brand that the corporation is trying to convey, which is fundamentally at odds with the difficulties tied to staying in shelters, such as limited access to a washer and dryer, and associated financial hardships.

At the same time, while the physical conditions of shelters hinder men's capacities to find and sustain work, the types of work available to men without a high school diploma and/or prior work experience are restricted. While these barriers force these men to work under particular conditions, physical limitations can contravene their efforts to work:

> John: I could lay carpet, I worked in a carpet complex for four years, and I've had good jobs. But certain types of jobs you know, you got to take a physical, and they found that my physical capabilities was, concerning my eyes, they don't want to take the risk. They don't want to take the risk; I mean I can't see out of this, I've got one eye …

Here John explains how his impaired vision is refigured as a risk. As a result of this physical disability, he, by extension, is constituted as a "risk" to potential employers. John confides that since his loss of vision he has been continuously deemed unemployable and a liability to potential employers. The effect of this discrimination is that any impairment in the neo-liberal flexible economy can be refigured as a risk, including an applicant's physical and mental disabilities. This is particularly acute among persons with criminal records, as their mental and physical disabilities are another risk factor that makes them unemployable (see Harding, 2003; Todd, 2004; Western, Kling, & Weiman, 2001).

## Risk, Insurance, and Security

Within the neo-liberal landscape, the management of risk associated with crime is placed on individuals and institutions (Beck, 1992; Garland, 2003). In relation to the latter, Ericson (2007) argues that the "vast majority of crimes are defined and responded to through the internal mechanisms of institutions other than criminal justice" (p. 2). Families, schools, healthcare, business enterprises, and insurance employ their own particular disposition to criminalization "based on its own private justice system and mobilization of the surveillant assemblage" (Ericson, 2007, p. 2). This is to say that in neo-liberal late capitalism, institutions must now manage their own risk of crime and criminal victimization and are linked into complex security networks that intensify the level of monitoring of crime. One area in which high levels of risk management and monitoring takes place is the nexus of insurance and business enterprises.

Carol Heimer (2003) has argued that insurers are moral actors and that "insurance works on both insurer and policy holder" (p. 298). Insurers discipline policy-makers through a series of mechanisms "that create communities of fate (e.g., through deductibles), make recovery contingent on attempts to reduce the magnitude of losses …, employ the services of third-party enforcers … and routinize the practices that insurers favour" (Heimer, 2003, p. 298). As such, governing bodies shape and control citizens and corporations by defining types of people and practices as either normal and acceptable, or as deviant and, therefore, unacceptable. In relation to the latter, hiring practices are refigured by insurance corporations as sites of control where particular types of people are constituted as risky and, therefore, not hireable. Consider Andrew's reflection on having a substance abuse charge and on the attendant struggle to acquire work despite having job skills:

Dale:     So you've got a lot of jobs skills, it's just a matter of getting in?

Andrew:   It's just a matter of connecting, okay, then I have a felony you know, the felony thing is there ... and what happens is I guess it depends on who you working for. And it's just because they see it, not so much is that they use it against you, it's just because it's there, uh, Chicago's a big thing on this insurance industry, so a lot of jobs won't even, won't touch you.... Well, say like if it's at the airport. It used to be if you had a record, you know and you just was cleared, so I mean yeah you could work at that airport, but now if you even, if it comes up, they won't touch you.

Dale:     Because of insurance?

Andrew:   The insurance companies pretty much telling employers if you got somebody that's a convict working for you, then uh ... they ... then uh ... that's going to be a liability to you.... Because I got the uh substance abuse charge, and this, this 13 years ago. And he's holding that against me, so therefore they ain't going to touch me ...

Andrew describes how he is blocked from employment at the airport through a chain of responsibilization that is inherent to the neo-liberal, late-capitalist economy. This concatenation is complemented by surveillance networks that allow employers to monitor and block employees with criminal records. Such information acts as a veritable shibboleth, where past criminal records, however minor, restrict access to employment. Without insurance the worker is translated into a liability, which is intolerable in risk-averse environments. The use of "touch" here is also particularly apt. The refusal to touch the former prisoner always implies an assertion of what the formerly incarcerated person is and what he is not yet, or will become. He is then coded not as a discrete person full of other potentialities (with skills and aptitudes), but instead is coded within a series of classifications that society must not touch. He is always *becoming criminal* through classifications based on his past transgressions of the law. Building on this concept, in the next section, I turn to consider the process of becoming criminal that so inhibits homeless males from becoming employed and reintegrating into society.

## Being Judged and Becoming Criminal

Employing the philosophy of Friedrich Nietzsche, George Pavlich (2008) demonstrates how such objects as "criminal" and "ex-convict" emerge as contingent "beings" only through ongoing patterns of "becoming" in a complex of power formations. These ongoing patterns of becoming criminal are intensely tied to practices of criminal accusation rather than the actual commission of crime (Pavlich, 2007). The act of judging someone based on past actions—rather than the present—ritualistically reaffirms "ex-convict" as a master status (Becker, 1963) that sticks to the individual. As shown by Charles, the ritualistic affirmation can be inscribed on the subjectivities of formerly incarcerated men:

> Charles: No doubt about it, they're going, you know you're going to get judged, you know ... people, people got to be people, I mean who wouldn't, I mean why not be leery of someone that's been in the penitentiary several times for several different things, I mean you're suppose to be leery, like I said to be aware is to be alive, um ... but these are our walks of life, you can't just look at somebody and tell what's going on with them till you know, till you talk to them, you know.... Been to the penitentiary several times ... been up and down basically, uh, right now I'm just trying to stay out of trouble, find a new apartment, get on with the rest of my life and it's been really hectic, but you know I can make it if I put my mind to it, I know I can do it, just looking for a change right now.

> Philip: Like in family housing, they don't want to deal with criminal background. And jobs don't want to deal with you because of background.

As evinced in his words, fear sticks to Charles in ways that he has no control over (Ahmed, 2004). He accepts the doxa that despite being incarcerated for *past* transgressions of the law, he is dangerous in the *present* for violence he may commit in the *future*. Despite being resolute about wanting to change and find stability, Charles faces the interpretation that he remains a criminal. This "criminal becoming" stands in the way of former prisoners' reintegration into society and their quest to acquire basic needs like housing.

Philip's response reveals how this mark of "criminal" sticks not only to him, but also has implications for his family and loved ones. The continuous process of "becoming criminal" is based on an interpretive framework that cannot view formerly incarcerated men in any other way. As formerly incarcerated men facing this interpretive framework explain:

Dennis: You know my life, I mean my life haven't really went nowhere, been like spiralling out of control all my youth, all my young hood I mostly spent ... just about half of my life in the penal system that, in the penitentiary, stuff like that, I mean I tried to, tried to grab hold of some type of supports in my life like go try to get a job or something, but most places won't let you uh work because your criminal background and stuff.... Yeah it does ... a lot of places don't want ex-felons working for them, you know I guess they're kind of scared of them or something, you know ... like I was, I applied for a job at uh UPS ... and I was getting ready to get the job, but then they did a background check and they told me man sorry but we don't hire ex-felons.

Jerome: Oh yeah. Especially the police. Yeah to them, they think I'm still a criminal when I haven't, I've been out of crime for like going close, next year it'll be five years for sure. Yeah, I was in trouble at 18 and 19 up to 20 and, and then from 20 till now it's be [sic] pretty well good and it's kind of hard to get a job with robbery with a firearm on your record and having a huge criminal record, lots of places don't want to hire you because you're a criminal.

Larry: Yeah, yes that still. Yeah, that's really going to stop me, so I'm kind of stuck between a rock and a hard place and they don't care how long ago it was, I mean this was even before they started doing the sex offender registry.

Here Dennis reflects on how he spent his youth, the impacts of engaging in criminal behaviours, and being incarcerated. He explains his lack of job opportunities and inability to acquire some semblance of stability due to the continued resistance of employers to hire formerly incarcerated men. Despite passing the formal interview process, Dennis has had the offer of employment revoked because of his criminal record (a situation also described in the first chapter by James Young). Jerome notes that he is subject to differential treatment both by police officers and by employers. Like for Dennis, the label of criminal sticks to him despite the fact that it has been over five years since he committed an offence. Larry, in a similar vein, sums up the situation of many formerly incarcerated men insofar as they are between "a rock and a hard place" without many, or indeed any, options: trying to survive in shelters and off the alms provided by drop-in centres, while being blocked from employment because of past crimes. Larry, however, is an extreme case as he was convicted and incarcerated for having sex with a minor. This is a charge that has branded him a sex offender, and thereby held as the worst of criminals (Brown, Deakin, & Spencer 2008; Ricciardelli, 2014; Ricciardelli & Spencer 2014; Spencer 2009). His prospects for finding living quarters, let alone work, are very poor.

## DISCUSSION AND CONCLUSION

Many men that I interviewed felt they had no voice, no say in being continuously labelled "ex-convicts," "criminals" and/or "felons." They felt the world was against them, forming a series of tangible and intangible barriers that kept them from reintegrating into society and finding meaningful work. Many found themselves hampered not only by having a criminal record, but by physical and mental afflictions that they had little to no capacity to remediate. The struggle to get back on track, to become reintegrated into society, felt like a line that was never there for them to walk in the first place.

In light of the stories in this chapter, it is rather curious that Hayek (2007), considered one of the principal architects of neo-liberalism and market liberation, was so very critical of the existential state of serfdom. The men in the present study, and many more like them, are in the current neo-liberal late-capitalist era denied even the economic and legal status that serfs had. The "road to serfdom" that Hayek thought so nightmarish—being full of state intervention and protectionism—may be more appropriately seen as a yellow brick road for the men in this study. They remain absolutely ravaged by market forces and sometimes even lack the capacity to acquire basic necessities. At the same time, the men in this study need not pull themselves up by their own bootstraps. If we are serious about the amelioration of the conditions that hinder formerly incarcerated men from reintegrating into society and finding employment, programmatic efforts by state and community actors must be oriented to providing the *means* to find work (including schooling and skills) and the active political arm to *combat* the pervasive discourse that a person who has been incarcerated is a lost cause or is a dangerous threat to society.

## NOTES

1　The Fordist production model is described as the system of mass production that was pioneered in the early 20th century by the Ford Motor Company and is most associated with the postwar mode of economic growth and its associated political and social order in advanced capitalism (Jessop, 1994).

2　See http://pbc-clcc.gc.ca/prdons/pardon-eng.shtml.

3　In this chapter I use the term "racialized" and "racialization" to denote the processes ascribing racial *identities* to a social group that does not identify itself as such (see Omi & Winant, 1994; Maldonado, 2006). The term "racialized" is a way of both noting that they are either Black or Indigenous men in this study, but also indicating that I understand that these very conceptions of Black/dangerous and Indigenous/ dangerous are the bi-products of processes that are symbolically violent and applied generically.

4  Only five participants stated that they did not have criminal records and had never been arrested. The remaining three participants did not want to talk about their experiences with the criminal justice system or their criminal record.

5  Here I am referring to forms of employment that are undervalued in Western cultures (in terms of remuneration) and are viewed as requiring less skill to carry out as compared to the "highly" skilled positions found in the technological sector.

## REFERENCES

Ahmed, S. (2004). *The cultural politics of emotion.* New York, NY: Routledge.

Anderson, N. (1923). *The hobo: The sociology of the homeless man.* Chicago, IL: University of Chicago Press.

Arrigo, B. (1999). Constitutive theory and the homeless identity: The discourse of a community deviant. In S. Henry & D. Milovanovic (Eds.), *Constitutive criminology at work: Application to crime and justice* (pp. 67–85). Albany, NY: SUNY Press.

Barbieri, P., & Scherer, S. (2009). Labour market flexibilization and its consequences in Italy. *European Sociological Review, 25,* 677–692. doi:10.1093/esr/jcp009

Bauman, Z. (2000). *Liquid modernity.* Cambridge, UK: Polity.

Bauman, Z. (2003). *Wasted lives: Modernity and its outcasts.* Cambridge, UK: Polity.

Beck, U. (1992). *Risk society: Towards a new modernity.* Thousand Oaks, CA: Sage Publications.

Becker, H. (1963). *Outsiders: Studies in the sociology of deviance.* New York, NY: Free Press.

Bell, D. (1976). *The coming of post-industrial society: A venture in social forecasting* (reissue ed.). New York, NY: Basic Books.

Berlant, L. (2011). *Cruel optimism.* Durham, NC: Duke University Press.

Bourdieu, P. (2010). *Sociology is a martial art.* New York, NY: New Press.

Bowen, R. (2012, June 21). Chicago panhandler laws and freedom of speech. *Chicago Panhandler Project.* Retrieved from http://chicagopanhandler.wordpress .com/2010/06/21/chicago-panhandler-laws-and-freedom-of-speech/

Bracken, D. C., Deane, L., & Morrissette, L. (2009). Desistance and social marginalization: The case of Canadian Aboriginal offenders. *Theoretical Criminology, 13*(1), 61–78.

Brisman, A. (2003). Double whammy: Collateral consequences of conviction and imprisonment for sustainable communities and the environment. *William and Mary Environmental Law and Policy Review, 28,* 423–475.

Brown, S., Deakin, J., & Spencer, J. (2008). What people think about the management of sex offenders in the community. *Howard Journal of Criminal Justice, 47*(3), 259–274.

Brown, W. (2015). *Undoing the demos: Neoliberalism's stealth revolution.* New York, NY: Zone Books.

Butler, J. (1990). *Gender trouble: Feminism and the subversion of identity.* New York, NY: Routledge.

Charmaz, K. (2014). *Constructing grounded theory: A practical guide through qualitative analysis*. Thousand Oaks, CA: Sage Publications.

Clear, T. R. (2009). *Imprisoning communities: How mass incarceration makes disadvantaged neighborhoods worse*. New York, NY: Oxford University Press.

Connolly, W. (2013). *The fragility of things: Self-organizing processes, neoliberal fantasies, and democratic activism*. Durham, NC: Duke University Press.

Coyle, A. (2005). Changing times: Flexibilization and the re-organization of work in feminized labour markets. *Sociological Review, 53*(s2), 73–88.

Deleuze, G., & Guattari, F. (1987). *Thousand plateaus: Capitalism and schizophrenia*. Minneapolis, MN: University of Minnesota Press.

Ericson, R. V. (2007). *Crime in an insecure world*. Cambridge, UK: Polity Press.

Flick, U. (2014). *An introduction to qualitative research* (5th ed.). Thousand Oaks, CA: Sage Publications.

Foucault, M. (1990). *The history of sexuality: An introduction*. New York, NY: Vintage.

Fraser, N. (2003). From discipline to flexibilization? Rereading Foucault in the shadow of globalization. *Constellations, 10*(2), 160–171.

Freeman, M. (2011). Validity in dialogic encounters with hermeneutic truths. *Qualitative Inquiry, 17*(6), 543–551.

Gadamer, H. (2004). *Truth and method* (2nd ed.). London, UK: Bloomsbury Academic.

Gaetz, S., Donaldson, J., & Gullver, T. (2013). *The state of homelessness in Canada 2013*. Toronto, ON: Canadian Homelessness Research Network Press.

Garland, D. (2001). *The culture of control: Crime and social order in contemporary society*. Oxford, UK: Oxford University Press.

Garland, D. (2003). The rise of risk. In R. V. Ericson & A. Doyle (Eds.), *Risk and morality* (pp. 48–86). Toronto, ON: University of Toronto Press.

Goudie, C., & Markoff, B. (2015, July 30). A story the city won't discuss: Homeless population explosion. *ABC7 Chicago*. Retrieved from http://abc7chicago.com/894464/

Graser, D. (2000). Panhandling for change in Canadian law. *Journal of Law and Social Policy, 15*(1), 45–91.

Hagan, J., & Dinovitzer, R. 1999. Collateral consequences of imprisonment for children, communities, and prisoners. *Crime and Justice, 26*, 121–162.

Hannah-Moffat, K. (2004). Gendering risk at what cost: Negotiations of gender and risk in Canadian women's prisons. *Feminism & Psychology, 14*, 243–249.

Harding, D. J. (2003). Jean Valjean's dilemma: The management of ex-convict identity in the search for employment. *Deviant Behavior, 24*, 571–595.

Hayek, F. A. (2007). *The road to serfdom: Text and documents. The definitive edition*. B. Caldwell (Ed.). Chicago, IL: University of Chicago Press.

Heimer, C. (2003). Insurers as moral actors. In R. V. Ericson & A. Doyle (Eds.), *Risk and morality* (pp. 284–316). Toronto, ON: University of Toronto Press.

Henry, M., Cortes, A., & Morris, S. (2013). *The 2013 Annual Homeless Assessment Report (AHAR) to Congress*. Washington, DC: US Department of Housing and Urban Development.

Huey, L. (2012). *Invisible victims: Homelessness and the growing security gap*. Toronto, ON: University of Toronto Press.

Hutchinson, S. (2006). Countering catastrophic criminology reform, punishment and the modern liberal compromise. *Punishment & Society, 8,* 443–467.

Jameson, F. (1992). *Postmodernism, or, the cultural logic of late capitalism.* Durham, NC: Duke University Press.

Jessop, B. (1994). Post-Fordism and the state. In A. Amin (Ed.), *Post-Fordism* (pp. 251–279). Oxford, UK: Blackwell Publishers.

Lash, S., & Urry, J. (1993). *Economies of signs and space.* Thousand Oaks, CA: Sage Publications.

Maldonado, M. M. (2006). Racial triangulation of Latino/a workers by agricultural employers. *Human Organization, 65*(4), 353–361.

Marshall, C., & Rossman, G. B. (2011). *Designing qualitative research* (5th ed.). Thousand Oaks, CA: Sage Publications.

Maruna, S. (2011). Reentry as a rite of passage. *Punishment & Society, 13*(1), 3–28.

Maruna, S., Immarigeon, R., & Lebel, T. (2013). Ex-offender reintegration: Theory and practice. In S. Maruna & R. Immarigeon (Eds.), *After crime and punishment* (pp. 3–26). New York, NY: Routledge.

Mauer, M., & Chesney-Lind, M. (Eds.). (2003). *Invisible punishment: The collateral consequences of mass imprisonment.* New York, NY: New Press.

Meyer, J., & O'Malley, P. (2005). Missing the punitive turn? Canadian criminal justice, "balance" and penal modernism. In J. Pratt, D. Brown, M. Brown, S. Hallsworth, & W. Morrison (Eds.), *The new punitiveness* (pp. 201–207). New York, NY: Willan Publishing.

Miller, B. L., & Spillane, J. F. (2012). Civil death: An examination of ex-felon disenfranchisement and reintegration. *Punishment & Society, 14*(4), 402–428.

Miller, J. G. (1996). *Search and destroy: African-American males in the criminal justice system.* Cambridge, UK: Cambridge University Press.

Miller, R. J. (2014). Devolving the carceral state: Race, prisoner reentry, and the micro-politics of urban poverty management. *Punishment & Society, 16*(3), 305–335.

Moody, K. (1997). *Workers in a lean world: Unions in the international economy.* New York, NY: Verso.

Moran, D. (2012). Prisoner reintegration and the stigma of prison time inscribed on the body. *Punishment & Society 14*(5), 564–583.

Murray, J. (2007). The cycle of punishment: Social exclusion of prisoners and their children. *Criminology and Criminal Justice. 7*(1), 55–81.

Omi, M., & Winant, H. (1994). *Racial formation in the United States: From the 1960s to the 1990s* (2nd ed.). New York, NY: Routledge.

Pavlich, G. (2007). The lore of criminal accusation. *Criminal Law and Philosophy, 1*(1), 79–97.

Pavlich, G. (2008). Being accused, becoming criminal. In D. Crewe & R. Lippens (Eds.), *Existentialist criminology* (pp. 51–69). Abingdon, UK: Routledge-Cavendish.

Petersilia, J. (2001). Prisoner reentry: Public safety and reintegration challenges. *Prison Journal, 81,* 360–375.

Portes, A. (2014). Downsides of social capital. *Proceedings of the National Academy of Sciences, 111,* 18407–18408.

Purcell, K. P. J. (1998). In-sourcing, outsourcing, and the growth of contingent labour as evidence of flexible employment strategies. *European Journal of Work and Organizational Psychology, 7*(1), 39–59.

Ricciardelli, R. (2014). *Surviving incarceration: Inside Canadian prisons.* Waterloo, ON: Wilfrid Laurier University Press.

Ricciardelli, R., & Spencer, D. (2014). Exposing "sex" offenders: Precarity, abjection and violence in the Canadian federal prison system. *British Journal of Criminology, 54*(3), 428–448.

Rose, N. (1999). *Powers of freedom: Reframing political thought.* Cambridge, UK: Cambridge University Press.

Ruddell, R., & Winfree, L. T. (2006). Setting aside criminal convictions in Canada: A successful approach to offender reintegration. *Prison Journal, 86,* 452–469.

Schwandt, T. A. (1999). On understanding understanding. *Qualitative Inquiry, 5,* 451–464.

Sennett, R. (2011). *The corrosion of character: The personal consequences of work in the new capitalism.* New York, NY: W. W. Norton & Company.

Spencer, D. C. (2009). Sex offender as homo sacer. *Punishment and Society, 11*(2), 219–40.

Spohn, C., & Holleran, D. (2000). The imprisonment penalty paid by young, unemployed Black and Hispanic male offenders. *Criminology, 38*(1), 281–306.

State Appellate Defender. (2015). *Expungement.* Retrieved from https://www.illinois.gov/osad/Expungement/Pages/Expungement-and-Sealing-General-Information.aspx." Illinois Government. *Criminal Expungement and Sealing.* Retrieved from https://www.youtube.com/watch?v=owlOTbVAibE

Tator, C., & Henry, F. (2006). *Racial profiling in Canada: Challenging the myth of "a few bad apples."* Toronto, ON: University of Toronto Press.

Tica, G., & Roth, M. (2012). Are former male inmates excluded from social life? *European Journal of Probation, 4*(2), 62–76.

Todd, J. (2004). It's not my problem: How workplace violence and potential employer liability lead to employment discrimination of ex-convicts. *Arizona State Law Journal, 36*(2), 725–764.

Tonry, M. (1995). *Malign neglect: Race, crime, and punishment in America.* New York, NY: Oxford University Press.

Tonry, M. (2012). *Punishing race: A continuing American dilemma* (reprint ed.). New York, NY: Oxford University Press.

Trimbur, L. (2013). *Come out swinging: The changing world of boxing in Gleason's Gym.* Princeton, NJ: Princeton University Press.

Vosko, L. F. (Ed.). (2006). *Precarious employment: Understanding labour market insecurity in Canada.* Montreal, QC: McGill-Queen's University Press.

Wacquant, L. (1998). Negative social capital: State breakdown and social destitution in America's urban core. *Journal of Housing and the Built Environment, 13*(1), 25–40.

Wacquant, L. (2001a). The penalisation of poverty and the rise of neo-liberalism. *European Journal on Criminal Policy and Research, 9*(4), 401–412.

Wacquant, L. (2001b). Deadly symbiosis: When ghetto and prison meet and mesh. *Punishment & Society, 3*(1), 95–133.

Wacquant, L. (2009). The body, the ghetto and the penal state. *Qualitative Sociology, 32*(1), 101–129.

Wacquant, L. (2014). Marginality, ethnicity and penality in the neo-liberal city: An analytic cartography. *Ethnic and Racial Studies, 37*(10), 1687–1711.

Western, B., Kling, J. R., & Weiman, D. F. (2001). The labor market consequences of incarceration. *Crime & Delinquency, 47*(3), 410–427.

Wormith, J. S., Althouse, R., Simpson, M., Reitzel, L. R., Fagan, T. J., & Morgan, R. D. (2007). The rehabilitation and reintegration of offenders: The current landscape and some future directions for correctional psychology. *Criminal Justice and Behavior, 34*, 879–892.

# CHAPTER 11

# Does the "Wrongful" Part of Wrongful Conviction Make a Difference in the Job Market?

Kimberley A. Clow

C anada currently lacks a database that tracks the number of national cases of wrongful conviction and the numerous factors that led to each of these miscarriages of justice. Innocence Canada has been involved in the exoneration of 20 individuals[1] (Innocence Canada, 2017), yet despite these relatively low numbers, wrongful conviction is an important issue in Canada given the severe ramifications of each incident (Department of Justice, 2015). As a result, Canada has launched multiple public inquiries into specific cases of wrongful conviction, as well as an inquiry into the criminal forensic cases of a former Toronto Sick Kids Hospital's employee, Charles Smith, who may personally have contributed to 12 wrongful convictions (Clow & Ricciardelli, 2014; Department of Justice, 2015; Goudge, 2008). Moreover, in a survey of defence lawyers in Ontario, Canada, 46.3 percent of the sample believed they had represented a factually innocent client who nonetheless was convicted (Doob, 1997). Precisely how large the problem of wrongful conviction is in Canada, however, is currently unknown.

In the United States, the National Registry of Exonerations (2015) maintains a database of over 1,700 wrongly convicted persons. Scholars and advocates warn, however, that identified cases represent a mere fraction of existing wrongful conviction cases (Findley & Scott, 2006; Kassin, 2015; Roach, 2012). For instance, many criminal justice personnel have estimated that 1–3 percent of all convictions in the United States are actually wrongful convictions (Ramsey & Frank, 2007; Zalman, Smith, & Kiger, 2008). Huff (2002) calculated that if only 0.5 percent of all index crimes that received convictions were wrongful, that would represent 7,500 wrongful convictions in the United States for index crimes in the year 2000 alone.

Indeed, the fact remains that the number of people who have been wrongly convicted remains unknown. What is known is that it is very difficult for an individual to establish their innocence, especially post-conviction (Findley & Scott, 2006; Krieger, 2011). In Canada, England, and the United States, once a person has been convicted, they generally need to exhaust all of their appeals before the case will be reviewed as a possible miscarriage of justice (Criminal Case Review Commission, 2015; Krieger, 2011; Roach, 2012). Even then, a case will not be reviewed unless new and significant evidence is discovered—evidence deemed so crucial that it would likely have changed the verdict of the original trial had the evidence been presented at the time (Criminal Case Review Commission, 2015; Scullion, 2004). Such new and significant evidence is neither easy to find nor does it typically emerge years (even decades) after a crime has occurred. For many, trying to prove one's innocence has been described as akin to Sisyphus ceaselessly (and unsuccessfully) trying to force a heavy boulder up a hill (Schehr, 2008).

Despite processes of "justice" resulting in the wrongful conviction of many innocent citizens, most governments (including Canada and the United States) do not currently offer specific community reintegration services for exonerees. Moreover, as some exonerees have discovered, the existing—but limited—services available for parolees may disqualify individuals who did not actually commit crimes from having access (Buck, 2004; Innocence Project, 2009). This leaves many exonerees as victims of injustice (Westervelt & Cook, 2009) and lacking the resources and assistance needed to recover from the trauma of wrongful imprisonment and challenges tied to re-entry (Curtiss, 2007; Grounds, 2004; Weigand, 2009).

Researchers have long documented the difficulties prisoners encounter when trying to reintegrate into society (Atkin & Armstrong, 2013; Harris & Keller, 2005; Petersilia, 2004). Exonerees, too, face these same obstacles (Curtiss, 2007; Westervelt & Cook, 2008) because of a crime they did not commit—or possibly, a crime that never occurred (e.g., accidental death or suicide misinterpreted as murder). In other words, exonerees have many of the same needs as parolees: they are expected to find housing and employment, adjust to technological and cultural changes that occurred during their incarceration, and they may lack family or social support due to the crime they were [erroneously] convicted of (e.g., individuals may have turned away believing the exoneree guilty of having murdered a family member) or owing to the challenges of maintaining relationships while incarcerated (Clow, Leach, & Ricciardelli, 2011; Westervelt & Cook, 2008). Also, like parolees, exonerees have a gap in their work history and suffer the consequences of a criminal record (Shlosberg, Mandery, & West, 2011)—even when the record solely involves the crime that they did not commit. Many employers are reluctant to hire individuals with criminal records (Atkin & Armstrong, 2013; Harris & Keller, 2005; Lam & Harcourt, 2003), and prison itself may be stigmatizing, regardless of someone's innocence (Clow, Ricciardelli, & Cain, 2012; Ricciardelli, 2014a). One of the most pronounced differences between exonerees and parolees is that exonerees face these obstacles without having committed an unlawful act, possibly increasing their feelings of frustration and injustice, preventing closure, and creating barriers to healing (Campbell & Denov, 2004; Weigand, 2009).

## EMPLOYER REACTIONS TO CRIMINAL RECORDS

Despite barriers to employment, research continues to find that work is invaluable for successful re-entry (Bahr, Harris, Fisher, & Armstrong, 2010; Cherney & Fitzgerald, 2014; Krienert, 2005). To investigate the barriers former prisoners face, Giguere and Dundes (2002) presented business owners and managers with a scenario of an articulate, motivated, and professionally dressed job applicant who was also a first-time offender convicted of selling crack cocaine. They found that 53 percent of employers claimed they would be willing to hire the individual (44 percent were unsure what they would decide and three percent said they would probably not hire him). Employers' biggest concerns, in order of importance, were that this job applicant would lack the necessary people skills; their customers would be uncomfortable if they knew convicted individuals were employed; co-workers would be uncomfortable working with someone who had been convicted of a crime; the applicant would lack appropriate training, not have had the chance to adequately adjust to life outside prison, and only work at the job for a short period of time; and/or the applicant might victimize the company (Giguere & Dundes, 2002). Thus, a number of factors were identified that employers might hold against individuals who had been convicted and incarcerated.

The relatively large percentage of employers agreeing to hire someone with a conviction in Giguere and Dundes' (2002) study, however, may have been due to the crime type presented in the scenario. Research has found that employers are more forgiving of drug crimes and traffic violations than violent crimes (Atkin & Armstrong, 2013; Giguere & Dundes, 2002). For example, Ricciardelli (2014b) found that even in an employment placement social enterprise designed to help former prisoners with employment during community re-entry, employers were still opposed to hiring men or women with sexual offence histories or more violent murder convictions. Unfortunately for exonerees, the bulk of known wrongful conviction cases involve homicide, sexual assault, and sexual abuse (National Registry of Exonerations, 2015; Roach, 2012). Thus, many exonerees have to deal with employers' reactions to their erroneous convictions for violent crimes, which are the types of crimes employers respond to more negatively.

An additional issue might be that business owners and managers were presented with a scenario in this study (Giguere & Dundes, 2002) and not a real employment decision. This would allow social desirability concerns to potentially have inflated employers' responses. Other researchers have found discrepancies in reported attitudes and actual behaviour as it relates to hiring individuals with criminal records (Pager & Quillian, 2005). Cohen and Nisbett (1997), for example, assessed companies in an actual employment context. The researchers mailed letters inquiring about employment and requesting a job application to 921 different businesses that belonged to five national chains located throughout the United States. Potential employers received a letter from a fictional applicant who had been convicted of a crime. The letter introduced the specific offence details midway, explaining that the applicant wanted to be open and honest, and in anticipation that the employer would likely request additional information before considering him, a brief explanation of the offence was presented. The letter then explained one of two scenarios: either that the applicant had discovered his fiancée had been cheating on him when it was announced at a bar in front of his friends by his fiancée's lover, and he had accidentally killed the lover in the fight that ensued (i.e., an honour killing); or that the applicant had stolen vehicles to provide money for his wife and children and to pay his bills.

Although only 12 percent of the letters were returned, there were a reasonably equal number of responses per condition. The responses revealed that organizations located in the southern and western parts of the United States were more likely to provide an application, and the tone of the return letter was more likely to be warm and understanding in the honour killing condition than were northern organizations from the same national chains. Organizations did not differ in their responses to the vehicle theft condition based on their geographic location. Thus, although the job applicant with a felony conviction did not receive many replies overall, it appears that certain types of crimes are viewed as more or less acceptable in different cultures, eliciting greater assistance and warmth when a culture is more understanding of the crime.

But what if the applicant was convicted of a crime they did not commit? Would employers be similarly understanding to someone who was wrongly convicted? Do people want to hire wrongly convicted individuals and treat them like any other citizen following their exoneration, or do people treat wrongly convicted individuals similarly to convicted individuals? In other words, do employers focus more on the fact they were "convicted" or the fact that the conviction was "wrongful" in the case of individuals wrongfully convicted? My research begins to empirically test these questions.

Exonerees have reported that the stigma surrounding wrongful convictions has blocked their efforts at employment (Clow et al., 2011; Westervelt & Cook, 2008). It is not clear, however, whether the discriminating experiences some exonerees have reported hold true on a wider scale. It is possible that with the recent economy being what it is, everyone—whether having been to prison or not—is encountering difficulties in the job market. If exonerees are systematically disadvantaged, however, greater empirical data to support exoneree's anecdotal evidence may assist in developing new policies to provide greater services for wrongly convicted individuals.

## METHOD

To better assess whether employers discriminate against wrongly convicted individuals, 1000 emails were sent to contact individuals responsible for Canadian job postings on popular job databases: Monster, Workopolis, and Job Bank. As it was not possible to respond to all postings, a random sample was used; more specifically, systematic random sampling was determined to be the most efficient strategy for a team of research assistants to document which postings had been responded to and which postings should be investigated next. Thus, every tenth posting listed on each of the databases the first day the study began was viewed. If that posting listed an email address to contact regarding the job, that job posting was selected and one of four different email inquiries was randomly selected to be sent to that contact person. If the posting did not list an email address for a contact person, or listed the same contact person as another selected posting, the next posting was viewed instead. Once an inquiry email was sent, the next tenth posting was selected and the same procedure was followed. This was done until 250 of each of the four inquiry emails were sent and spanned from March 2010 until April 2011.

I chose to send emails inquiring for further information on the posted jobs (as Cohen and Nisbett [1997] did), as opposed to submitting job applications or resumés, for a number of reasons. Foremost among them was an interest in minimizing the impact the study had on the already busy schedules and hiring processes of the companies contacted. As most professionals reply to dozens of emails every day, sending an email to companies did not seem to be a greater inconvenience than employers would encounter in their day-to-day lives. Moreover, using an email inquiry allowed the stimuli to be kept constant across companies, with the exception of the specific information manipulated across email conditions (i.e., convicted, wrongly convicted, out of the workforce, control). To actually apply for the posted jobs would have required creating unique resumés for each job posting (as each job varied in specific qualifications), thereby making it more difficult to assume that the applicant was equally qualified across conditions, or even within a condition. In addition, if actual applications were sent, companies would potentially be expending more time on the study's fictional applicants.

A key distinguishing feature between my study and Cohen and Nisbett's (1997) is that I was not able to contact multiple stores or businesses from the same chain, as they did. At the time of this study, most national or multinational chains had one particular contact person, as opposed to separate contact individuals per store/business. Sending multiple emails would therefore have increased the likelihood of exposing the research study. As the companies could not be kept consistent in each condition, a diverse range of organizations, both small and large, representing hundreds of different occupations (e.g., stylist, construction worker, financial analyst) were contacted.

As stated earlier, there were four versions of the email, with 250 emails of each version being sent to potential employers. The first version was the control condition. It read as follows:

> Dear [insert contact name], I would like to inquire about [insert job] at [insert company]. My educational background and relevant work experience have made me results-oriented and confident working either independently or as part of a team. My references will confirm that I am very hard working and detail-oriented. I am also able to successfully multitask, prioritize work, and meet deadlines.
>
> I would greatly appreciate if you would send me any further information you have about the position and provide me with an application. If you have a number where I can reach you, we can discuss my application further. The best way to contact me is by email [provided email address]. Thank you for your time and consideration.
>
> Sincerely,
>
> Jason Stewart

The second version of the email had an additional paragraph informing the company that the potential job applicant had committed a crime. The additional paragraph explained that the job applicant had "one thing I must explain, because I want to be honest and I do not want there to be any misunderstandings." The paragraph continued, revealing that he had been convicted of manslaughter, had served four years in prison, and was now ready to "resume a productive role in society. I believe working for [insert company name] would be an important step in reaching this goal." The language for this paragraph was modeled after Cohen and Nisbett (1997), but without the details of the actual crime. I did not want to provide the specific details of the case, as this could limit the generalizability of the findings.

In the third version of the email, a similar paragraph was used to explain that the fictional potential job applicant had been wrongly convicted. This email claimed that he had been wrongly convicted of manslaughter, "however, I served four years before DNA evidence exonerated me and I am now ready to resume a productive role in society." The email ended with the same sentence about working for the particular company being an important step toward reaching that goal. Manslaughter was chosen for the convicted and wrongly convicted conditions to keep the study parallel to Cohen and Nisbett's (1997), and because the majority of known exonerations to date involve erroneous homicide convictions (National Registry of Exonerations, 2015).

A fourth version of the email was created, in light of concerns that the email inquiry may be more negatively interpreted in the control condition than in the conviction and wrongful conviction conditions, as the job applicant in the control condition inquired about the job rather than following the instructions for applying.[2] A secondary control condition was created where the fictional job applicant felt he should disclose that he had been out of the workforce for the same amount of time as the job applicants in the convicted and wrongly convicted conditions, writing: "There is one thing I must explain, because I want to be honest and I do not want there to be any misunderstandings. I have been out of the workforce for the past four years." Otherwise, the paragraph ended as it did in the convicted and wrongly convicted versions, where he was ready to be productive again and believed that working for the company would help in working toward that goal.

The applicant, Jason Stewart, remained the same across each of the four study conditions. For this first exploration into employer reactions to exonerees, I chose to focus on a male applicant and I did not wish to manipulate race or any other demographic variables. Among known cases of wrongful conviction, men far outnumber women as exonerees (Innocence Canada, 2017; National Registry of Exoneration, 2015). Thus, it was appropriate to start with a male applicant. Moreover, most known Canadian exonerees are Caucasian or their ethnicity is not specified (e.g., Steven Truscott, Guy Paul Morin, David Milgaard, Thomas Sophonow). For this preliminary exploration, I picked the name Jason Stewart, as based on an informal survey among a group of undergraduate research assistants, it was not regarded as stereotypical of any particular racial minority group.

## Data Preparation

As the inquiry emails requested further information and an application for the posted position, coding included whether or not the email responses provided this information. In addition, each email was coded regarding whether it indicated it was an automated message or appeared to be (i.e., indicated the contact person was out of town, thanked the individual for applying when the applicant had merely inquired about the job, told the individual that his/her resumé had been received when no resumé was submitted); outlined necessary qualifications; asked Jason to submit his resumé or otherwise apply for the job; suggested arranging a meeting, phone call, or interview; rejected Jason outright; or acknowledged Jason's story in any way. If an automated response and then a personal response were received (which happened occasionally), we did not code the response as automated but coded the personal response instead, as someone put in effort beyond the automated response.

The primary dependent variable was whether or not (*yes* = 1; *no* = 0) a company responded to the supposed job applicant's inquiry email. For the remaining dependent variables, the presence (1) or absence (0) of each variable was tabulated within each email response. The data are frequency counts, thus chi-square tests were conducted to determine if the potential job applicant's condition (control versus wrongly convicted versus convicted versus out of the workforce) appeared to influence the dependent variables.

## RESULTS

Of the 1000 email inquiries sent, 313 replies were received (31.3 percent). Within these 313 responses, approximately 8 percent appeared or claimed to be automated responses, without a personal or relevant follow-up email. Typically, these responses simply acknowledged the receipt of the application (which was not true for the supposed applicant, as he had inquired about the job without submitting a resumé or application package), but occasionally automatic out of office alerts were received. As expected, the chi-square test revealed that these automatic replies did not differ across conditions ($\chi^2$ = 3.60, $p$ = .31).

Although the automated messages were not significantly different by condition, overall employer responses were. In the control condition, the job applicant received an email response 39 percent of the time, but the same inquiry email received a response only 24 percent of the time when the applicant mentioned having a criminal record, and 28 percent of the time when the applicant mentioned being wrongly convicted ($\chi^2 = 14.67, p = .001$). The number of responses in the convicted and wrongly convicted conditions was not significantly different ($\chi^2 = 1.04, p = .31$). Thus, being convicted of manslaughter—even if it was a crime for which DNA evidence indicated an individual was innocent—led to potential employers being more likely to ignore the job inquiry.

This discrimination in responses was not due to the four-year gap in work history that the conviction (or wrongful conviction) caused. In the secondary control condition, where the potential applicant explained that he had been out of the workforce for four years, responses were received 34 percent of the time. Although fewer responses were received in this condition than the original control condition, the difference was not significant ($\chi^2 = 1.46, p = .28$). This lack of a significant difference suggests that potential employers were not reacting to a gap in work history significantly differently than they reacted to the control applicant. Granted, that may not be the case the longer the gap became and/or if the gap was associated with a lack of relevant job skills, which are variables future research may wish to explore. Moreover, the out of the workforce control condition did receive significantly more responses than the convicted and wrongly convicted conditions ($\chi^2 = 6.19$, $p = .05$). Although research has suggested that employers may interpret gaps in work history as being due to incarceration (e.g., Pogarsky, 2006), this did not appear to be the case in the present study, as employers were significantly more likely to respond in the out of the workforce condition than in the conviction condition. Thus, although convicted individuals do have a gap in their work history, that gap in employment does not appear to be the largest obstacle to being encouraged to apply for a job.

Although the response rate in this study was low (31.3 percent), it was higher than the 12 percent response rate Cohen and Nisbett (1997) received. There are two likely reasons for this difference. One, I included non-convicted control groups in the study that did in fact receive more responses, which raised the overall response rate. Two, given that the processes for applying for jobs today relies heavily on the use of computers and email, potential employers in this study could simply hit reply and compose an email, which may be more appealing than printing a letter and mailing it, as was necessary in Cohen and Nisbett's (1997) research.

Despite the higher response rate compared to Cohen and Nisbett (1997), the low response rate in this study overall may be reflective of the sheer volume of applications employers receive. Even in the control condition, the email was replied to less than half of the time (39 percent). In these times, employers may have the luxury of ignoring anyone who does not follow their application procedures, without seriously limiting the quality or quantity of their applicant pool. Nonetheless, employers were still more likely to encourage Jason to apply when he did not mention a conviction or wrongful conviction than when he did. Thus employer apathy—or applicants failing to follow application instructions—cannot account for the differential condition findings (i.e., more replies in the control conditions than the convicted or wrongly convicted conditions), as these issues would hold true across conditions or should more seriously affect the control conditions (where they received more responses rather than fewer).

Of the 313 companies that did reply, only 11.5 percent actually provided further information, as requested, about the posting (or where to find it), an application, or explained that there was no application form for the position. This response rate is similar to what Cohen and Nisbett (1997) found. The most common response in the email replies received, which may have been viewed as an answer to the inquiry about an application form, was to ask the applicant to provide a resumé (19 percent).[3] An incredibly small proportion of replies (2 percent) asked to arrange a meeting or interview, asked if the applicant had specific qualifications (3 percent), or rejected the applicant because the position had already been filled and/or the applicant did not sufficiently fit the position (1 percent). None of these characteristics significantly differed across conditions.

A few of the replies did imply that an inquiry rather than a full application was perceived negatively. For instance, one employer in the out of the workforce control said:

> I normally don't take the time to respond to job applicants. If you are going to get anywhere in your job search, you must provide all the information possible ...

Another reply (in the wrongful conviction condition) said:

> Generally I won't respond to an email that didn't give me a resumé or expects me to do the work for you i.e. send you more info when the info is on our website. I'm assuming that you didn't send a resumé up front because your four year gap in work looks bad without an explanation so why bother ...

Thus, it is possible that the control condition received fewer responses than it would have had applications been submitted rather than email inquiries, as the applicant may have appeared lazy or ignorant for not simply applying properly. If this was the case, however, it suggests that the discrimination faced by convicted and wrongly convicted individuals may have been underestimated in this study.

Upon reading the email responses received, two issues were striking: (1) very few replies acknowledged the disclosure of the conviction or wrongful conviction ($n = 18$); and (2) those who did acknowledge the disclosure were often positive. Even among the individuals who took the time to reply to the potential applicant, the typical approach appeared to be to ignore the disclosed information and respond as if he was any other applicant (e.g., tell him to submit a resumé, direct him to the website). This is not to suggest that they blatantly ignored the information—as the difference in response rates suggests otherwise—but that the disclosed information was rarely referred to in employers' replies. This was possibly due to litigation concerns or employers' discomfort. Future research may seek to investigate the reasons behind acknowledging (or failing to acknowledge) private information that applicants choose to disclose.

The rare individuals who did acknowledge the disclosed information sometimes thanked the applicant for his honesty, indicated if there were security checks involved in the job or application procedure, or occasionally encouraged Jason to apply. Although rare, this acknowledgement was not significantly different across convicted ($n = 5$) and wrongly convicted ($n = 13$) conditions ($\chi^2 = 2.23$, $p = .14$). The emails were further categorized into sympathetic/positive responses or not, where sympathetic responses apologized for the situation, thanked Jason for his honesty, or otherwise responded in an understanding or positive manner. The entire response did not have to be sympathetic; responses were coded as sympathetic if at least one phrase was positive or understanding. For example, one sympathetic reply in the convicted condition began "I certainly appreciate your honesty ...," but later indicated that a pardon would be necessary for the job. Another sympathetic reply, this time in the wrongful conviction condition, read "sorry to hear your story, glad you got out. Have you ever worked in this field, as we require someone with min. 2 years experience? Please advise." Other replies were more encouraging. In the convicted condition, one reply began with "Thanks for your honesty. We at Company X believe in allowing a person a second chance ..." Another in the wrongful conviction condition read "Thanks for sharing your story with us. I have approached our CEO with your story and you will be considered for a role. Please submit your resumé for consideration. We look forward to receiving it."

These positive replies were not representative of the typical response, nor were they proof that Jason would have received a job in either condition. They do, however, symbolize hope that there are understanding and sympathetic individuals who are responsible for hiring decisions. Sympathetic responses did significantly differ across the two conditions ($\chi^2 = 4.63, p = .03$). Of the 70 email responses in the wrongful conviction condition, 10 appeared sympathetic or positive, whereas only two of the 60 email responses in the convicted condition did so. Thus, although Jason did not receive significantly more email responses when he was wrongly convicted than when he was convicted, he was significantly more likely to receive sympathetic or positive comments in the email replies he did receive.

## CONCLUSION

These findings suggest that wrongly convicted individuals are not treated the same as average applicants on the job market. The fictitious applicant received fewer replies to his inquiry email in the wrongful conviction condition than the control conditions. Although the present study focuses on being wrongly convicted (or convicted) of manslaughter, future research may wish to examine the generalizability of the findings. For instance, would an exoneree be similarly disadvantaged in the job market as a female applicant, if wrongly convicted of a different crime, or based upon their ethnicity?

Consistent with exonerees' reported difficulties finding employment post-incarceration (Clow et al., 2012; Westervelt & Cook, 2008), significantly fewer people were interested in assisting Jason Stewart in his job search, or encouraging him to apply, when he had been wrongly convicted of manslaughter than when he had simply been out of the workforce for the same number of years. Exonerees—like former prisoners—cannot begin to rebuild their lives without financial independence, yet few of them receive compensation; compensation, if it is received, is generally available years after re-entry; and exonerees are not provided automatic expungement, which may further impede their job prospects (Shlosberg et al., 2011; Weigand, 2009; Westervelt & Cook, 2009). Thus these research findings are particularly discouraging. When a justice system puts the wrong individual in prison, morality dictates that the government responsible for that system should therefore be responsible for providing for the wronged individual and assisting them until that person has, at a minimum, attained a place in society approximate to where they would likely have been if the injustice had not occurred. Clearly, that is not occurring. My results, however, empirically demonstrate that exonerees are in worse positions than if time had simply stood still. It is not the gap in their work history that is so damaging—as the applicant who was out of the workforce did not receive significantly fewer replies than the more normative control condition. What seems to be damning to wrongly convicted individuals is the false conviction (e.g., doubts about whether the person is truly innocent), prison time (e.g., the negative impact prison may have had on the person), or both. Currently, the Canadian and American governments are not doing enough to address these issues.

The potential applicant in this study did receive more replies with positive or sympathetic sentiments when he was wrongly convicted than when he was convicted. Although this finding has negative implications for parolees, it may be positive for exonerees—granted, sympathy is not the same as a job offer. Moreover, the sympathetic responses in this study were very rare. That being said, it only takes one understanding person to offer someone a chance, and the emails received in this study suggested that such individuals exist for former prisoners, and perhaps even more so for individuals who have been wrongly convicted.

## NOTES

I would like to thank Amy Leach for her ideas and insights in the planning phase of this research. I would also like to thank the many research assistants, and the Social Sciences and Humanities Research Council of Canada, who made this research possible.

1  Innocence Canada was formerly known as the Association in Defence of the Wrongly Convicted (AIDWYC).
2  Whereas the applicant in the other conditions could be seen as asking whether or not they should bother applying, given their circumstances.
3  These were not coded as answering the inquiry unless they specified that submitting a resumé was all he had to do to apply or the email also provided (or directed) him to additional information about the job.

## REFERENCES

Atkin, C. A., & Armstrong, G. S. (2013). Does the concentration of parolees in a community impact employer attitudes toward the hiring of ex-offenders? *Criminal Justice Policy Review, 24*(1), 71–93. doi:10.1177/0887403411428005

Bahr, S. J., Harris, L., Fisher, J. K., & Armstrong, A. H. (2010). Successful re-entry: What differentiates successful and unsuccessful parolees. *International Journal of Offender Therapy and Comparative Criminology, 54*(5), 667–692. doi:10.1177/0306624X09342435

Buck, G. (2004). They took my life: His wrongful arrest led to 12 years in jail. David Shephard can't make up for the lost time—but he's determined to try. *Reader's Digest.* Retrieved from http://www.rd.com/content/printContent.do?contentId=28504&KeepThis=true&TB_iframe=true&height=500&width=790&modal=true

Campbell, K., & Denov, M. (2004). The burden of innocence: Coping with a wrongful imprisonment. *Canadian Journal of Criminology and Criminal Justice, 46*(2), 139–163.

Cherney, A., & Fitzgerald, R. (2014). Finding and keeping a job: The value and meaning of employment for parolees. *International Journal of Offender Therapy and Comparative Criminology, 60*, 1–17. doi:10.1177/0306624X14548858

Clow, K. A., Leach, A-M., & Ricciardelli, R. (2011). Life after wrongful conviction. In B. L. Cutler (Ed.), *Conviction of the innocent: Lessons from psychological research* (pp. 327–341). Washington, DC: American Psychological
Association.

Clow, K. A., Ricciardelli, R., & Cain, T. L. (2012). Stigma-by-association: Prejudicial effects of the prison experience for offenders and exonerees. In
D. W. Russell & C. A. Russell (Eds.), *The psychology of prejudice: Interdisciplinary perspectives on contemporary issues* (pp. 127–154). New York, NY: Nova
Science Publishers.

Clow, K. A., & Ricciardelli, R. (2014). Public perceptions of wrongful conviction.
*Canadian Criminal Law Review, 14,* 183–198.

Cohen, D., & Nisbett, R. E. (1997). Field experiments examining the culture of
honor: The role of institutions in perpetuating norms about violence. *Personality and Social Psychology Bulletin, 23*(11), 1188–1199.

Criminal Case Review Commission. (2015). *About the criminal case review
commission.* Retrieved from http://www.ccrc.gov.uk/making-application/
how-it-works/

Curtiss, J. J. (2007) *Reentry challenges faced by the wrongly convicted* (unpublished
thesis). Northern Arizona University (Flagstaff, AZ). Retrieved from http://
www.jjay.cuny.edu/Wrongly_Convicted_Thesis_10.5.07.pdf

Department of Justice (2015). Canadian commissions of inquiry. From the *FTP
Heads of Prosecutions Committee Report of the Working Group on the Prevention of Miscarriages of Justice.* Retrieved from http://www.justice.gc.ca/eng/
rp-pr/cj-jp/ccr-rc/pmj-pej/p3.html

Doob, A. N. (1997) *An examination of the views of defence counsel of wrongful
convictions.* Toronto: Centre of Criminology.

Findley, K. A., & Scott, M. S. (2006). The multiple dimensions of tunnel vision in
criminal cases. *Wisconsin Law Review, 2,* 291–397.

Giguere, R., & Dundes, L. (2002). Help wanted: A survey of employer concerns
about hiring ex-convicts. *Criminal Justice Policy Review, 13*(4), 396–408.
doi:10.1177/088740302237806

Goudge, S. T. (2008). *Inquiry into Pediatric Forensic Pathology in Ontario.* Retrieved
from http://www.attorneygeneral.jus.gov.on.ca/inquiries/goudge/index.html

Grounds, A. (2004). Psychological consequences of wrongful conviction and
imprisonment. *Canadian Journal of Criminology and Criminal Justice, 46*(2),
165–182.

Harris, P. M., & Keller, K. S. (2005). Ex-offenders need not apply: The criminal background check in hiring decisions. *Journal of Contemporary Criminal Justice,
21*(1), 6–30. doi:10.1177/1043986204271678

Huff, C. R. (2002). Wrongful conviction and public policy: The American Society of Criminology 2001 presidential address. *Criminology, 40*(1), 1–18. doi:
10.1111/j.1745-9125.2002.tb00947.x

Innocence Canada (2017). Retrieved from http://www.aidwyc.org/cases/historical/

Innocence Project. (2009). *Making up for lost time: What the wrongfully convicted
endure and how to provide fair compensation.* Report for the Innocence Project. Benjamin N. Cardozo School of Law, Yeshiva University.

Kassin, S. M. (2015). The social psychology of false confessions. *Social Issues and
Policy Review, 9*(1), 25–51.

Krieger, S. A. (2011). Why our justice system convicts innocent people, and the challenges faced by innocence projects trying to exonerate them. *New Criminal Law Review, 14*(3), 333–402. doi: 10.1525/nclr.2011.14.3.333

Krienert, J. L. (2005). Bridging the gap between prison and community employment: An initial assessment of current information. *Criminal Justice Studies, 18*(4), 293–303. doi: 10.1080/14786010500157409

Lam, H., & Harcourt, M. (2003). The use of criminal record in employment decisions: The rights of ex-offenders, employers, and the public. *Journal of Business Ethics, 47*, 237–252.

National Registry of Exonerations. (2015). *Exonerations by year and type of crime.* Retrieved from https://www.law.umich.edu/special/exoneration/Pages/Exoneration-by-Year-Crime-Type.aspx

Pager, D., & Quillian, L. (2005). Walking the talk? What employers say versus what they do. *American Sociological Review, 70*, 355–380.

Petersilia, J. (2004). What works in prisoner reentry? Reviewing and questioning the evidence. *Federal Probation, 68*(2), 4–8.

Pogarsky, G. (2006). Criminal records, employment, & recidivism. *Criminology and Public Policy, 5*(3), 479–482.

Ramsey, R. J., & Frank, J. (2007). Wrongful conviction: Perceptions of criminal justice professionals regarding the frequency of wrongful conviction and the extent of system errors. *Crime & Delinquency, 53*(3), 436–470. doi:10.1177/0011128706286554

Ricciardelli, R. (2014a). *Surviving incarceration: Inside Canadian penitentiaries.* Waterloo, ON: Wilfrid Laurier University Press.

Ricciardelli, R. (2014b, April). *Evaluation of Klink Coffee Social Enterprise.* Prepared for Human Resource and Skills Development of Canada and St. Leonard's Society of Toronto, ON.

Roach, K. (2012). Wrongful convictions in Canada. *University of Cincinnati Law Review, 80*(4), 1465–1526.

Schehr, R. (2008). Shedding the burden of Sisyphus: International law and wrongful conviction in the United States. *Boston College Third World Law Journal, 28*(1), 129–165.

Scullion, K. (2004). Wrongful convictions and the criminal conviction review process pursuant to section 696.1 of the Criminal Code of Canada. *Canadian Journal of Criminology and Criminal Justice, 46*(2), 189–195.

Shlosberg, A., Mandery, E., & West, V. (2011). The expungement myth. *Albany Law Review, 75*(3), 1229–1241.

Weigand, H. (2009). Rebuilding a life: The wrongfully convicted and exonerated. *Public Interest Law Journal, 18*, 427–437.

Westervelt, S. D., & Cook, K. J. (2008). Coping with innocence after death row. *Contexts, 7*(4), 32–37. doi:10.1525/ctx.2008.7.4.32

Westervelt, S. D., & Cook, K. J. (2009). Framing innocents: The wrongly convicted as victims of state harm. *Crime, Law, and Social Change, 53*(3), 259–275. doi:10.1007/s10611-009-9231-z

Zalman, M., Smith, B., & Kiger, A. (2008). Officials' estimates of the incidence of "actual innocence" conviction. *Justice Quarterly, 25*(1), 72–100. doi:10.1080/07418820801954563

CONCLUSION

# Employment Reintegration

Rose Ricciardelli and Adrienne M. F. Peters

**M**ost people who have been in prison in Canada, as often is the case in other countries, including the United States, will eventually return to the community (Andress, Wildes, Rechtine, & Moritsugu, 2004; Travis, 2005; Visher & Travis, 2003), where they are inevitably expected to resume typical daily responsibilities. In Canada specifically, each federal prisoner is likely to be released, either on parole after serving one-third of their federal sentence or on statutory release after serving two-thirds. Given the indisputable importance of employment for most former prisoners' successful reintegration into society, why must it be so challenging for this population to seek, acquire, and retain employment? And why is employment that provides a decent living wage, and is enjoyable and challenging, but neither precarious nor unsafe, impossible to find, let alone acquire?

Community and employment reintegration is negotiated by well over 100,000 former prisoners—parolees, probationers, or simply releasees—annually in Canada alone (Dauvergne, 2012). Securing employment is essential for most releasees if they are to be successful in the community in desisting from crime, as evinced across the contributions in this collection, (Harding, 2003; Visher, Winterfield, & Coggeshall, 2005). We have witnessed too many times in the course of our research, work, or lived experiences, instances wherein former prisoners have chosen to return to prison because they have felt unable to succeed in society. Many are resilient, but even so, how many times are we to expect a former prisoner to have a door slammed in their face, an opportunity removed, or experience being outwardly shunned or rejected before ever having a chance? How much resiliency can one person have?

Recognizing the challenges, the stigma (Goffman, 1963), and disgust (Agamben, 1995), or simple negative views and attributes too often ascribed to former prisoners, it is not surprising that some prefer, or at least feel more comfortable in, prison. It is perhaps difficult to comprehend that for many, the volatile, hard, and saddening environment which is prison (see Ricciardelli, 2014), is nevertheless a more accepting environment for prisoners than the larger free society in which the public lives (see Giddens, 1991).

In a society that fails to accept those with a criminal history or record, employment can appear unattainable. Yet it would benefit former prisoners by heightening their self-esteem, feelings of independence, financial stability, and pro-social responsibility (Rahill-Beuler & Kretzer, 1997; Rosenfeld, Petersilia, & Visher, 2008; Uggen, 2000). Of course, even precarious employment or odd-job labour is not always readily available for releasees, and fulfilling, gainful employment—whatever that looks like—seems to be an unattainable dream (Scott, 2010; Visher, Debus-Sherrill, & Yahner, 2008). As evinced through the pages of this collection, men, women, and youth, after incarceration, must navigate the stigma of their criminal past and/or mental illness, the gaps in their employment history or the complete absence of law-abiding employment experience, and the limited social networks on which they must rely to find work. They must also manage the realities of their parole/probation conditions, the inaccessibility of pardons, and the demands of programming and treatment, as well as technological and societal changes when seeking work.

In this concluding chapter we first revisit classical theories of criminality to contextualize the theoretical and empirical tie between employment and community reintegration for prisoners. Next, we draw on contributions from the authors in this edited collection to speak to the realities of employment for releasees, the perspectives of employers, and the policies and practices that hamper or advance the quest for successful employment for diverse prisoner populations after incarceration.

## THEORETICAL UNDERPINNING: REVIEWING THE CLASSICS

Several leading sociological and criminological theorists link engagement in criminal activities with employment or, more specifically, unemployment (Agnew, 2001; Cohen & Felson 1979; Gottfredson & Hirschi, 1990; Hirschi, 1969; Laub & Sampson 2003; Moffitt, 1993; Sampson & Laub, 1997). Rational choice theorists, for example, purport that persons who commit criminal acts are hedonistic and less likely to offend *if* the potential losses or consequences tied to the commission of an offence outweigh the anticipated gains or rewards (Beccaria, 1963; Clarke & Cornish, 1985). In this sense, it has been outlined in theories of deterrence for well over half a century that people with more to lose are less likely to risk this loss and thus refrain from participating in criminal activity (see Loughran et al., 2009). As such, and in light of the human aptitude for making rational decisions, employment can motivate individuals to follow a "straight and narrow" path rather than risk losing their job, income, and financial stability for themselves and their family. Indeed, Merton's (1938) classic theory of strain reveals how the disjuncture between goals and means can result in deviance, including criminal behaviours. Later, Agnew (1992) proposed general strain theory to evince the link between offending behaviour and employment. Specifically, unemployment is argued to represent an individual's failed attempts to achieve their positively valued goals. The associated financial instability—or lack of money—and the humbling experience of being terminated from a job, together, can foster feelings of frustration and anger, and encourage illegitimate coping strategies. Experiences of job loss, particularly when compounded with the stresses of searching for employment anew or coming down from the stresses of their former work environment, can considerably increase the potential for more deviance and more serious offending.

From youth to adults, researchers demonstrate that various crimes can, at least partially, be explained by the strains and negative emotions that result from unemployment, monetary dissatisfaction, and relative deprivation (Baron, 2006; Cernkovich, Giordano, & Rudolph, 2000). The link between property crimes and unemployment more specifically reveals that the motivations behind many criminal behaviours are tied to financial strains, be they framed as needs or desires (Aaltonen, Macdonald, Martikainen, & Kivivuori, 2013). Of course, being known to have engaged in any criminal act results in the label of "offender" being applied to the individual—under nearly any circumstances, no matter what the justification or perceived need (see Becker 1963; Lemert, 1967).

Said processes of labelling are known to both influence a labelled person to internalize an ascribed label, which may encourage subsequent criminal involvement and, in consequence, lead to "cumulative disadvantage" (Sampson & Laub, 1997). Or, as evinced in the application of Sutherland's (1947) differential association theory to explain youth participation in property and violent crimes, exposure to criminal associates can increase their interest in committing said crimes (e.g., Alarid, Burton, & Cullen, 2000). A substantial number of researchers have been dedicated to testing this theory, including Morselli, Tremblay, and McCarthy (2006) who revealed that only a minority of persons, aged 18 to 63,[1] in their sample were introduced to criminal behaviours through someone they esteemed and viewed as a mentor. Persons with low self-control and raised in a home with two parents employed full-time were indicated as more likely to be influenced by a criminal mentor. The authors suggest that older/experienced "offenders" may seek out risk-taking, minimally supervised youth to engage with in criminal activities.[2] However, another possible explanation is that children whose parents are working, and who are thus less supervised, may have more time and opportunity to be encountered by said older/experienced youth. Whatever the reasons, it is clear that prolonged exposure to criminally active individuals is recognized to perhaps not be an ideal way to motivate people oriented toward crime in a different direction.

Social control theorists and contemporary developmental theorists have also served to assist in our understanding of the relationship between employment and criminal behaviours. Looking back to Hirschi's (1969) classic social bonding theory, for example, he purported that individuals will be inhibited from engaging in crime in the presence of strong social bonds—something that is revisited in more recent theories of desistance today. Said bonds include attachment to conventional others, including family, teachers, and peers; involvement in and commitment to conventional activities; and belief in the prevailing social norms and laws. Conventional employment then fosters social cohesion and bonding with pro-social employers. Gottfredson and Hirschi (1990) attributed unemployment and financial difficulties to an individual's low self-control, contending that many criminalized persons have instability in their employment patterns, which results from employment that is neither secure nor sustainable. Again, this is a reality evident among releasees seeking or trying to maintain work. Theorists contend that deficiencies in self-control are thought to contribute to opportunities for crime because these individuals are more likely to eschew traditional, legitimate work settings where employees are supervised and controlled by their employers. Less supportive of such claims, we instead argue that former prisoners are less likely to be able to acquire adequate employment which then leaves them at a disadvantage and more likely to turn back to crime rather than desist from it. Gainful, legitimate employment can divert individuals from seeking illegitimate sources of money and status, as well as encourage significant reductions in recidivism among youth and adult offenders when compared to those without employment (e.g., Skardhamar & Telle, 2012).

Finally, we draw attention to Sampson and Laub's (1993) life-course framework that incorporates elements of many classical works (largely on social control, rational choice, strain, and learning theories). They argue that employment can expand relationships in society (see also Mortimer, 2003), increase investment in social capital, or in valued social institutions, and thereby prevent involvement in criminal behaviours. In their research, Sampson and Laub (1990) examined the role of adult relationships and established that, while delinquency in adolescence was a valid predictor of the persistence of offending into adulthood, strong attachment to family (i.e., marriage) and the workplace (i.e., job stability) redirected these individuals' offending trajectories, and even reduced deviant behaviours like excessive drinking. They found that formerly criminally active persons who had become committed to their jobs and experienced job stability committed fewer crimes as adults; these results were even more pronounced when the sample was divided into persistent offenders and desisters from crime (Sampson and Laub, 1990, 1993). This model also found that marital attachment reduced the continuation of offending. Like Sampson and Laub (1990, 1993), Uggen's (2000) results also reveal that employment has significant positive effects (i.e., fewer arrests) for older (i.e., 26 years of age and older) former prisoners, drug users, and high school dropouts when compared with younger adults and adolescents (under the age of 26). These findings suggest that important life transitions or turning points occur as individuals mature, invest in more meaningful relationships, and assume more adult roles, thereby being provided with stronger motivation to work and maintain a job. Four general types of turning points that may contribute to desistance are:

1) new situations that "knife off" the past from the present;
2) new situations that provide both supervision and monitoring as well as new opportunities of social support and growth;
3) new situations that change and structure routine activities; and
4) new situations that provide the opportunity for identity transformation. (Sampson & Laub, 2005, pp. 17–18)

What is undeniable then is that employment, or rather unemployment and underemployment, is a significant factor in the current understanding of crime and processes of desistance from crime.

### Employees: Why Is Employment so Vital for Men, Women, and Youth after Imprisonment?

Scholars have repeatedly verified that unemployment and underemployment are associated with recidivism rather than desistance from crime (Berg & Huebner, 2011; Bushway, 2011; Snyder & Sickmund, 2006; Visher et al., 2008; Uggen & Staff, 2001). Desistance, despite a lack of agreement on a conclusive definition of the process, is generally understood as the "process by which offenders give up criminal activity and become law-abiding citizens" (see

Sampson & Laub, 1992, 1995; Weaver, 2013). While desistance can therefore include a decline in offending frequency, reduced seriousness of offending, and/or ultimately total cessation, recidivism is typically only measured for a set period which, in much research, has been a maximum period of two years. As such, it can be challenging to draw comparisons between each of these outcome measures or view them as direct opposites of one another (see Zara & Farrington, 2016). Scholars nevertheless have long documented the value of employment for persons who are working toward exiting criminal activity. It is argued, and empirically validated, that as individuals develop stakes in conformity or community ties, such as employment or marital and family relationships, which all seem to go hand in hand, desistance is encouraged. Individuals become committed to free society and to persons and opportunities outside of prison or illegal activities. However, neither marriage nor employment alone solidify pathways for desistance; said processes also require the desister themselves to have a strong commitment to their relationships and their new self-identity as a law-abiding citizen and labour market contributor. This includes structure and self-monitoring, which, when coupled with emotional support, is the foundation for desistance.

Shadd Maruna (2001), to exemplify, employed narrative theory to examine the psychology of desistance beyond the age-out theory and discovered that successful prevention of recidivism depended on the personal narratives individuals developed. Specifically, he found that desisters create redemption scripts, where they claim their past criminal activity resulted from external factors beyond their control, while recidivists developed condemnation scripts that embody a fatalistic viewpoint and doubt their ability to change. Desisters from crime, he further found, played a role in their reformation process—which for many includes successfully seeking or continuously trying to solidify employment. For releasees, then, it is prudent for criminal justice policy to clearly highlight the *end* of their punishment and provide some means of signalling their redemption and re-inclusion within their communities. One step toward this end, however, is for the former prisoner to rewrite their past into a necessary prelude to a productive and "worthy" life. This self-reconstruction is not a deletion of one's history, but rather a reinvention of one's self—the creation of a new identity, with which comes the possibility, aptitude, and desire to acquire and maintain employment. Indeed, current understanding supports that recidivism is related to key risk factors, like criminal associates, substance misuse, and unemployment (Andrews & Bonta, 2010), and involves changes in lifestyle and opportunities, and a renewed interest in rejoining the community and developing human and social capital.

Not surprisingly then, researchers like Motiuk and Vuong (2005) who conducted research on a Canadian adult correctional sample, reveal that unemployment was one of the most reliable variables associated with reoffending (see Arditti & Parkman, 2011; Visher, Debus-Sherrill, & Yahner, 2011; Visher et al., 2008; Visher & Travis, 2003). Internationally, researchers' findings have noted that criminal engagement or prior incarceration limits individuals' ability to obtain employment and thus be independent (Arditti & Parkman, 2011), reduces their income and/or probability of obtaining employment (Waldfogel, 1994) especially for offenders whose pre-conviction jobs apparently require trust or for offenders who are sent to prison. Significant conviction effects on income are large compared with state-imposed penalties, and makes fewer types of jobs, or jobs of more limited duration, available to them (Harding, 2003).

Former prisoners with poor mental health are even more disadvantaged in gaining employment after incarceration. This was further unpacked by Krystle Martin, in her contribution, as she drew on her clinical experiences to evince how former prisoners with mental illness have explicit and unique barriers to labour force participation. Such challenges are tied to their psychiatric symptoms, to stigma, and to hiring policies/legislation (see chapter 3).

Another population that experiences vast and unique barriers to employment post-release are, as put forth by Dale Spencer (see chapter 10), homeless, formerly incarcerated men. Researchers have documented that former prisoners or criminalized persons with stable housing are more likely to engage meaningfully in rehabilitative programming, gain and sustain employment, and successfully abide by their community conditions, thus reducing the likelihood of recidivism and a return to jail compared to those who are homeless or experience housing instability (see Altschuler & Brash, 2004; Metraux & Culhane, 2004; Roman & Travis, 2004). Unstable housing is predictive of continued problems related to employment and offending. It contributes to disruptions across multiple facets of an individual's life, including social capital, i.e., the social support and networks that can provide access to employment opportunities (see Hook & Courtney, 2011). Spencer, in chapter 10, outlines how homeless men in Canada and the United States struggle to find employment in our neo-liberal, late-capitalist society and unpacks how the mark of their criminal record as well as the associated challenges of living rough (i.e., on the streets) makes the transition from the streets to work even more impossible.

Interestingly, it is not only those with criminal pasts who have difficulties finding employment after incarceration. Kimberley Clow, in her chapter, explores the negative impact that being wrongfully convicted has on individuals' job market participation and acceptance. She empirically examined if potential employers discriminate against wrongly convicted persons (see chapter 11). She found that respondents, who represented potential employers, provided similar rates of possible interest to job candidates in the wrongly convicted and rightly convicted conditions, all who had emailed queries in response to job advertisements. However, she noted that the tone of the received emails were more likely to be sympathetic in the wrongly convicted than the rightly convicted condition. Although wrongly convicted persons receive more sympathetic responses from possible employers than rightly convicted, they are not more frequently given job opportunities. Clow argues, therefore, that even wrongfully convicted persons face challenges acquiring employment after prison. Thus, simply being a former prisoner and having the label of "offender" tied to a criminal record are disadvantaging for further employability and the ability to maintain employment (LeBel, 2012; Waldfogel, 1994; Western, 2002, 2007; Western & Pettit, 2005).

After incarceration, releasees have limited social capital and relationships, both central needs for successful reintegration and employment. For example, Berg and Huebner (2011) examined the relationship between social capital and employment using a sample of 401 formerly incarcerated adult males in the United States whose average age was 32 years at release from prison. Employing measures of parental ties and ties to other relatives, they found that former prisoners who had developed strong attachment to relatives had a higher likelihood of being employed. This also diminished the likelihood to reoffend for males who had ties both to parents and other relatives. Employment itself had the greatest impact on recidivism, as the variables representing ties to participants' family members were only significant in models that excluded employment (Berg & Huebner, 2011). The researchers further demonstrated that joblessness among former prisoners was linked to frequent periods of past unemployment, but for individuals who had positive relationships with relatives the link was not as strong. The inclusion of family in program provision may hence be incredibly beneficial for individuals seeking employment following their release from custody.

Researchers assessing the effectiveness of re-entry programs for an adult serious/violent offender sample found that offenders were more likely to experience program failure if they were unable to secure employment both in the facility prior to their release and in the community post-release (Listwan, 2009). This finding underscores the significant barriers that offenders encounter even when they are enrolled in re-entry programming designed to assist in their reintegration. Ricciardelli and Mooney, consistent with Listwan (2009), also showed in their contribution (chapter 5) that the inability of releasees to secure employment was tied, to some degree, to a lack of education or employment experience. Further they noted the challenges releasees face, including when participating in re-entry programming, because seeking employment can be a source of stress—a reality that could be mediated by strong family supports. Unfortunately, family support is not available to all former prisoners. Family, as well as friends and acquaintances, can expose individuals to extended networks and job prospects (Lin, 2001)—this has been supported in more recent research specific to offenders (Visher et al., 2008)—yet for releasees without family connections or support there is no such assistance when pursuing employment. Connectedness to family may encourage the attainment of a conventional job, as suggested in previous research (e.g., Maruna, 2001).

## EMPLOYERS

Much scholarly attention focuses on how a former prisoner's failure to obtain employment has detrimental effects (Visher et al., 2008), including an increased risk of recidivism, and on how employers are genuinely concerned about hiring former prisoners. For example, Graffam Shinkfield, Lavelle, and McPherson (2008) surveyed employers, employment service workers, corrections workers, and prisoners in Australia to understand their views of former prisoners' abilities in the workforce, including if they had the skills and characteristics needed to get and hold a job. They found that employment service workers and correctional workers all have a shared low level of confidence in former prisoners' abilities to display the relevant skills and characteristics required to do well on the job. However, despite having evinced that employers feel and express numerous concerns when considering the hiring of former prisoners or persons with a criminal history, few researchers have systematically assessed whether said concerns are valid. An exception is Harmon and his co-authors, who show in chapter 6 that among their sample of former prisoners, disciplinary rates and rates of termination did not differ based on employees' past convictions, be they felonies or other indictable convictions. In doing this, they challenge the stigma of criminalization by empirically showing that there is no support for the assumption that "former prisoners will be trouble at work." They argue that "second-chance" businesses are needed to help reduce rates of recidivism through encouraging and assisting employers in hiring people with a criminal history.

Further, reports from the United States and the United Kingdom reveal that many former prisoners want to improve their image and themselves— they are seeking to change. Thus, many exude a high level of commitment, loyalty, honesty, and reliability, more so than the average person seeking work (Devaney, 2011; Gardiner, 2012; Gill, 1997; Jolson, 1975). By employing former prisoners, who tend to have much to prove and much on the line through work—even staying on parole rather than being sent back to prison with revoked freedom—employers also can take solace in their efforts toward fulfilling their corporate social responsibility to give former prisoners a second (or third or fourth) chance. In some cases, employers may also be given financial incentives to hire former prisoners, such as targeted wage subsidy programs[3] (see Gill, 1997). Second-chance organizations, like social enterprises or not-for-profits, may be available to offer expert guidance and/ or training to help prepare former prisoners for the workforce and even absorb a majority of the hiring costs associated with hiring former prisoners. In some cases, as Adrienne Peters discussed in her contribution on youth employment re-entry (see chapter 8), the first ten weeks of wages for a formerly incarcerated employee may be supplemented by an external agency as a means to encourage employers' willingness to hire formerly incarcerated persons, and build foundational relationships, which, in successful cases, can lead to longer-term employment and desistance. A secondary element to such an approach, Peters outlined, incorporates employer mentoring that can further build individuals' self-confidence and self-efficacy, as well as their preparation to assume greater responsibilities and positions.

## POLICY AND PRACTICES

Skill training and pre-employment readiness are recognized needs of former prisoners. It is known that working with formerly incarcerated youth one-on-one is more beneficial than group-based programs (Lipsey, 2006). Further, customized program elements based on the service recipient's unique needs can contribute to program effectiveness for both adults and youth. Of course, practices proven to be effective should be modified rather than removed completely, as certain skills learned and rehearsed through employment programs have been found to be more effective than others (Liu, Huang, & Wang, 2014). Undoubtedly, former prisoners would benefit from tracked pre-employment training, both in prison and post-release, as well as education and job skills training more generally. This training should incorporate elements of evidence-based approaches. Also important, however, is ensuring that correctional staff, parole officers, probation officers, community service providers, and any other positive supports (e.g., family, peers, colleagues) in the individual's life maintain open communication throughout each stage of the re-entry process. These diverse sources of assistance must be prepared to support not only the former prisoner, but also one another during any setbacks or newly presented obstacles.

One central evidence-based practice that should be collaboratively applied in former prisoner case management and re-entry strategizing is the risk–need–responsivity model. As Ashley Brown outlined in chapter 9, for populations identified as high-risk the risk–need–responsivity principles recommend high-intensity interventions, which target criminogenic needs and offer individualized approaches conducive to former prisoners' learning styles (Andrews, Bonta, & Hoge, 1990). In consideration of the extant research on the ineffectiveness of high-intensity interventions for low-risk offenders, and researchers' findings revealing that this can indeed increase individuals' likelihood to recidivate (Andrews & Bonta, 2006; Andrews et al., 1990; Lowenkamp & Latessa, 2005), re-entry/employment-related service providers can benefit greatly from following the risk–need–responsivity principles in cooperation with one another. Brown expands on complementary practices for assisting former prisoners in attaining work in her chapter. She discusses the importance of positive therapeutic relationships and strength-based approaches—following the responsivity principle of the risk–need–responsivity model—both offered by the Crossroads Day Reporting Centre's case-management and pre-employment programs. The application of these strategies not only provides releasees with positive relationships, but also improves their self-concept and agency, thereby providing tools to help releasees overcome stigma and obtain long-term employment.

Diverse suggestions have also been offered across time and place to encourage employers to hire former prisoners or to help former prisoners acquire work. These range from the aforementioned government incentives and subsidized wages for employers, to notions of "corporate" social responsibilities, to simple stigma reduction programs and skills training. Of course, one reality here is the matter of disclosure for former prisoners in relation to their criminal record. In Europe, like in Canada, individuals do not by law have to disclose their criminal history, with the exception of when applying for jobs that require pre-employment screening. Given that many employers unknowingly hire people with a criminal record, Gill (1997) notes that discrimination towards former prisoners is illogical. Instead, he suggests that employers should work towards fostering an inclusive environment where individuals are encouraged to be open about their diverse experiences, including their incarceration history (Gill, 1997).

Anazodo, Chan, and Ricciardelli, in their contribution (chapter 2), reveal the role of employment in social and community reintegration post-incarceration; specifically, they detail the "mark" a criminal label imposes on a releasee (Pager, 2003), the consequential experiences of devaluation and stigmatization, and the associated barriers in their quest for lifestyle changes that result from said mark. The authors clearly outline the value of employment for releasees—its fundamental value in determining one's ability to success-fully desist from crime—yet, they argue, the barriers to labour market par-ticipation make getting a job nearly impossible for these men and women.

Samantha McAleese explains the ways in which having a criminal record is a significant and often insurmountable barrier to acquiring and maintain-ing employment (see chapter 4). For many jobs, employers are increasingly requesting background checks when making new hires, although in more precarious types of employment—like construction, seasonal, and temporary positions—employers are less likely to spend the money and time doing back-ground checks (see chapter 5). In Canada, it has become more difficult for former prisoners to expunge or seal their criminal history in light of recent changes to the pardon system (see McAleese's contribution in chapter 4). Now, instead, the new record suspension program actually appears to be a step backward, not forward, as it makes it even more difficult to find employ-ment for those with records or histories of criminal behaviours. England and Wales appear also to have complicated the policies and practices available to assist former prisoners as they re-enter society and the job market, as Chris-tine Hough demonstrates in chapter 7 on South Asian/Muslim offenders. The Conservative government introduced a Transforming Rehabilitation (TR) agenda that has ushered in changes to the probation model. Alongside these changes are what Hough presents as increasing barriers in access to community-based employment programs for former prisoners, particularly those of minority ethnic groups and of the Muslim faith. On the other hand, Samantha McAleese, and Mark Harmon and his colleagues draw attention to more positive trends happening in the United States, specifically campaigns and emergent policies like "Ban the Box" that strive to remove the barrier of a criminal record.

It is imperative to revisit the former "pardon" processes and to advocate for positive change. Why need it be so difficult to seal a record? At what point should one be able to have a second chance? As Ricciardelli (2014) questioned before, if Canada—as a country and society—is opposed to both capital and corporal punishment, should that not suggest we as a nation believe in the decency of humanity and in affording others an opportunity to change them-selves and their lives? This leads to a second question: when is a person no longer the same person who committed the original crime? A decade or two or three or four after a person committed their crime(s), are they still the same person capable of committing said criminal acts? Is a man who commits a robbery at 17 still the same person 30 years later? Would they still be open to committing a robbery at 47? At what point are we no longer punishing the person who committed the crime? At what point is a person no longer who they once were? Why can we not as a society give people a genuine second chance, with employment and a genuine possibility to succeed?

## NOTES

1 The youngest age for which background information was provided was 14.
2 Morselli and colleagues (2006) report as well that other research has illustrated alternative forms of informal social controls for youth with limited parental supervision who are instead indirectly supervised by other positive mentors (see Basso, Graham, Pelech, DeYoung, & Cardey, 2004).
3 See for example Ontario's Targeted Wage Subsidy: http://www.myocca.ca/programs _government-incentives-results.php?id=7&height=400&width=600.

## REFERENCES

Aaltonen, M., Macdonald, J. M., Martikainen, P., & Kivivuori, J. (2013). Examining the generality of the unemployment–crime association. *Criminology, 51,* 561–594.

Agamben, G. (1995). *Homo sacer: Sovereignty and bare life.* (D. Heller-Roazen, Trans.). Stanford, CT: Stanford University Press.

Agnew, R. (1992). Foundation for a general strain theory of crime and delinquency. *Criminology, 30*(1), 47–88.

Agnew, R. (2001). Building on the foundation of general strain theory: Specifying the types of strain most likely to lead to crime and delinquency. *Journal of Research in Crime and Delinquency, 38,* 319–361.

Alarid, L. F., Burton, V. S. Jr., & Cullen, F. T. (2000). Gender and crime among felony offenders: Assessing the generality of social control and differential association theories. *Journal of Research in Crime and Delinquency, 37,* 171–199.

Altschuler, D. M., & Brash, R. (2004). Adolescent and teenage offenders confronting the challenges and opportunities of reentry. *Youth Violence and Juvenile Justice, 2,* 72–87. doi: 10.1177/1541204003260048

Andress, D., Wildes, T., Rechtine, D., & Moritsugu, K. P. (2004). Jails, prisons, and your community's health. *Journal of Law, Medicine and Ethics, 32*(4), 50–51.

Andrews, D. A., & Bonta, J. (2006). *The psychology of criminal conduct* (4th ed.). Newark, NJ: LexisNexis.

Andrews, D. A., & Bonta, J. (2010). Rehabilitating criminal justice policy and practice. *Psychology, Public Policy, and Law, 16*(1), 39–55. doi:10.1037/a0018362

Andrews, D. A., Bonta, J., & Hoge, R. D. (1990). Classification for effective rehabilitation: Rediscovering psychology. *Criminal Justice and Behavior, 17,* 19–52.

Arditti, J. A., & Parkman, T. (2011). Young men's reentry after incarceration: A developmental paradox. *Family Relations, 60*(2), 205–220. doi:10.1111/ j.1741-3729.2010.00643.x

Baron, S. W. (2006). Street youth, strain theory, and crime. *Journal of Criminal Justice, 34,* 209–223.

Basso, R. V. J., Graham, J., Pelech, W., DeYoung, R., & Cardey, R. (2004). Children's street connections in a Canadian community. *International Journal of Offender Therapy and Comparative Criminology, 48,* 189–202.

Beccaria, C. (1963). *On crimes and punishments.* New York, NY: Macmillan. (Original work published 1764).

Becker, H. (1963). *Outsiders: Studies in the sociology of deviance.* New York, NY: Free Press.

Berg, M. T., & Huebner, B. M. (2011). Reentry and the ties that bind: An examination of social ties, employment, and recidivism. *Justice Quarterly, 28,* 382–410. doi:10.1080/07418825.2010.498383

Bushway, S. D. (2011). Labor markets and crime. In J. Q. Wilson & J. Petersilia (Eds.), *Crime and Public Policy* (pp. 183–209). New York, NY: Oxford University Press.

Cernkovich, S. A., Giordano, P. C., & Rudolph, J. (2000). Race, crime and the American dream. *Journal of Research in Crime and Delinquency, 37,* 131–170.

Clarke, R. V., & Cornish, D. B. (1985). Modeling offenders' decisions: A framework for research and policy. *Crime and Justice, 6,* 147–185.

Cohen, L. E., & Felson, M. (1979). Social change and crime rate trends: A routine activity approach. *American Sociological Review, 44,* 588–608.

Dauvergne, M. (2012). *Adult correctional statistics in Canada, 2010/2011.* (Catalogue no. 85-002-X). Juristat. Ottawa, ON: Statistics Canada. Retrieved from http://www.statcan.gc.ca/pub/85-002-x/2012001/article/11715-eng.pdf

Devaney, T. (2011, July 4). Feds recommend ex-cons for hard-to-fill jobs. *Washington Times.* Retrieved from http://www.washingtontimes.com/news/2011/jul/4/ex-cons-recommended-for-hard-to-fill-jobs/?page=all

Gardiner, T. (2012, May 4). Prisoners can be honest and motivated workers, Ken Clarke tells business as he urges the High Street to give ex-offenders jobs. *Daily Mail Online.* Retrieved from http://www.dailymail.co.uk/news/article-2139390/Prisoners-honest-motivated-workers-Ken-Clarke-tells-business-urges-High-Street-ex-offenders-jobs.html

Giddens, A. (1991). *Modernity and self-identity: Self and society in the late modern age.* Stanford, CA: Stanford University Press.

Gill, M. (1997). Employing ex-offenders: A risk or an opportunity? *Howard Journal, 36,* 4, 337–351.

Goffman, E. (1963). *Stigma: Notes on the management of spoiled identity.* Englewood Cliffs, NJ: Prentice-Hall.

Gottfredson, M., & Hirschi, T. (1990). *A general theory of crime.* Stanford, CA: Stanford University Press.

Graffam, J., Shinkfield, A., Lavelle, B., & McPherson, W. (2008). Variables affecting successful reintegration as perceived by offenders and professionals. *Journal of Offender Rehabilitation, 40*(1–2), 147–171.

Harding, D. J. (2003). Counterfactual models of neighborhood effects: The effect of neighborhood poverty on dropping out and teenage pregnancy. *American Journal of Sociology, 109,* 676–719.

Hirschi, T. (1969). *Causes of delinquency.* Berkeley, CA: University of California Press.

Hook, J. L., & Courtney. M. E. (2011). Employment outcomes of former foster youth as young adults: The importance of human, personal, and social capital. *Children and Youth Services Review, 33,* 1855–1865.

Jolson, M. A. (1975). Are ex-offenders successful employees? *California Management Review, 17,* 65–73.

Laub, J. H., & Sampson, R. J. (2003). *Shared beginnings, divergent lives: Delinquent boys to age 70*. Cambridge, MA: Harvard University Press.

LeBel, T. P. (2012). If one doesn't get you another one will: Formerly incarcerated persons' perceptions of discrimination. *Prison Journal, 92*, 63–87.

Lemert, E. (1967). *Human deviance, social problems and social control*. Englewood Cliffs, NJ: Prentice-Hall.

Lin, N. (2001). *Social capital: A theory of social structure and action*. New York, NY: Cambridge University Press.

Lipsey, M. (2006). The effects of community-based group treatment for delinquency: A meta-analytic search for cross-study generalizations. In K. A. Dodge, T. J. Dishion, & J. E. Lansford (Eds.), *Deviant peer influences in programs for youth: Problems and solutions* (pp. 162–184). New York, NY: Guilford Press.

Listwan, S. J. (2009). Reentry for serious and violent offenders: An analysis of program attrition. *Criminal Justice Policy Review, 20*, 154–169.

Liu, S., Huang, J. L., & Wang, M. (2014). Effectiveness of job search interventions: A meta-analytic review. *Psychological Bulletin, 140*, 1009–1041. doi:10.1037/a0035923

Loughran, T. A., Mulvey, E. P., Schubert, C. A., Fagan, J., Piquero, A. R., & Losoya, S. H. (2009). Estimating a dose–response relationship between length of stay and future recidivism in serious juvenile offenders. *Criminology, 47*, 699–740.

Lowenkamp, C. T., & Latessa, E. J. (2005). Increasing the effectiveness of correctional programming through the risk principle: Identifying offenders for residential placement. *Criminology and Public Policy, 4*, 263–290.

Maruna, S. (2001). *Making good: How ex-convicts reform and rebuild their lives*. Washington, DC: American Psychological Association.

Merton, R. K. (1938). Social structure and anomie. *American Sociological Review, 3*, 672–682.

Metraux, S., & Culhane, D. P. (2004). Homeless shelter use and reincarceration following prison release. *Criminology and Public Policy, 3*(2), 139–160.

Moffitt, T. E. (1993). Adolescence-limited and life-course-persistent antisocial behavior: A developmental taxonomy. *Psychological Review, 100*(4), 674–701.

Morselli, C., Tremblay, P., & McCarthy, B. (2006). Mentors and criminal achievement. *Criminology, 44*, 17–43.

Mortimer, J. T. (2003). *Working and growing up in America*. Cambridge, MA: Harvard University Press.

Motiuk, L., & Vuong, B. (2005). Offender employment: What the research tells us. *Forum of Corrections Research, Offender Employment, 17*(1). Retrieved from http://www.csc-scc.gc.ca/research/forum/Vol17No1/v17n1e-eng.shtml

Pager, D. (2003). The mark of a criminal record. *American Journal of Sociology, 108*(5), 937–975.

Rahill-Beuler, C. M., & Kretzer, K. M. (1997). Helping offenders find employment. *Federal Probation, 61*(1), 35–37.

Ricciardelli, R. (2014). *Surviving incarceration: Inside Canadian prisons*. Waterloo, ON: Wilfrid Laurier University Press.

Roman, C. G., & Travis, J. (2004). *Taking stock: Housing, homelessness, and prisoner reentry*. Urban Institute. Retrieved from http://www.urban.org/sites/default/files/alfresco/publication-pdfs/411096-Taking-Stock.PDF

Rosenfeld, R., Petersilia, J., & Visher, C. (2008, June). The first days after release can make a difference. *Corrections Today*, 86–87.

Sampson, R. J., & Laub, J. H. (1990). Crime and deviance over the life course: The salience of adult social bonds. *American Sociological Review, 55*, 609–627.

Sampson, R. J., & Laub, J. H. (1992). Crime and deviance in the life-course. *Annual Review of Sociology 18*, 63–84.

Sampson, R. J., & Laub, J. H. (1993). *Crime in the making: Pathways and turning points through life.* Cambridge, MA: Harvard University Press.

Sampson, R. J., & Laub, J. H. (1995). Understanding variability in lives through time: Contributions of life-course criminology. *Studies on Crime and Crime Prevention 4*, 143–58.

Sampson, R. J., & Laub, J. H. (1997). A life-course theory of cumulative disadvantage and the stability of delinquency. In T. P. Thornberry (Ed.), *Developmental Theories of Crime and Delinquency.* New Brunswick, NJ: Transaction.

Sampson, R. J., & Laub, J. H. (2005). A life-course view of the development of crime. *Annals of the American Academy of Political and Social Science, 602*, 12–45.

Scott, T. (2010). Offender perceptions on the value of employment. *Journal of Correctional Education, 61*, 46–67.

Skardhamar, T., & Telle, K. (2012). Post-release employment and recidivism in Norway. *Journal of Quantitative Criminology, 28*, 629–649.

Snyder, H. N., & Sickmund, M. (2006). *Juvenile offenders and victims: 2006 national report.* Washington, DC: U.S. Department of Justice, Office of Justice Programs, Office of Juvenile Justice and Delinquency Prevention. Retrieved from http://www.ojjdp.gov/ojstatbb/nr2006/downloads/NR2006.pdf. See more at: http://youth.gov/youth-topics/juvenile-justice/references

Sutherland, E. (1947). *Principles of criminology* (4th ed.). Philadelphia, PA: Lippincott.

Travis, J. (2005). *But they all come back: Facing the challenges of prisoner reentry.* Washington DC: Urban Institute Press.

Uggen, C. (2000). Work as a turning point in the life course of criminals: A duration model of age, employment, and recidivism. *American Sociological Review, 67*, 529–546.

Uggen, C., & Staff, J. (2001). Work as a turning point for criminal offenders. *Corrections Management Quarterly, 37*, 347–368.

Visher, C., Debus-Sherrill, S. A., & Yahner, J. (2008). *Employment after prison: A longitudinal study of releasees in three states.* Washington, DC: Urban Institute.

Visher, C., Debus-Sherrill, S. A., & Yahner, J. (2011). Employment after prison: A longitudinal study of former prisoners. *Justice Quarterly, 28*, 698–718. doi:10 .1080/07418825.2010.535553

Visher, C. A., & Travis, J. (2003). Transitions from prison to community: Understanding individual pathways. *Annual Review of Sociology, 29*, 89–113. doi:10.1146/annurev.soc.29.010202.095931

Visher, C. A., Winterfield, L., & Coggeshall, M. B. (2005). Ex-offender employment programs and recidivism: A meta-analysis. *Journal of Experimental Criminology, 1*, 295–315.

Waldfogel, J. (1994). Does conviction have a persistent effect on income and employment? *International Review of Law and Economics, 14*(1), 103–119.

Weaver, B. (2013). Desistance, reflexivity and relationality: A case study. *European Journal of Probation, 5*(3), 71–88.

Western, B. (2002). The impact of incarceration on wage mobility and inequality. *American Sociological Review, 67,* 526–546.

Western, B. (2007). The penal system and the labor market. In S. Bushway, M. A. Stoll, & D. F. Weiman (Eds.), *Barriers to re-entry? The labor market for released prisoners in postindustrial America* (pp. 335–360). New York, NY: Russell Sage Foundation.

Western, B., & Pettit, B. (2005). Black–white wage inequality, employment rates, and incarceration. *American Journal of Sociology, 111,* 553–578.

Zara, G., & Farrington, D. P. (2016). *Criminal recidivism: Explanation, prediction and prevention.* Abingdon, UK: Routledge.

# ABOUT THE AUTHORS

**KEMI SALAWU ANAZODO** is a lecturer at the Goodman School of Business at Brock University and a doctoral candidate in Human Resource Management at York University. Her current research interests include employment re-entry, identity management, marginalized populations, and organizational inclusion.

**ALEXANDRA M. ARNESON** recently completed her MS in Criminology and Criminal Justice at Whitman College. She received a BA from University of Portland. She is interested in Social Justice and has worked in child welfare.

**ASHLEY BROWN** is a case manager at the Crossroads Day Reporting Centre (CDRC) with the St. Leonard's Society of Toronto. She earned a BA in Psychology through University of Western Ontario, a Bachelor of Social Work from the University of Victoria, and has worked with criminalized men and women since 2006 in both community and residential settings. Her work at the Crossroads Day Reporting Centre focuses on stabilizing high-risk offenders who are newly released into the community. Ms. Brown has previously written on topics such as the need for trauma-informed care when working with offending populations, as well as the benefits of the therapeutic alliance. She can be reached by email at abrown.jhst@outlook.com.

**CHRISTOPHER CHAN** is an Associate Professor in Human Resource Management at York University, Honourary Research Fellow at the Australian Catholic University and visiting Associate Professor at the Université de Rennes 1. His main research interests include interfaces between religiosity, spirituality and HR/business practices; work–family conflicts and enrichment; and cross cultural management.

**KIMBERLEY A. CLOW** has a PhD in psychology from the University of Western Ontario. She is an Associate Professor in the Forensic Psychology program at the University of Ontario Institute of Technology. Her research focuses on stereotypes and prejudice. Currently, her main line of research investigates the stigma of wrongful conviction and looks for ways to decrease the stigma that exonerees experience.

**ASHLEY M. HANSEN** received both her BA and MS in Criminology and Criminal Justice from Portland State University. She is interested in addiction and counselling.

**MARK G. HARMON** has a PhD in Sociology from University of Oregon and is an Assistant Professor in the Department of Criminology and Criminal Justice in the Hatfield School of Government at Portland State University. He studies the interconnection between race, politics, and the criminal justice system. His recent research has focused on the effects of state-level sentencing reforms on various components of sentencing including the impacts on people of colour. Other recent research has focused on reducing barriers to maintaining employment of previously incarcerated individuals, and research into racial disparities in prosecutorial decision making. Dr. Harmon has also worked on developing more robust quantitative methods in criminal justice research.

**LAURA J. HICKMAN** has a PhD in Criminology and Criminal Justice from University of Maryland, is a Criminology & Criminal Justice Professor at Portland State University, and an adjunct Behavioral Scientist with the RAND Corporation. The focus of Dr. Hickman's work is evaluating and improving criminal justice policy and practice. She has lead and co-lead multi-million-dollar, multi-site experimental evaluations, employing original data collection, rigorous methodology, and advanced statistical techniques. Her work has focused on a range of policy-oriented topics, including domestic violence, law enforcement policy and practice, federal capital punishment, immigration, correctional programming supervision, and children exposed to violence.

**CHRISTINE VICTORIA HOUGH** has a PhD in Education Policy from the University of Lancaster, UK. She is a Senior Lecturer at the University of Central Lancashire, in the School of Social Work, Care and Community. She is the module leader for the compulsory work-based modules on the Children Schools and Families BA Honours degree program and teaches the Data Analysis module on the Educational Doctorate program. She is currently a co-researcher for a research project funded by the Barrow Cadbury Trust, entitled Faith, Family and Crime, which will explore the impact of the criminal justice system on Muslim families, due to a family member's involvement with the criminal justice system.

**KRYSTLE MARTIN** is a Clinical and Forensic Psychologist registered with the College of Psychologists of Ontario. She received her PhD in Counselling Psychology from the Ontario Institute for Studies in Education at the University of Toronto (OISE/UT). Dr. Martin has provided clinical services in both correctional facilities and forensic psychiatric hospitals. Currently, she is a Research Scientist and Advanced Practice Psychologist at Ontario Shores Centre for Mental Health Services in Whitby, Ontario. Her research interests include dynamic risk assessment, length of stay, psychopathy, and how individuals' beliefs about the future are related to risk for reoffending.

**SAMANTHA MCALEESE** is a PhD candidate in Sociology at Carleton University in Ottawa. She is interested in understanding experiences of prisoner re-entry considering recent changes to Canadian penal policies. More specifically, her work examines the changes made to Canada's pardon system and the impact of these changes on people with criminal records and on the work of non-profit organizations that provide re-entry supports to formerly incarcerated individuals. McAleese has worked frontline in adult education, employment, and community reintegration programs, and has been an active member of the Criminalization and Punishment Education Project since 2012.

**TAYLOR MOONEY** is a research associate at the Canadian Institute of Public Safety Research and Treatment (CIPSRT) and an instructor in the Department of Sociology at Memorial University of Newfoundland. Her research interests include post-incarceration employment, community corrections, and policing in Canada.

**ADRIENNE M. F. PETERS** is an Assistant Professor in the Department of Sociology at Memorial University of Newfoundland. Her research areas include young offender treatment, programming, and rehabilitation; serious and violent youth offending; mental health and delinquency; youth justice legislation and policy; policing; and collaborative crime reduction strategies.

**ROSE RICCIARDELLI** is an Associate Professor and the Coordinator of Criminology in the Department of Sociology at Memorial University of Newfoundland. She is an Associate Scientist at Ontario Shores Centre for Mental Health, a Senior Research Fellow with Correctional Services Canada, a Research Fellow with B Division of the Royal Canadian Mounted Police, and Chairs the Corrections pillar of the Canadian Institute of Public Safety Research and Treatment, where she also serves a member of the Scientific

Leadership Council. She has published in a range of academic journals including *British Journal of Criminology, Sex Roles,* and *Theoretical Criminology.* She has published three books, her first entitled *Surviving Incarceration: Inside Canadian Prisons* (Wilfrid Laurier University Press, 2014), explores the realities of penal living for federally incarcerated men in Canada. Other books include *Violence, Sex Offenders, and Corrections* (with Dale Spencer, Routledge). She has also published three edited collections, including *Engaging with Ethics in International Criminological Research* (Michael Adorjan, Routledge). Her primary research interests include evolving conceptualizations of masculinity, and experiences and issues within different facets of the criminal justice system. Her current research looks at prison culture, desistance, and the coping strategies, risk perception, and lived experiences of prisoners, prison officers, and police officers.

**DALE C. SPENCER** is an Associate Professor in the Department of Law and Legal Studies at Carleton University. His main interests are violence, victimization, policing, youth, and conceptions of homelessness, domicile, and the law. He has published three books, *Violence, Sex Offenders, and Corrections* (with Rose Ricciardelli, Routledge), *Reimagining Intervention in Young Lives* (with Karen Foster, University of British Columbia Press) and *Ultimate Fighting and Embodiment* (Routledge), and three edited volumes, *Emotions Matter* (with Kevin Walby and Alan Hunt, University of Toronto Press), *Fighting Scholars* (with Raul Sanchez Garcia, Anthem Press), and *Reconceptualizing Critical Victimology* (with Sandra Walklate). His work can be found in a number of journals, including *Theoretical Criminology, Body and Society, Punishment and Society,* and *Ethnography.*